Spirituality and Religion in Counseling and Psychotherapy

Diversity in Theory and Practice

Eugene W. Kelly, Jr., Ph.D.

Spirituality and Religion in Counseling and Psychotherapy

10 9 8 7 6 5 4 3 2 1

American Counseling Association
5999 Stevenson Avenue
Alexandria, VA 22304

Acquisitions and Development Editor
Carolyn Baker

Managing Editor
Michael Comlish

Cover design by Brian Gallagher

Library of Congress Cataloging-in-Publication Data

Kelly, Eugene W.
    Spirituality and religion in counseling and psychotherapy :
diversity in theory and practice / Eugene W. Kelly, Jr.
        p.   cm.
    Includes bibliographical references.
    ISBN 1-55620-148-6 (alk. paper)
        1. Counseling.   2. Counseling—Religious aspects.
    3. Psychotherapy—Religious aspects.   4. Religion and psychology.
    I. Title.
B   BF637.C6K4324   1995
    158′.3—dc20   95-5668
                                                                      CIP

To my father and mother,
Gene and Beverly Kelly,
whose love and guidance opened me
to the spiritual/religious dimension

About the Author

Eugene W. Kelly, Jr., Ph.D., is professor of counseling, Department of Counseling/Human and Organizational Studies at The George Washington University, where he also served as director of the GWU Counseling Laboratory from 1988 to 1993. He was previously dean of the GWU School of Education and Human Development from 1979 to 1987. He is a licensed professional counselor and psychologist in Virginia, a National Certified Counselor, and a clinical member of the American Association of Marriage and Family Therapy. He is listed on the National Register of Health Service Providers in Psychology, and he has served as chair and vice-chair of the Virginia Board of Professional Counselors. Dr. Kelly received his Ph.D. from the University of South Carolina, where he was an NDEA Fellow, and his M.Div. from the Pontifical College Josephinum. His areas of special interest are counselor education and supervision, developmental counseling/therapy, values in counseling, and family and relationship counseling. His most recent book is *Relationship-Centered Counseling: An Integration of Art and Science* (Springer, 1994). He has also written several book chapters and numerous articles in professional journals on counseling and related topics.

Acknowledgements

I thank in a special way my wife and colleague, Joan F. Kelly,
Ph.D., for her many valuable and substantive suggestions in thinking through and writing this book.

I also thank the library staffs at the Gelman Library of The
George Washington University and the Bishop Payne Library of
the Virginia Theological Seminary for their valuable assistance in
locating and obtaining reference and research material.

Table of Contents

CHAPTER ONE

Spirituality and Religion: Diversity and Importance

1

CHAPTER TWO

Spirituality and Religion in Life Development and Personal and Social Well-Being

45

CHAPTER THREE

The Counseling/Therapeutic Relationship: Spiritual and Religious Implications
87

CHAPTER FOUR

Assessing the Spiritual/Religious Dimension in Counseling
131

CHAPTER FIVE

Counseling Approaches and Techniques: Treatment Intervention and the Spiritual/Religious Dimension
189

Preface

Steve was seeing the counselor for follow-up counseling after several episodes of manic-depressive behavior, including a brief but terrifying period of paranoid hallucinations. Steve spoke with relief and gratitude about the skillful counseling, reassuring manner, and timely psychiatric consultation that had resulted in his considerable and sustained improvement. However, he also mentioned his disappointment that neither his counselor nor his psychiatrist responded with any interest when he mentioned to them that he also thanked God for his recovery.

Lisa spoke to the counselor about how she first chose a particular counselor specifically because her referral source had said that the counselor would be receptive to discussing issues in a religious context. However, when she tried to talk about her difficulties in a religious framework, the counselor led her away from the religious perspective. She soon terminated.

Henry was a counselor colleague with whom I consulted about a client who was painfully stressed by intense guilt and anger tied to her father's literal interpretations of the Bible and frightening portrayals of a punishing, vindictive God. Henry was a skilled, insightful, and sensitive counselor. But he also spoke to me about his discomfort, occasional annoyance, and frustration at how the client seemed to be gripped, emotionally and cognitively, in a literalistic and guilt-inducing form of religion. Not only was the client's debilitating religiosity a problem for her, it was also becoming a negative block to Henry's conceptualizing and dealing effectively with the client's emotional pain and self-defeating behavior.

Robert, a client in his mid-20s, came to a beginning counselor with problems relating to persons at work and constant arguing with his parents. He said that the arguments with his parents had been aggravated over the past year because he had stopped going to church and had become interested in meditative and spiritual practices, with a special interest in Buddhism. The client said these spiritual interests and activities represented serious changes in his life; however, the counselor, herself a regular member of a mainstream Christian church, was puzzled and uncomfortable with this line of thought. She found it difficult to respond in ways that might help the client explore the meaning and behavioral consequences of his newly emergent spiritual concerns.

These incidents in themselves do not, of course, prove anything about the sensitivity or insensitivity of all or even most counselors toward religious or spiritual issues in counseling. However, they suggest that some counselors *outside of religious settings* may hesitate to try or be uncertain about incorporating the spiritual and religious dimensions of clients' lives and problems into the counseling process. Ethical concerns about improperly influencing clients' values, a strong opinion about the privacy of religious beliefs, reservations about discussing religious issues in a publicly funded counseling setting, lack of knowledge about or skill in dealing with the spiritual or religious aspect of clients' issues, uncertainty about the relevance of clients' spiritual beliefs to their developmental and mental health issues—all these may cause counselors, even those who personally value spirituality and religion, to avoid including clients' spiritual beliefs in the counseling process.

A fundamental thesis of this book is that a client's spiritual and religious beliefs and values, like any other set of personal beliefs and values, are potentially legitimate considerations in the counseling process. To the extent that they are pertinent to clients' issues in counseling, they deserve the same respectful, ethical, and skillful attention as any other relevant values. The particular setting in which counseling occurs may set certain limitations; however, setting-specific requirements should not be generalized as a limitation inherent in the counseling process itself. Thus, building on the fundamental thesis about the legitimate role of spirituality and religion in counseling, this book seeks to provide a knowledge base about spirituality and religion vis-à-vis counseling and to describe various practical ways for counselors to ethically and effectively include clients' religious and spiritual concerns in the counseling process.

This book is written from the perspective of spirituality and religion *in* counseling and not from the perspective of *religious counseling*. The latter refers to counseling guided by assumptions taken from religious belief systems (Worthington, 1986). The primary perspective of this book, in contrast, is what might be called secular counseling, that is, counseling as it is generally derived from the behavioral and social sciences and practiced in a contemporary, pluralistic society (Genia, 1994). It is within this perspective that spirituality and religion are discussed as pertinent and sometimes important elements of the general counseling process.

Survey evidence repeatedly points to the importance that many persons attach to spirituality and religion. However, the *actual effect* of spirituality and religiousness on human development and human behavior, and not just the magnitude of religious profession, is especially pertinent to how counselors will respond to these elements in the course of counseling. Spirituality and religion may be either beneficial or problematic for human development, depending on the form and force they take in peoples' lives, and any comprehensive approach to dealing with spirituality and religion in counseling will have to come to grips with these diverse effects. The diversity of effects of spirituality and religion on individuals' life development and functioning is also reflected in the diverse opinions that researchers and theoreticians hold regarding the value and validity of religion. These opinions, as well as related research data, must be assessed fairly in our understanding of spirituality and religion vis-à-vis counseling.

In anticipation of a full and balanced discussion later in this book, I note here that my own basic point of view is that spirituality and religion, while occurring in some respects as limiting or negative influences in human development and behavior, nonetheless represent essentially positive, vital forces for personal and social development. In this book the recognition of spirituality and religion's ambivalent effects, including negative effects, is subsumed within a larger view that spiritual and religious attitudes and behaviors are not purely psychological constructs but also signify existentially significant and essentially positive dimensions of reality. At the same time, it is recognized that many personal and social manifestations of spirituality and religion fall short of being constructive, and some are in fact debilitating.

Insights associated with this negative view have practical importance in clarifying the potential, and all too often actual, distortions of spirituality and religion. Critical assessments of spirituality and religion can help counselors understand and work with clients whose difficulties are tied up with debilitating expressions of spirituality and religiosity. However, what these essentially negative assessments of religion cannot do—and what the essentially positive affirmation of this book does do—is to provide an important opening for counselors to value clients' spirituality and religion as elements with potentially beneficial developmental and healing power.

The terms, religion and spirituality, have overlapping meanings insofar as they both point to a transcendent, meta-empirical dimension of reality. However, they also represent, in certain respects, divergent approaches to this reality. Although definitions differ, spirituality generally signifies an affirmation of and participation in the in-depth, transcendent, holistically connected, and inherently meaningful dimension of reality. Religion in its fuller meaning embraces spirituality, but also generally signifies specific modes and systems of belief, imaging, and practice that are often institutionalized in creeds, rituals, and moral codes; religion is embodied in religions. For convenience, in many parts of this book I will use the double term, spirituality/religion, or the phrase, the spiritual/religious dimension, to convey the overlapping but divergent meanings noted above. The perspective that guides the presentation of spirituality/religion vis-à-vis counseling in this book is that spirituality and religion have counseling implications that are substantially convergent, but also divergent in certain respects.

The primary audience for this book is professional counselors and psychotherapists in general and specialty practice, as well as other helping professionals, such as social workers and professional psychologists, who function in all types of secular settings. This book is also intended for use by counselor and therapist educators and counselors-in-training in college, university, and specialized counselor preparation programs. Although this book is relevant to the work of pastoral and religious counselors, it is not primarily oriented toward these counselors, but toward professional counselors and therapists in secular settings. Persons who function in adjunctive counseling and therapeutic positions in a variety of community and agency settings should also find this book helpful.

The book presents and discusses major and recent theory and research on spirituality and religion with regard to counseling and psychotherapy. Many aspects of this issue are examined with balanced consideration for the substantial diversity inherent in this topic. Within the context of these diverse perspectives, this book builds on the premise that spirituality and religion deserve coun-selors' sensitive regard, informed understanding, and, as ethically and therapeutically appropriate, skillful integration into effective counseling treatment.

I have written this book with an openness and respect for the diversity of religious and spiritual traditions and expressions. Given my own upbringing, education, and professional experience within a Western and largely Judeo-Christian environment, the book reflects to some extent this perspective. However, it certainly does not advance this perspective as normative nor does it imply any evaluative ranking of life philosophies for professional coun-seling, either religious or secular. Every reasonable effort is made to approach the issues of spirituality and religion in a way that is respectful of and relevant to the spiritual/religious dimension as expressed in diverse traditions.

Introduction

As an introduction to the primarily practical orientation purpose of this book, the first two chapters present information, concepts, and background knowledge that undergird counseling approaches, skills, and techniques. Chapter 1 discusses relevant contextual and definitional subjects that help frame our approach to the spiritual/religious dimension in counseling. Chapter 2 presents theory and research bearing on the relationship of spirituality and religion to human development and mental health. I realize that these two chapters may tax the patience of readers focused on practice; however, I invite readers' patient attention to these chapters because they provide important background for the directly practice-oriented aspects of subsequent chapters.

Chapter 3 focuses on the relationship dimension of counseling and discusses principles and practices for relating the spiritual/religious dimension to the counseling relationship. Chapter 4 discusses systematic approaches for evaluating the appropriateness of including spiritual and religious issues in counseling and methods of assessing the spiritual/religious dimension. Chapter 5 addresses a variety of treatment approaches and techniques for working with clients' spiritual and religious concerns.

This book presents a growing body of knowledge and practical application that can help counselors move from what is often a respectful but hesitant neutrality to a knowledgeable, skilled, and action-oriented sensitivity toward their clients' spirituality and religiousness. Applying this knowledge and sensitivity for the therapeutic benefit of the client, counselors can use available approaches and methods to work ethically and effectively with the positive potential and negative impact of spiritual and religious issues.

CHAPTER ONE

Spirituality and Religion: Diversity and Importance

An appreciation of the role of religion and spirituality in counseling begins with a twofold challenge: to achieve reasonable clarity in organizing the many different meanings that people attach to the terms, religion and spirituality, and to understand the importance that spirituality and religion carries for many people. A microcosm of this blend of diversity and significance can be illustrated from a class on counseling, religion, and spirituality that I teach for graduate and upper-division undergraduate students, including women and men of diverse backgrounds ranging in age from their early 20s to their late 50s. Even the initial, tentative ways that students introduce themselves show a many-sided assortment of religious and spiritual beliefs.

The majority of Christian and Jewish students in the course display a complex, and sometimes fuzzy, set of beliefs. These beliefs run the gamut from traditional and fundamental beliefs in a personal God and a spiritual realm to nontheistic and rationalistic beliefs with considerable uncertainly about any notion of God or any nonmaterial realm. As students speak about their beliefs, many struggle to articulate what they believe and to adjust to the challenge that they feel as others describe different beliefs. This experience of diversity broadens further when, for example, an Arab-American speaks of her Muslim faith, or a young woman tells of her disenchantment with her Christian upbringing and her current participation in Buddhism, or a young man tells of his return to faith in a noninstitutional 12-step program, or a middle-aged woman describes her commitment to the Baha'i faith, or a young man says that he has no religious or spiritual belief but is curious about the course. A prerabbinical student wonders aloud how anybody can*not* believe in God and the value of religion, while a visiting professional social worker says that her Judaism is for her a secular culture. A mature professional woman describes her very traditional Roman Catholic upbringing in Argentina, while another woman describes her growing up in a Buddhist family and society in Cambodia. A young African-American woman from a Black southern Baptist background speaks about the importance of her personal faith in Jesus, while another African-American woman working on her doctorate in business describes her deep faith in the Episcopal church.

Spirituality and religion

Shared and Distinctive Meanings

Common core of meaning. These examples illustrate that the effort to define and distinguish between spirituality and religion is a complex and thorny issue, full of differences and disputes. Catherine Albanese (1992) sums up this definitional quandary as follows:

> Why is it that so common a feature of human life proves so baffling? Is the inability to define, like the optical illusion, simply caused by staring too long into the religious landscape? Or are there other problems as well, intrinsic to the nature of religion? . . . A definition means an end or a limit—a boundary. A definition tells us where some reality ends; it separates the world into what is and what is not that reality.
>
> Religion cannot be defined very easily because it thrives both within and outside of boundaries. The boundaries of religion are different from the logical boundaries of good definitions. In the end, religion is a feature that encompasses *all* of human life. . . . [italics in original]. (p. 3)

Using this notion of boundaries, Albanese identifies two major dimensions of religion: "extraordinary" religion that "involves an encounter with some form of otherness . . . and helps people to transcend and move beyond their everyday culture and concerns" (pp. 7, 6); and "ordinary" religion that is "more or less synonymous with culture. . . . the source of distinguishable cultural forms and the background out of which the norms arise that guide us in our everyday life" (p. 6).

The notion of boundaries, especially as associated with what Albanese calls "extraordinary," provides a useful starting point to identify the most universal core of meaning common to virtually all definitions of spirituality and religion. These definitions contain as a minimum an almost universal, although quite diverse, understanding of spirituality and religion as grounded in a dimension of reality beyond the boundaries of the strictly empirically perceived, material world. Elaborations beyond this critical minimum are great. However, this critical minimum—this meta-empirical belief—is important in distinctively identifying the spiritual and religious in comparison with the nonspiritual and nonreligious. Religion and spirituality are grounded in an affirmation of transcendence or "otherness" that is reflected within the boundaries of everyday culture and manifested in identifiable religious forms pointing beyond the boundaries of the ordinary and tangible.

Among the many different understandings of transcendence, there is a broad, twofold difference of opinion that has some special importance for counseling. For those who adhere to religion and spirituality in their more traditional and typical expressions, this transcendental realm is objectively real and legitimately expressed in a variety of religious and spiritual forms and practices. Others, though, value spirituality and religion only as a psychological reality, potentially beneficial constructs of the human mind and heart. As we will see from survey data cited below, the former view is far more prevalent among the general population in the United States. On the other hand, the view of the transcendent as a psychological phenomenon has been prominent in the history of psychology and has had influence in the development of psychotherapy and counseling. These differing views will be discussed more fully in Chapter 2, and implications for counseling practice will be presented in later chapters.

Distinctive meanings. Having identified the affirmation of a transcendental, meta-empirical dimension of reality as constituting the core element of spirituality and religion, we can next describe how spirituality and religion may be distinguished from each other. A typical distinction between religion and spirituality is found in a demarcation between spirituality as a personal affirmation of a transcendent connectedness in the universe and religion as the creedal, institutional, and ritual expression of spirituality that is associated with world religions and denominations (Bergin & Jensen, 1990; Ingersoll, 1994; Shafranske & Gorsuch, 1984; Shafranske & Malony, 1990a, 1990b). Although this distinction is used in this book, we should note that several major conceptualizations of religion (e.g., Allport, 1950; Eliade & Couliano, 1991; James, 1902/1961; H. Smith, 1991) are either very close to what some prefer to define as spirituality or they incorporate spirituality within the domain of religion.

In line with this basic distinction, Shafranske and Gorsuch (1984) offer the following definition of spirituality:

> It has been said that spirituality is the "courage to look within and to trust." What is seen and trusted appears to a deep sense of belonging, of wholeness, of connectedness, and of openness to the infinite. (p. 233)

Elkins, Hedstrom, Hughes, Leaf, and Saunders (1988) offer a complementary definition:

> Spirituality, which comes from the Latin, *spiritus*, meaning "breath of life," is a way of being and experiencing that comes about through awareness of a transcendent dimension and that is characterized by certain identifiable values in regard to self, others, nature, life, and whatever one considers to be the Ultimate. (p. 10)

Based on a review of many different writers, they suggest that the "identifiable values" of spirituality include confidence in the meaning and purpose of life, a sense of mission in life and of the sacredness of life, a balanced appreciation of material values, an altruistic attitude toward others, a vision for the betterment of the world, and a serious awareness of the tragic side of life. Spirituality also means living out these values with discernable effects on oneself, others, and nature and on one's relationship with "whatever one considers to be the Ultimate" (p. 12).

Seen in this light, spirituality involves an active search, a spiritual quest, involving an "innate capacity . . . and tendency to seek to transcend one's current locus of centricity [i.e., the primary psychological position from which one experiences and evaluates life events, such as egocentricity, relational/community-centricity, etc.] . . . toward greater knowledge and love"

4

(C. K. Chandler, Holden, & Kolander, 1992, p. 169). The spiritual search according to Gerald May (1982b) is rooted deeply in the very essence of our humanness and is a "search for an experiential appreciation of the meaning of life" (p. 32), moving us toward transcendent connectedness in love, belonging, and being—from the being of just who we are and into the oneness of ultimate Being.

The term *religion* has come to signify for many the codified, institutionalized, and ritualized expressions of peoples' communal connections to the Ultimate. Corbett (1990) defines it as follows:

> A religion is an integrated system of belief, lifestyle, ritual activities, and institutions by which individuals give meaning to (or find meaning in) their lives by orienting them to what is taken to be sacred, holy, or the highest value. (p. 2)

In this book the term, religion, is used primarily in this sense. However, it is important to note that for many persons religion signifies in concept and practice a profound spirituality that finds expression in shared meanings, rites, and institutional forms. The religious scholar Huston Smith (1991) writes: "authentic religion is the clearest opening through which the inexhaustible energies of the cosmos enter our lives, . . . [then] moving outward through myth and rite [and] symbol" (p. 9). "Taken in its widest sense, [it is] a way of life woven around a people's ultimate concern. . . . [While] in its narrower sense [it is] a concern to align humanity with the transcendental ground of its being" (p. 183). H. Smith's notion of "moving outward" from religion's core connection with the ultimate to a people's or culture's expression of its ultimate concern in myth, rite, and symbol provides a way of understanding religion in a distinctive sense while retaining its inherent connection with spirituality. Recognizing its groundedness in authentic spirituality, we can then let religion primarily signify an "institutionalized system of attitudes, beliefs, and practices" (*Merriam-Webster's Collegiate Dictionary*, 1993) through which people manifest their faith and devotion to an ultimate reality or deity. Religion in this sense is expressed in such world religions as Judaism, Christianity, Islam, Hinduism, Buddhism, Confucianism, and Taoism as well as the many institutionalized variations—denominations, sects, cults—within each of these. The great variety of religions displays even more complexity when one considers the personal twist that each person gives to his or her own religious belief.

Distinctions made by laypersons and professionals. Although spirituality and religion are closely associated with one another in their core meaning and content, research indicates that many people do make distinctions between the two. For example, in a recent national study of participants in various small groups, many with a spiritual/religious orientation, Wuthnow (1994) found that 55% of the respondents highly agreed that one's spirituality does not depend on being involved in a religious organization. A 1993 West Coast survey identified "spiritual seekers" whose belief in God, existential questioning, and spiritual longings were similar to those in traditional religions, but who pursued their spiritual longing in personal ways that draw eclectically on diverse religious and philosophical traditions and generally avoid religious dogmas and traditional churches (Lattin, 1993). In a study of hospice workers, Millison and Dudley (1992) found that although these caregivers considered themselves religious, they rated their spirituality as stronger than their religiosity, which suggests that for some their spirituality was not attached to religion.

The distinction between spirituality and religion is striking among mental health professionals. In a national survey of professional counselors, counselors showed considerable disagreement about certain elements of traditional religiousness but expressed a highly consensual affirmation of values stated in spiritual terms (E. W. Kelly, in press). In a national survey of clinical psychologists, Shafranske and Malony (1990b) found that less than one in five respondents agreed that organized religion was the primary source of their spirituality, with the majority of respondents characterizing their spiritual beliefs and practices as an alternative spiritual path that is not part of an organized religion. Other surveys of such mental health professionals as psychologists, psychiatrists, and social workers have found much the same results (Bergin & Jensen, 1990; Shafranske & Gorsuch, 1984).

For many people, the two terms appear to mark a significant difference between, on the one hand, a personal affirmation of the transcendent with a commitment to spiritual/humanistic values and, on the other hand, an affiliation with and allegiance to organized religion. Given this currently common (although by no means unanimous) understanding of the two terms, both terms are generally used in this book according to this distinction, with, however, the equally important understanding that religion in its authentic, intrinsic sense is grounded in a life-guiding spirituality (Allport & Ross, 1967; Gorsuch & McPherson, 1989).

Although a distinction between spirituality and religion is useful for conveying perceptual and practical differences about transcendental beliefs and practices, a sharp and judgmental separation between the two, especially for counselors, is neither sound nor constructive. Such a separation finds at one extreme spiritually oriented people who apparently see only the manifold institutional and ritualistic aspects of religions, especially in forms that appear to have little spiritual depth or human warmth. These "spiritual" individuals want to avoid a seeming bazaar of religions, as well as what they perceive as the hypocrisy and clubbiness associated them. However, the problem with avoiding religion, or oversimplifying it as a defective form of religiosity or churchiness, is that one runs the danger of misconstruing the positive and deeply spiritual involvement that many persons have with organized religion. Nonaffiliated spiritually oriented people, including counselors, may be more comfortable with noninstitutional spirituality. Nevertheless, counselors need to take care that a personal discomfort with the earthiness and sometimes quirkiness of concrete religions does not blind them to other peoples' positive regard for and involvement in traditional religions and religious practice.

At the other extreme of a judgmental separation between spirituality and religion are some traditional religionists who view all forms of nonaffiliated spirituality as suspect, even dangerous, forms of syncretism. Observing unchurched spiritual seekers manifesting their spirituality in a variety of forms taken from diverse religious and philosophical traditions, traditional religionists fault, even sometimes condemn, spiritual beliefs and practices that appear to water down scriptural teaching, traditional dogma, and religious laws. In this traditionally religious view, all nontraditional spirituality tends to be lumped together as spiritualistic beliefs that promote strange, selfish, and potentially immoral practices. The problem with simplistically associating nontraditional spirituality with its esoteric and occult manifestations is that one is apt to miss or misconstrue the deeply religious and humanly benevolent attitude toward others and the universe that nonaffiliated but spiritually committed people hold. Traditionally religious counselors in particular may have to take care that their own religious convictions do not lead them to devalue the integrity and motives of spiritual seekers who are outside traditional religious affiliations.

Therefore, to readers who very likely represent a wide variety of religious and spiritual traditions as well as no religious tradition at all, please remain open to the generally positive use throughout this book of spirituality and religion. Both terms are used to represent somewhat distinctive but inherently positive ways of people manifesting their personal and communal beliefs in the transcendental dimension of reality. To omit either, to artificially separate them, or to confuse their special meanings would be to distort or trivialize the deep and diverse religious/spiritual attitudes that so many people hold and bring to counseling. In practical terms, a counseling approach that is sensitive to religious and spiritual diversity builds on an ecumenical attitude and pursues an eclectic approach that can accommodate the pluralistic manifestations of religion and spirituality (Bergin & I. R. Payne, 1991).

Varieties of religious and spiritual traditions

A full treatment of the varieties of religious and spiritual traditions is beyond the scope of this book. Nonetheless, any effort to effectively incorporate the spiritual/religious dimension into counseling must be informed with a reasonably broad recognition of the major religious and spiritual traditions in which individuals travel their own spiritual journeys. A reasonably comprehensive organization of major categories of spirituality and religion provides counselors with a conceptual framework for an informed sensitivity to the wide range and general content of beliefs that spiritually and religiously oriented persons may bring to counseling. This broad knowledge is becoming increasingly important as the cultural and religious diversity of countries like the United States continues to grow.

Groupings of Religions and Spiritualities

Religions. A logical starting place for framing a broad knowledge of religion and spirituality is with the world's major religions, defined as those religious traditions that have a long and identifiable history, have a large number of adherents, and are more or less found all across the world. Using these criteria, Huston Smith (1991) identifies Hinduism, Buddhism, Confucianism, Taoism, Islam, Judaism, and Christianity, and within each of these "differences that are too numerous to be delineated in a single chapter" (p. 2). The Western reader in particular may be struck by at least two aspects of this list. First, the two predominant religions historically associated with Europe and the Americas, namely Christianity and Judaism, are but two of the world's seven great religions according to Smith. Until relatively recently in the West, especially in the Americas, the religions of the Near and Far East tended to have little or no influence on most Americans' views of religion and spirituality (Corbett, 1990; Ghayur, 1993). Even Islam, the third great Abrahamic religion along with Judaism and Christianity, was for the most part an exotic, even suspect, form of faith for many Americans and Europeans (Briggs, 1993).

In the mainstream popular culture of the United States, the predominant Judeo-Christian perspective long cast an obscuring shadow over knowledge and appreciation, not only of the great religious and spiritual traditions of the East but also those of indigenous peoples. This neglect of indigenous spiritualities is a second striking aspect of Huston Smith's (1991) list of world religions. Smith, however, does not entirely neglect indigenous religions; he discusses them in a final chapter on "the primal religions," which are characterized by oral rather than written traditions, are local rather than universal in scope, and are focused on atemporal causal forces rather than historically embedded sequential events. Given a rising awareness of the cultures and rights of indigenous peoples—for example, the native peoples of the Americas—an initial schema for appreciating religious diversity needs to include a category for the religions and spirituality of indigenous people.

The inclusion of indigenous or "primal" religions takes us a step beyond the major categories of the world religions. For example, surveying religion and spirituality as systems of thought and practice across time (history) and place (geography), Eliade and Couliano (1991) describe 33 world religions. These include still active religions associated with specific peoples and regions (e.g., the religion of the Yoruba practiced by more than 15 million people in Nigeria and the shamanistic religion of the indigenous peoples of the North American plains) and religions that have passed into history. To be sure, many of the religious systems described by Eliade and Couliano have little or no practical relevance for counselors in the United States. However, others certainly do, and even a summary recognition of the scope, diversity, and complex-

9

ity of these many religions adds another important element to the counselor's conceptual framework for a ready openness to the potential range and subtlety of clients' religious issues.

Spiritual movements. Another step in completing a broad framework for a flexible sensitivity to religion is to include a category for spiritual movements generally outside the traditional universal and indigenous religions. To speak of spiritual movements outside traditional religion is not altogether satisfactory. In the American experience, 19th-century transcendental spirituality was one of the forerunners of current spiritualities. Represented especially by Ralph Waldo Emerson and emphasizing nature as the sacred place where the individual's inner eye perceived the presence of the divine in nature, this spirituality grew out of the liberal traditions of American Protestantism (Albanese, 1992). Other predecessors to present-day spiritualities include 19th-century occult and metaphysical movements represented, for example, in spiritualism (contact with the spirits of the dead) and theosophy (special or occult knowledge leading to universal brotherhood and salvation through a disciplined life).

Today in America there is a vast array of alternative spiritualities, many loosely associated with the New Age movement. As noted above, many conservative Christians view New Age as a set of dangerous beliefs and practices. For others, however, New Age represents a legitimate and vital form of spirituality. R. Chandler (1988) describes it this way:

> New Age is a hybrid mix of spiritual, social, and political forces, and it encompasses sociology, theology, the physical sciences, medicine, anthropology, history, the human potentials movement, sports, and science fiction. New Age is not a sect or cult, per se. Identifying individuals as "full-blown" New Agers is baffling. Some subscribe to certain portions of New Age, some to others; some dissociate themselves from the movement altogether, though they embrace core aspects of its thinking. . . . [and] may simply think of it as a pragmatic, humanistic philosophy of life. (p. 17)

Within this hybrid of New Age movements, key premises are the following: everything is one vast interconnected process; humanity is one, with a hidden inner self that reflects and is connected to the divinity of the universe; through enlightening practices like yoga and meditation, humans can tap the divine energy and transform reality; and reincarnation allows the soul to progress toward this transformation through many life cycles (R. Chandler,

1988). These premises do not, of course, constitute any kind of New Age creed, but they do make up a more or less widely shared set of beliefs undergirding much of New Age.

Major elements of the spirituality of New Age can be seen in the spirituality described in psychological literature (see, e.g., Elkins, Hedstrum, Hughes, Leaf, & Saunders, 1988, and Shafranske & Gorsuch, 1984). This is not to say that the spirituality described in the psychological literature is a product or a part of New Age. But it does point to the interweaving of various expressions of spirituality and assorted forms of religions, and it highlights the difficulty of distinctly identifying specific models of spirituality or clearly separating spirituality from the diverse systems of religion. An alert sensitivity to spiritual and religious issues in counseling requires the counselor at the most basic level to have an appreciative understanding of how diversely these issues can be manifested across a remarkable variety and intermixing of religious and spiritual beliefs.

An expression of spirituality with particular relevance to counseling is that nested in the 12 steps of Alcoholic Anonymous (AA), a recovery program that is now widely used for many different kinds of addictions and dependencies and adapted across cultural differences (Buxton, D. E. Smith, & Seymour, 1987; D. E. Smith, 1994; D. E. Smith, Buxton, Bilal, & Seymour, 1993). The 12-step program and the related 12 traditions of AA are deeply infused, historically, conceptually, and practically, with a spirituality of trust in a benevolent transcendence ("a Power greater than ourselves" [Step 2], "God *as we understand Him*" [Steps 3 and 11]), caring human connections (making amends to all persons we have harmed [Steps 8 and 9], the "common welfare" of "A.A. unity"), and an action-oriented spiritual awareness ("a spiritual awakening" leading to helping others [Step 12]) (Alcoholics Anonymous World Services, 1992; Kurtz, 1988). Twelve-step spirituality is not without controversy and varying interpretations in the mental health field (Ellis, 1985; Khantzian & Mack, 1994); however, especially when distinguished from the particularities of religion, 12-step spirituality is widely regarded as a core, integral part of the recovery program (D. E. Smith, 1994). The spirituality of the 12-step program is connected especially with the acceptance of a power (Higher Power) greater than oneself, providing "a connection with an unknown reality beyond the manifest one and a higher self both within and outside the person"

(Khantzian & Mack, 1994, pp. 90–91), and "the tapping of an unexpected inner resource and identification of this resource as their own conception of a Power greater than themselves" (D. E. Smith, 1994, p. 111). The success of the 12-step program, including for many its spiritual aspects, makes self-help groups that use it an important adjunctive helping resource for counselors (Humphreys, 1993).

Differences within Religious and Spiritual Traditions

The broad categories of major religious and spiritual heritages give the counselor a way to view religious belief and practice *across* traditions and cultures. A further refinement in knowledge calls for complementing this broad perspective with some appreciation of the significant differences that exist within major groupings of religions and spirituality. The counselor is not, of course, expected to have expert knowledge about the great variety of intrareligious differences; however, an appreciation that many important nuances exist can help the counselor avoid falling into stereotypical thinking.

Some idea of the multiple diversity of American religions is conveyed in the following introductory statement from the 1993 edition of the *Encyclopedia of American Religions* (Melton, 1993):

> The United States is currently home to more than 1,500 different primary religious organizations—churches, sects, cults, temples, societies, missions—each seeking to be the place of expression of the primary religious allegiances and sentiments of its members and adherents. The majority of these organizations are Christian churches, and the overwhelming majority of Americans who engage in any outward religious activity are members of one of the more than 900 Christian denominations. Prior to the 1880s, the Christian churches had little competition, except for Native American religions. . . . [Since then] the church has been rent with schism (from 20 denominations in 1800 to more than 900 in 1988), while at the same time having to face competition from the literally hundreds of different varieties of the great world religions and an imposing assortment of new innovative American faiths, including a revived and assertive Native American spirituality. (p. 1)

Christianity. Christianity includes by far the largest group of religious groups and religious adherents of any religion in America. Melton (1993) identifies 19 major religious families, with 57 subdivisions within American Christianity alone. While the larger body of Christian and Jewish scriptures and tradition represents the principal common ground of these religions, the divisions among them highlight their different emphases in belief and practice. Such diversity can be overwhelming without an intelligible scheme for conceptually organizing groups according to significant commonalities and differences. Two initial crosscutting categories for helping counselors bring a degree of conceptual and practical clarity to their understanding of Christian religion are: (a) a grouping according to mainstream religion, Eastern Orthodoxy, sectarian churches, and universalist-humanistic churches (Corbett, 1990; Melton, 1993) and (b) a grouping according to liberal, conservative, and fundamentalist religious orientation (Corbett, 1990). Cults are considered in a separate category of marginal religious, quasi-religious, and magic-oriented groups.

Mainstream Christian religion in America includes the major Protestant groups (Baptists, United Methodists, Lutherans, Presbyterians, and Episcopalians) and Roman Catholics. (Mainstream religion in America also includes Judaism, which is discussed below.) These major traditional Christian groups—although certainly diverse in several important creedal, institutional, and ritualistic ways—share certain common characteristics that distinguish them from nonmainstream or sectarian forms of religion. They generally share a common religious heritage in the Bible (Christian and Jewish scriptures), a belief in a creative and saving God and the central role of Jesus in the relationship of humanity and God, a morality of personal spiritual growth and social caring inspired by biblical tenets and tradition, and an affirmation of the God-connected destiny of human beings. In addition to these directly religious tenets, the mainstream churches are characterized by a generally culture-affirming stance, relatively open and welcoming membership requirements, tolerance and friendliness toward other religious groups, the forming of voluntary associations across religious groups to carry out large and mutually acceptable projects, and toleration of diversity of opinion within religious groups (Corbett, 1990). Mainstream religions draw much of their membership from middle- and upper-class American society and usually employ highly educated, full-time ministers. These characteristics of the mainstream churches, while important to an understanding of their social and personal effects, constitute no more than a broad-stroke picture; when observed more closely, they reveal a number of important or subtle differences.

13

Nonetheless, these general characteristics offer counselors one important lens through which they may *initially and partially* view clients from mainstream religions.

Eastern Orthodox churches in America have been characterized religiously by their rich liturgical worship and focus on contemplative practice, both of which reflect traditional Christian beliefs in the divinity of Christ and the Trinitarian nature of God. Culturally, the Orthodox churches have been closely identified with their traditional ethnic and cultural groups of Eastern Europe, Russia, and the eastern Mediterranean countries. Orthodoxy in America, largely because of its Eastern European, Russian, and Near Eastern heritage as well as its liturgically distinctive form of worship, has not been generally thought of as part of mainstream Christianity in the United States. However, in recent times efforts toward unity in the Orthodox Church in America and the general Americanizing of second- and third-generation Orthodox families have led Orthodoxy toward mainstream American Christianity (Albanese, 1992; Corbett, 1990). Depending on their generational standing in the United States, clients who come to counseling with an Orthodox religious background will more or less reflect an adherence to traditional Christian belief and an attachment to the cultural mores of those countries with which Orthodoxy is closely associated.

The sectarian religions, a number of which are "newmade" in America (Albanese, 1992, p. 219), differ from the mainstream religions in several key ways (Corbett, 1990). The term, sectarian, is used here not with a negative connotation but in an expanded sociological sense to identify religious groups representing, in relation to established mainstream religion, newer, often more intense (Marty, 1993) religious groups. The sectarian religions emphasize some ideal expression of Christianity, either enhanced with new revelations or intensified by a return to what is considered original or primitive belief and practice (Albanese, 1992). Although there are substantial differences in belief and practice among these churches, they share several common elements that distinguish them from mainstream churches. In contrast to mainstream religion, a number of these so-called sectarian religions, each according to its particular tenets, tend in varying degrees to foster a sense of separation from the world and the mainstream culture and make greater demands in life-style change for their members. There is a tendency among many of these churches to encourage socializing exclusively within their own groups. The sectarian churches typically have writings, often of their founders, whose authority is equal to and/or strongly complements that of the Bible. These extrabiblical sources, as well as distinctive emphases on different aspects of scripture and Christian tradition, play an important part in certain striking differences in beliefs, practices, and attitudes among these churches.

The grouping of sectarian religions prominently includes the following diverse kinds of churches: (a) the Holiness and Pentecostal churches (e.g., the Assemblies of God), which grew out of movements within the Methodist and Baptist traditions, emphasize the Bible as the literal word of God, and focus on the experience of God's saving power (including enthusiastic charismatic experiences such as speaking in tongues) to make persons holy in spirit and nonworldly in life-style; (b) the European Free-Church denominations like the Mennonites and Amish, whose tradition of deep piety is marked with tolerance of and a communal separation from the world, and the Quakers, whose stress on the spark of divinity in all persons is frequently expressed in social activism and peace work; (c) the Seventh-Day Adventists, whose general Protestant faith is complemented with beliefs about the imminent return and reign of Christ, the primacy of the Saturday Sabbath, and an emphasis on healthy life-style and health care; (d) the Jehovah's Witnesses, whose great stress on Bible-based belief highlights the soon-coming Kingdom of God, the need for repentance, and a worship of God that is not by contaminated image worship (e.g., a national flag) but is also consistent with an interest in secular community affairs; (e) the Latter-Day Saints (Mormons), whose distinctively Christian beliefs about a newly restored apostolic church based on the visionary life and writings of their founder Joseph Smith are complemented by an optimistic, healthy, morally upright, and family-oriented life-style; and (f) the Christian Scientists, whose allegiance to basic Christian tenets is characterized by belief in the basic goodness and rationality of all creation, the locating of sickness and sin in the erring human mind rather than in nature itself, and the power of God to directly effect healing through the fundamentally harmonious order of the world as originally intended by God (Corbett, 1990; Melton, 1993).

Brief characterizations like these are only sketchy illustrations to help counselors to *begin* to cognitively prepare themselves to work with clients who present with religious issues from these religions. Counselors cannot let these characterizations, either of mainstream or sectarian religion, become stereotypes or categories for pigeonholing individual clients. The theology of these churches is far more complex, diverse, and nuanced than can be presented here. Moreover, the way in which individuals interpret and live their religion adds great personalized differences in religious belief and practice. The value of understanding principal differences and commonalities among mainstream and sectarian religion is that it adds to counselors' overall attitudinal and cognitive readiness to explore more deeply, with their clients and in further study, the potential relevance and impact of the spiritual/religious dimension.

The Black church. Although ethnicity has played an important role in many churches in the United States, the particular experience of African Americans deserves special attention (Albanese, 1992; Corbett, 1990; Marty, 1993). An adequate treatment of African Americans' original condition of slavery in America, of efforts to suppress their native cultures and religions, and of their experience of social and economic oppression is beyond the scope of this book. It must be noted, however, that the distinctive history of African Americans has played an important role in the development of religious belief and expression that has come to characterize the Black churches of America. Again, we must take care to avoid stereotypes. African Americans, historically and currently, have participated to a greater or lesser extent in many of the mainstream and sectarian religions noted above. For example, many Africans who came early to Louisiana, and to a lesser extent to Maryland, became members of the Catholic church. Currently, African Americans are reintroducing some of the traditional beliefs and practices associated with African religions and cultures from which they were violently cut off at the time of the slave trade. Other African Americans have risen to positions of high leadership in traditionally Euro-American churches, for example, becoming bishops in the Episcopal church. In many respects, the religious diversity of African Americans reflects the diversity of American religion in general.

Nonetheless, the identification of many African-Americans with Protestantism, especially the Baptist, Methodist, and Pentecostal and Holiness churches, has given rise to a distinctive Black church in America. The Black church understood in this sense has come to incorporate an understanding and practice of Christianity that focuses on God's support in this life's trials; God's promise of salvation in the life to come; the building of a religiously grounded community for social and personal support; and God's current will for justice, freedom, and personal dignity for an oppressed people in the midst of a society very much dominated by Euro-Americans and negatively influenced by racist attitudes and stereotypes. Certainly not all African Americans belong to the historical Black churches, but those who do tend to reflect, according to the extent of their commitment, the core biblical beliefs typical of the Baptist and Methodist churches (e.g., personal salvation in Jesus, the power of God's spirit for comfort and salvation, and the promise of eternal life for those who are saved in faith), the importance of the church community as a place of support and help, and a strong belief in God's intention for the freedom and dignity of everyone, expressed in the struggles and programs of African Americans toward their equal and rightful status in American society.

Judaism. "Being Jewish has always meant being a people as well as serving a God" (Albanese, 1992, p. 55). The largest non-Christian minority in America, numbering approximately six million, Judaism is a religion deeply rooted in the Jewish religious experience of a long history of ongoing and sometimes contentious dialogue with God. This religious history is embedded especially in the written laws and guides of the Torah and Talmud and set forth in prophecy, poetry, and historical stories in the Hebrew scriptures (the *Tanach*, or generally what Christians refer to as the Old Testament). Judaism is also observed in rituals (e.g., Sabbath, Passover, Rosh Hashanah, Yom Kippur) that bind the community in memory of its covenanted history with God and call Jews in their covenant with God to lives of moral goodness and justice toward others.

Religious Judaism is represented in three main categories: Orthodox, representing the modern close observance of traditional Jewish belief and practice; Reform, a modern adaptation of Jewish practice to the contemporary world; and Conservative, representing a middle-ground observance of Jewish tradition. Judaism is also a culture; indeed, Lovinger (1990) maintains that "Judaism may be better understood as a culture than a religion, for the family is the crucible of character formation and socialization to

17

the norms and values of the group" (p. 70). "Industriousness, adult study, educational accomplishment, familial devotion, enjoyment of legitimate pleasure, careful observance of both ritual and ethical practices, and a concern for the needy are traditional values inculcated in the child, through parental behavior, the synagogue, and the Jewish school" (Lovinger, 1990, p. 71). The formal divisions within Judaism (Orthodox, Reform, and Conservative) are suggestive of the even greater diversity among individual Jews whose lives and outlooks are as diverse as America itself and make a lie of stubborn stereotypes. For the counselor, an initial appreciation of religious and cultural aspects of Jewish clients provides an open-minded sensitivity to the likelihood of values focused on achievement, altruism, and concern for family and children, along with internalized pressures to achieve according to these values. As with every other client, the counselor's informed respect for Judaism provides a loose framework of knowledge for an individualized understanding of each Jewish client, not for predetermined expectations for all clients.

Native American religion. After years of authoritarian missionary activity and European cultural imperialism that resulted in most Native Americans' currently being Christian, Native American religion is now experiencing a revival of traditional rituals, practiced in exclusively Native American forms as well as being blended with Christian forms (Wax & Wax, 1993). Before the arrival of the Europeans, Native American religion was diverse across peoples and represented many traditions. However, it is possible to identify a traditional worldview with common characteristics that run through most Native American religions. Albanese (1992) describes this worldview as follows:

> In general, Native American religions possessed a strong sense of continuity with the things that people held sacred. Both in space and time, Native Americans saw what they conceived as holy and mysterious as very closely related to their daily existence. . . . Native Americans thought of a world to which they were bound by ties of kinship. There were the Grandfathers who were Thunder Beings; there was Grandmother Spider; and there was Mother Corn. There were animals who took on human form such as Coyote the Trickster or sacred birds or sacred buffalo. There were gifted human beings such as shamans—holy people who, as sacred healers, mystics, and magicians incorporated into one, were said to fly as birds and talked to the animals. . . . The world, in short, was a huge extended family network,

with the Indians existing as younger and humbler brothers and sisters among their more venerable relations. (p. 27)

This traditional worldview still has considerable influence in the religion of contemporary Native Americans. However, contact with other cultures over time has resulted in basically three variations on this core worldview: (a) the maintaining of traditional beliefs and practices but adding elements for a syncretistic blending of Christian elements into the Native American religious traditions; (b) the forming and taking up of new religions based on new visions that modify the traditional Native American views with Christian concepts (e.g., the imminent end of the world with the birth of a new world); and (c) an accepting of Christian beliefs within established Christian denominations while maintaining some aspects of traditional views and practices (Albanese, 1992). With this in mind, a sensitively informed approach to counseling with respect to the religiousness of Native American clients involves an awareness of the potential influence of a traditional worldview as described above along with a recognition of different degrees of attachment and devotion to various Christian religious and spiritual beliefs and practices. To the extent that the traditional Native American worldview is influential in the client's life, the counselor is likely to find that the client is responsive to an approach that respects the spiritual connectedness of reality and the value of traditional rituals.

Islam. Although there is no accurate count of the number of Muslims in America, carefully calculated estimates place the number at about 3.3 million in the 1980s (Stone, 1991; Haddad & Lummis, 1987), making Islam the second largest American religious minority after Judaism. Furthermore, it is growing rapidly with increased immigration from traditionally Islamic countries (Bagby, 1994; Melton, 1993). Islam, as is true of the other great religions, is marked with considerable diversity. However, fundamental Islamic beliefs and practices constitute a rich religious and cultural commonality, which Haddad and Lummis (1987) describe as follows:

Beyond the variety of practices and customs that may distinguish one Islamic culture from another and one individual Muslim from another, a basic commonality is provided by the overall structure of Islam that binds the adherents together. Belief that the Qur'an is the final revelation of God to humanity and adherence to its specific injunctions is the cornerstone of the common identity. In addition to the Qur'an, the collections of traditions (*hadith*), which are believed to be sayings from and about the Prophet Muhammad as remembered and written down by his followers, are an integral part of Islamic teaching. Together, the Qur'an and the *hadith* provide a common bond for all Muslims and are the basis for the Islamic law or shari'a, which sets out a complete way of life. (p. 16)

According to Islamic belief, the Qur'an contains God's final universal message to humankind through the prophet Muhammad. It completes the partial revelations given through Abraham, Moses, and Jesus and calls all persons to the worship of the one and all-supreme God, *Allah*. In practice it calls for five specific acts of worship ("five pillars of Islam") that shape the lives of Muslims. These are, first, the affirmation that there is no God but Allah and that Muhammad is His prophet; second, ritual prayer performed five times a day; third, the sharing of wealth with the needy; fourth, fasting from sunrise to sunset during the Islamic month of Ramadan as a way of increasing one's consciousness of God; fifth, a pilgrimage to Mecca (Muhammad's birthplace) at least once in one's lifetime, finances permitting.

Differences among Muslims stem in part from historical, political, and theological controversies. For example, there are within Islam five major schools of Islamic jurisprudence that apply the vast body of Islamic law to all aspects of life (Haneff, 1979; Schimmel, 1992). Another distinction that is sometimes made within Islam is that of the Sunnis and Shiites, based on differences of opinion about successorship to Muhammad and the legitimate sources of tradition and teaching. However, in America many Muslims consider this distinction between Sunni and Shiites an unnecessary carryover from political disputes elsewhere in the world and unhelpful in the understanding and practice of Islam (L. Bakhtiar, personal communication, March 7, 1994; Haneef, 1979). Another major tradition in Islam includes those who follow the Sufi order, which represents a variety of disciplines and intellectual endeavors rooted in the mystical tradition of Islam.

Of special importance in the United States are the Black Muslims, represented today in two major divisions. One is the American Muslim Mission, which the son of Elijah Muhammad, longtime leader of the Nation of Islam, has now guided into Islamic orthodoxy; the other is the newly resurrected Nation of Islam representing a reassertion of Elijah Muhammad's heterodox ideas about Blacks' favored but now oppressed place in God's plan and

Black nationalism/separatism, as well as a strict code of personal moral behavior (Mamiya, 1993; Melton, 1993). African Americans now constitute about 42% of the American Muslim population (Bagby, 1994).

In addition to these theologically and historically based differences, Muslims in America today "exhibit a range of responses in their understanding of what constitutes the essentials of Islam and Islamic law and what is required to be a good and responsible Muslim" (Haddad & Lummis, 1987, p. 24). Muslims in America, representing in many cases first- and second-generation immigrants from predominantly Muslim countries, express varying degrees of concern about the potential negative effects of integration into American society on Islamic belief and practice. This is especially true of conservative or strictly traditional Muslims who note serious differences between America's secular materialistic culture and the tenets of Islam. For example, the Western values that undergird modern counseling (e.g., individualistic self-fulfillment, materialistic success, free self-determination, and ethical relativity with the rationalization of guilt feelings) are seen to be at odds with such Islamic values as a God-centered sense of altruistic collective responsibility, personal actualization as a holistic consonance of the person with God's pleasure, free choice in line with God's law, and corrective repentance to modify guilt-inducing sinful acts (Badri, 1979; Jafari, 1993).

Of course, the degree to which an individual Muslim adheres to his or her religion affects the extent to which a counselor needs to incorporate traditional Islamic values in the counseling process. However, for Muslim clients whose Islamic observance is strict or moderate (46% and 36%, respectively, according to Haddad and Lummis's [1987] findings for a sample of mosque members), the counselor needs to understand and respect the client's Islamic values of God's primacy, God's laws for righteous behavior, and the requirements of religious practices to the extent that these values have a bearing on the therapeutic and developmental welfare of the client.

Religions of the Far East: Hinduism and Buddhism. Hinduism and Buddhism are two distinct world religions originating in India (and in the case of Buddhism, prevalent across Asia), but they share a special emphasis on personal knowledge and enlightenment through practices such as meditation and physical discipline

21

(e.g., yoga) that aim toward higher forms of consciousness for spiritual peace and a transcendent oneness with the power and harmony of the universe. This aspect of Hinduism and Buddhism is especially congenial with the mostly noninstitutional transcendental movements in 19th-century American history and the current popularity of nontraditional forms of spirituality and religious syncretism in the United States.

However, Hinduism and Buddhism also differ in important ways from one another and are quite diverse within themselves (Albanese, 1992). For example, in addition to the ways of enlightenment that are characteristic of such practices as Transcendental Meditation or yoga associated with Hinduism and the Tibetan or Zen observances of Buddhism, there are also the "church" forms of Hinduism and Buddhism. These latter are maintained by devotional communities of believers who worship and practice according to religious traditions brought from India, China, Japan, and Southeast Asia. In those parts of the United States where there has been a rise in immigrants from these areas in recent years, these "church" forms of Hinduism and Buddhism have also increased, accompanied in some cases by changes reflecting the perspectives of new North American adherents (Fields, 1992). For the vast majority of American counselors whose cultural and religious heritage is Western and Judeo-Christian, a readiness to work effectively with clients of traditional Hindu or Buddhist faith calls for an openness to a non-Western worldview that emphasizes a spiritually holistic understanding of life. This holistic perspective is associated with diverse forms of religious devotion, enlightenment, and discipline aiming toward moral goodness in this life and a transformation into an eternal oneness with the spiritual power of the universe.

Contemporary American spirituality: a bridge between religion and humanism. One major direction that the expansive diversity of religion has taken is toward a noncreedal, nondogmatic, often noninstitutionalized affirmation of basic humanistic values (e.g., altruistic involvement in improving the worldly conditions of human existence for all persons) and basic transcendental values (e.g., an active appreciation of humanity's connectedness with all nature and the destiny of the universe). Originating within the Christian tradition, the Universalist Unitarian Association is an example of a noncreedal congregational or "church" form of humanistic spirituality guided by principles affirming the dignity of all, the freedom and responsibility of each person to search for knowledge and meaning, the interconnectedness of all life, and the ethical importance of justice and compassion in building one world of peace. The wisdom of all world religions is affirmed as contributing to these life-guiding principles, and tolerance toward diversity in personal beliefs is emphasized (Corbett, 1990). Another expression of universalist, humanistic spirituality is Baha'i, which arose primarily out of the Islamic heritage in contact with new religious movements. Baha'i affirms the equality of all human beings and all races, with the goal of unifying all human beings in a universal peace. While affirming the developmental value of all religions for the earlier stages of history, Baha'i offers itself as a mature religion for an emerging age of unity and peace (Albanese, 1992).

It is a small step from the "church" or "religious" forms of universalist, humanistic spirituality as manifested in Universalist-Unitarianism and Baha'i to the nonchurch-affiliated humanistic spirituality that characterizes a wide range of people outside organized religion. Spirituality in this sense represents the transcendent, interconnected dimension of existence and a way of achieving meaning according to values for improving human life and respecting all creation in relation to what one considers the Ultimate. Like members of the "church" forms of humanistic spirituality, those who affirm a noninstitutional spirituality may be theistic, agnostic, or atheistic. They may express their spirituality in philosophical or religious terms taken from disparate sources in the world religions, ancient and contemporary schools of philosophy, mythology, and science. The client with a nonaffiliated spiritual worldview will generally be open to counseling interventions that recognize the healing effect of increased self-awareness connected with a spiritual, transcendent, or metaphysical dimension of meaning, as, for example, in certain forms of meditation and yoga. At the same time, such clients are likely to be averse to any spiritually oriented interventions that are packaged in terms of organized religious beliefs and practices. For counselors, spirituality understood in this sense constitutes a kind of core noncreedal orientation to the spiritual/religious dimension, the broadest form of spiritual belief that the counselor may use as an ethical and therapeutic point of connection for spiritually oriented counseling interventions.

For clients who profess no spiritual or religious beliefs or values influenced by spirituality even in the broadest sense, the inclusion of spirituality in counseling becomes moot. This situation has ethical and therapeutic implications for how counselors, in practice, implement their understanding of human development and human well-being, especially when such understandings include a spiritual dimension (see, e.g., Witmer & Sweeney, 1992). This question of diverging client-counselor spiritual beliefs will be addressed in Chapter 3.

Cults. At the margins of religion are the groups whose extreme divergence from mainstream religion and spirituality causes them to be identified as cults. Unlike sects that have often grown from mainstream religions and have found more or less long-standing success and acceptance within society, cults represent relatively new and intense groups with beliefs and practices that strike most persons as strange and deviant, even dangerous. Of course, what is strange, deviant, and dangerous is to some extent in the eye of the beholder, so that the term "cult" carries a pejorative connotation that is sometimes applied without careful discrimination to a wide variety of groups that persons of other groups disapprove of. This loose and typically pejorative use of the term cult as well as the difficulties involved in clearly specifying the major commonalities of these deviant, intense religious groups have led some authorities to suggest that the term lacks adequate descriptive clarity and might be replaced with terms such as marginal religions (Corbett, 1990) or intense group belief systems (Levine, 1989). Perhaps reflecting this dissatisfaction with the term cult, Melton (1993), in his extraordinarily comprehensive cataloguing and description of American religions, does not use cult to describe a specific religious group.

Nonetheless, the term continues to be widely used to describe intense, new, marginal religious groups that are not part of the dominant religious tradition. Typical characteristics of most cults are intensely shared and bonding beliefs, often involving religious expectations about a dramatic world change, and a high degree of group cohesiveness and social regimentation within an authoritarian structure, headed by a charismatic leader and requiring members' sharp separation from nongroup members (Corbett, 1990; Galanter, 1989b). Although cults often represent a deviant form of religious belief involving in many cases idiosyncratic revelations of a supernatural or occult nature, "some have no more than an ill-defined ideological orientation" (Galanter, 1989c, p. 6). "Many cults do not offer a sufficiently complete theology to qualify as religions, but instead are limited to providing magical services or to propagating myth and amusement" (Bainbridge & Stark, 1992, p. 290). With this understanding of cults, specific examples usually include groups with highly modified versions of the mainstream Christian view such as the Unification Church (so-called Moonies), Faith Assembly, and the Way International; groups with Eastern roots such as Krishna Consciousness; and groups with a magical worldview like Witchcraft, Neo-Paganism, Voodoo, and Satanism (Corbett, 1990; Melton, 1993).

Especially relevant to counseling, some cults are known to attract highly dissatisfied, religiously distressed, or even emotionally troubled persons. Many are middle class, between the ages of 18 and 25, and are searching for certainty in belief and structure in living (Corbett, 1990; Galanter, 1989b). Recent reports show that cults are also attracting large numbers of people over 50—a group whose members' accumulated life savings makes them attractive candidates for unscrupulous cult recruiters who take advantage of those who may be lonely or sick and looking for spiritual support (Collins & Frantz, 1994). Such individuals are psychologically vulnerable for responding sympathetically to a cult's intensely delivered message of clear teachings and to acceptance into a tightly knit social group; young or old, they not only will join the cult but may also cut off past relationships for a new life within the group.

The vulnerability of the recruit, combined with the persuasiveness of a charismatic leader and the authoritarian regimentation of the group, has led to charges of brainwashing and coercion to keep people within the group. This has led to dissatisfied adherents and their families at times to take extraordinary measures (e.g., deprogramming, lawsuits) to get the adherent away from the cult. It may be inaccurate to characterize *all* cults as mind-controlling and coercive. However, individual cases of people trying to extricate themselves from cults as well as the dramatic horror of group murder-suicide at the People's Temple in Jonestown, Guyana, in 1978; the still lingering questions of the deadly siege of the Branch Davidian compound at Waco, Texas, in 1993; and the conflagration of buildings and adherents of the Order of the Solar Temple in Switzerland in 1994 raise legitimate concerns about the adverse emo-

25

tional effects of some cults. These events also point to the dangers of religious and spiritual beliefs that become isolated from critical dialogue and of practices that are hidden from ordinary view.

Experts of American religion advise against alarmist stigmatizing of all cults—a caution for counselors not to stereotype all cults or marginal religions as dangerous in their strangeness. On the other hand, the clear negative effects of cults on many people call for counselors to be prepared to assess potentially adverse impacts (e.g., destructive social deviancy and antisocial behavior, personally self-destructive or self-defeating ways of thinking) of cult involvement on a cult-client's problems. This issue will be addressed in Chapter 5.

Conservative, Fundamentalist, and Liberal Religion

Religious attitudes can be understood not only in terms of the content of peoples' beliefs and the religious groupings that institutionalize these beliefs but also in terms of how closely and literally individuals and groups adhere to the traditional formulations of these beliefs. Considering religion in this latter perspective leads us to three different ways in which the content of religious belief is interpreted, with differential effects on peoples' attitudes and behaviors. These three ways of believing are typically described as conservative, fundamental, and liberal. Although this categorization cannot capture fully the complexity of religious belief and behavior and needs to be applied with care, it does reflect significant, influential differences among religious believers. Fundamentalism, conservatism, and liberalism in religion generally represent a continuum from strict, literal adherence to orthodox, traditional formulations of beliefs, through more moderate but nonetheless close and firm belief in traditional teaching and doctrine, to a far more flexible stand in interpreting traditional belief and practice according to human advances in science, rational enlightenment, and contemporary life-styles.

Christianity. A specific, major example of differences among these three broad approaches to belief is the way in which Christians interpret the Bible (Corbett, 1990). Fundamentalists believe that the Bible is without error of any kind and that it is to be understood literally—every word being the unerring word of God. The Bible is the infallible guide for knowing and living. All other sources of knowledge and all life-styles are judged in the light of the unerring, literal teaching of the Bible. Conservatives believe that the Bible is the inspired word of God, conveying God's revealed message as the standard of belief and practice; they do not insist, however, on the literal interpretation of the Bible in every respect or its influence in all matters outside religious belief and practice (e.g., with regard to details about secular history or geography). For liberals the Bible is a book of collected human writings (e.g., historically and nonhistorically based stories, poems, allegories, ethical teachings, religious interpretations of nature and life) that convey valuable religious and ethical lessons. The Bible is understood in the light of human scholarship, science, and rational inquiry. Based on this particular criterion, Corbett's (1990) analysis of opinion data from 1972 through 1987 indicates that between 40 and 50% of American Christians are conservative, about 40% are fundamentalist, and about 10 to 15% are liberal.

Parallel to differences in biblical belief, conservative Christian believers hold closely to traditional formulations of belief and are cautious about innovations in belief, practice, and ethics: "Conservatism or traditionalism takes the position that the historic faith ought to be preserved insofar as possible, with only minimal regard for changes in the secular world" (Corbett, 1990, p. 184). Christian fundamentalists take an absolutist stand on the infallibility of literal biblical belief, finding such belief completely incompatible with secular humanism, liberalism, modernism, and scientific or rationalistic interpretations of the Bible. Fundamentalists see a sharp distinction between true believers who are saved and nonfundamentalists whose accommodations to this world show them to be the nonsaved who require conversion to fundamentalist belief to avoid eternal damnation. At the other extreme are the religious liberals for whom traditional formulations of belief are open to many interpretations guided by reason, science, and Christianity's core message of the golden rule (the second of the two great Judaic commandments of love of God and neighbor as reaffirmed by Jesus): "Faith and reason, in other words, are understood as partners in a common quest" (Corbett, 1990, p. 186) toward a more enlightened, humanitarian world. Religious liberals are tolerant and open to the belief and practices of many religions and philosophies as being different expressions of an essentially similar message for moving humanity toward a just unity and peace.

While helpful in organizing our understanding of diversity among Christians, the distinctions among fundamentalist, conservative, and liberal Christians are not without their problems and potential pitfalls. Although these distinctions are characteristic of major subgroups within Christianity (e.g., the Assemblies of God Church and the Liberty Baptist Fellowship are institutionally fundamentalist; the Roman Catholic church and Lutheran churches are institutionally conservative; the Universalist-Unitarian church is an institutionally liberal church), they cannot be understood to characterize rigidly all members of any particular religion or church. Especially within mainstream churches like the Episcopal, Methodist, Presbyterian, and Catholic, one finds individual conservative, liberal, and fundamentalist members, as well as those who represent a mixture of one or more of these belief perspectives. Another problem with this distinction is that those unfamiliar with fundamentalist Christians tend to blur distinctions of belief and practice that exist between fundamentalist and evangelical Christians (Marty & Appleby, 1991). Although both exalt the Bible and insist on the primacy of its authority for belief and practice, evangelicals have become more accommodating to modern-day science and more cooperative with nonevangelicals in social, political, and humanitarian concerns.

Judaism and Islam. These brief descriptions of Christian fundamentalism, conservatism, and liberalism can be extended to understand similar divisions in other great world religions. For example, the diversity within Judaism according to Orthodox, Conservative, and Reform movements represents varying degrees of attachment to and practice of traditional Jewish beliefs with varying degrees of accommodation to modern and liberal secular life-styles. Within Islam there are differences of opinion, sometimes obscured by political and religious disputes, that are reflected in varying degrees of literal or nonliteral interpretations of traditional Islamic teaching and varying degrees of accommodation of traditional Islamic practice to modern secular life-styles (Haddad & Lummis, 1987). These differences show up between Islamic fundamentalists who insist on literal understandings and practice of traditional Islamic teaching in contrast to conservative Muslims whose faith, while deeply traditional, is more moderate in application to the modern world. One can also identify liberal Muslims for whom Islam is primarily a rich, religiously grounded culture that can coexist accommodatingly with other religious and secular cultures, not to mention the liberal perspective of adherents of the universalist Baha'i faith.

Spiritualities. The distinction of conservative, fundamental, and liberal is not directly applicable to spirituality outside organized or traditional religions. Indeed, as viewed from the point of view of traditional religionists, nonreligious spirituality of all forms is likely to be viewed as liberal. On the other hand, spirituality outside of traditional religion comes in a variety of forms. These include: (a) theistic, agnostic, and nontheistic forms of existentialism; (b) a wide array of New Age spiritualities including such mind-over-matter practices and phenomena as channeling (acting as an intermediary for spiritual messages), holistic medicine, yoga, telekinesis (moving objects without physical contact), and transcendental meditation; and (c) the personal spiritualities of individuals who affirm in varying degrees and without any institutional connections or New Age practices the transcendental connectedness of all reality and humanistic as well as environmental values related to the individual's sense of an ultimate meaning. In this variety of spiritualities we can see what we might call the more "conservative" perspectives of spiritual individuals who maintain a theistic and/or other-world perspective and/or who are associated with some line of tradition (e.g., Eastern religions or ancient magic rites) in contrast with the more "liberal" perspectives of nonaffiliated individuals whose spirituality complements their primarily empirical, scientific, and rationalistic perspective of reality.

Personal differences in belief. The counselor's knowledge of a client's conservative, fundamentalist, or liberal religious orientation, along with some understanding of the content of the client's spiritual and religious belief, provides an increasingly elaborate schema that the counselor may refine and use to understand each client's individual, idiosyncratic spiritual or religious attitudes as these are relevant to counseling. For example, a counselor's appreciation of a Catholic client's religious concern about a problematic pregnancy also needs to be informed as to the degree of the client's personal openness and flexibility (strict to liberal) with regard to official Catholic teaching about abortion. A counselor's sensitive understanding of a Baptist client's adherence to biblical belief with regard to the role of women also needs to be informed as to the degree of the client's personal fundamentalist, evangelical, or conservative understanding of how the traditional biblical role of women is understood in light of movements toward human equality. A counselor's respect for a Jewish client's concern about an adult child's self-absorbed drift away from traditional Jewish practice in the family also needs to be informed as to the degree that religious belief in God and Jewish religious practice are important in the client's understanding of his or her own Judaism. These are but a few of myriad variations on how religiously and spiritually alert counselors may *begin* to orient themselves to clients whose counseling needs appear to have a therapeutically relevant spiritual/religious dimension.

Culture and Religion

Religion and culture are intimately intertwined. Religion is a part of culture, which makes up and expresses a group's overall pattern of living: "A society's tools, techniques, customs, beliefs, institutions, laws, morality, religion, and art—in short, everything that is uniquely human . . . [by which] members of a society interpret their experience and interact with one another, their environment, their past, and their future" (Vanderburg, 1985, pp. xxii–xxiii). Religion is, in one respect, a separate part of society; this is its "extraordinary" aspect, representing a special, often institutionalized, way of contacting the divine or transcendental. In another important respect, religion is also "ordinary . . . more or less synonymous with culture" (Albanese, 1992, p. 6), and as such it exercises a very important influence on the "customs, laws, beliefs, institutions, morality" of the culture of which it is a part.

Oneness of American religious culture. The interweaving of religion in the larger culture of the United States is very complex, reflecting both a "manyness" and a "oneness" of religion (Albanese, 1992). On the one hand, the oneness of religion in American culture has been formed historically by Calvinist and Puritan Christianity, giving importance to such practical virtues as hard work, frugality, and commitment, and stressing ideals of freedom of conscience, personal morality, individual responsibility, and achievement. In this perspective, worldly success gradually came to be seen as a sign of one's virtuous living. A strong recurring religious theme of looking for a transformed, new future (as represented, e.g., in religious millenialism and utopianism based on biblical and extrabiblical revelations) became reflected in an American ideal of progress. Although many early American religionists were not noted for respectful acceptance of other religious groups, the ideals of freedom (expressed religiously and humanistically) and the requirements for different groups to live together gradually led to increasing religious tolerance, enshrined constitutionally in the separation of church and state.

With the escalating separation of church and state, the religious themes of early America became a prominent part of a kind of American civil or secular religion, an "ordinary" cultural religion of tolerance and freedom, democratic equality, individualism, hard work and material success, and activist progressivism. Despite the incorporation of these religious values into the larger American culture, however, the separation of church and state has led to a highly secularized culture, with nonreligious life-styles increasingly at odds with traditional religious beliefs and practices. Thus the religiously inspired values of the larger American society (i.e., the "oneness" of American religion) have become mixed with secular practices (e.g., the exploitation of sex, violence, and personal privacy for monetary profit) that few religious persons would want to follow.

Manyness of American religious culture. The "oneness" of religious influence in American culture contrasts with the "manyness" of religion in America. The "manyness" of spirituality and religion has grown into an expanding number of more or less distinct denominations and religions, some largely culture-affirming, with many others, however, stressing ideas and practices that are in opposition to or in tension with the values pervasive in the larger culture. In this sense, these different denominations or religious groups represent subcultures within the larger culture, where "extraordinary" religion flourishes in diverse beliefs and practices. The specifically cultural aspect of these religious groups is intensified as new immigrant groups come with religious traditions deeply ingrained in their cultures (Hinduism in Indian immigrant culture, Buddhism in the cultures of Southeast Asia, and Islam in Arab and Pakistani cultures). The previous review of some of these religions highlighted the diversity of these religious and spiritual subcultures.

31

Implications for counseling. Counselors need to be alert to the extraordinary and denominational as well as the ordinary and mainstream cultural aspects of religion and spirituality in the lives of their clients. Corbett (1990), following the thought of the American theologian Reinhold Niebuhr, summarizes the interaction of culture and religion in three categories: (a) primarily oppositional to one another, (b) primarily affirming of one another, or (c) a more balanced mixture of mutual opposition and affirmation. Especially to the extent that a client's religious or spiritual values are in opposition to one or more prominent values of mainstream American culture, counselors need to help clients clarify how and to what extent their culturally divergent values are personally important for their development and mental health. For example, the counselor may help the client explore—within the context of the client's own religious or spiritual beliefs—the therapeutic and developmental ramifications of culturally divergent values and beliefs. These might include, for example, premarital abstinence from sexual intercourse, nonviolent reactions to violence, frequent communal prayer and dietary rules, women's subordinate role to men, or mind-over-matter healing—all of which contrast with practices and perspectives typical of American society, such as casual or early sexual experiences, the use of violence as a solution to violence, a separation of religious practice from everyday secular life and pleasure, the equality of women and men, and the general reliance on medical science for healing.

Given the pluralism of American values and the diversely personalized expressions of mental health, the counselor's first responsibility is to enter with understanding into the world of the client's *personal* spiritual/religious belief system. It is from this vantage point that the counselor helps the client to clarify and apply personal beliefs in ways that express the client's own religion or spirituality and are conducive to the client's psychosocial development and well-being. For some this may mean living counterculturally in the midst of the larger culture (see, e.g., Witmer's [1988] discussion of Amish life), balancing the demands of religious practice with secular demands (see, e.g., Haddad and Lummis's [1987] discussion of the Islamic observance of Ramadan), or reevaluating traditional beliefs in the light of scientific knowledge (see, e.g., Albanese's [1992] discussion of modern-day evangelicals). In each case, the role of the counselor is, first, to understand the meaning of specific beliefs and practice in the light of the client's larger and/or growing understanding of his or her own religion and, second, to help the client expand personal awareness and make developmentally positive decisions based on clarified religious values. In this case neither the counselor nor the client will benefit from being culturally encapsulated or rigidified. Rather, the counselor helps the client to explore positive and negative implications that the client's religion or spirituality may raise for the individual's psychosocial development, spiritual and religious development, and relationship with culture.

Thus, the practical impact of a knowledgeable structuring of major categories of religion and spirituality, as outlined above, is to give the counselor an informed sensitivity to the diversity of clients' spiritual/religious beliefs and a base for flexibility in managing spiritual/religious issues in counseling. Clearly, such categorization of religions is only a first step toward appreciating the complexity and contextual nuances within major religious and spiritual traditions, not to mention the personal differences in religious belief. However, these schemas for understanding religion and spirituality in their many different manifestations constitute an initial knowledge base for the counselor's open-minded respect for the spiritual/ religious dimension of clients—an informed cognitive perspective for avoiding religious encapsulization. These schemas are also the foundational blocks for counselors to expand their knowledge of religion and spirituality through continued study specific to the spirituality of their clientele and through careful listening to the personal slant that each client puts on his or her religious and spiritual beliefs.

Importance of religion and spirituality in the general population

Survey Data

Over many years large numbers of Americans have reported that religion is important to them. Assuming that potential clients are representative of the general population, the implication for counselors is that a substantial proportion of their clients may have religious beliefs, attitudes, and practices that potentially affect their personal development and problem solving. The importance of religion for large numbers of people has shown up again and again in Gallup polls since the 1950s. In a 1993 Gallup poll (Gallup & Bezilla, 1994), 59% of those interviewed said that religion was very important to them, down from a high of 75% in 1952 but up from a low of 52% with the same view in 1978. An additional 29% in the 1993 poll said that religion was "fairly important" in their lives, while 12% responded that religion is "not very important" to them. There are some significant differences among the population in rating religion as very important. For example, Gallup's 1993 poll showed that women (65%) are more likely than men (52%) to consider religion as very important; African Americans (87%), more likely than whites (56%); persons 65 or older (76%), more likely than persons under 30 (less than 50%); and persons with incomes of less than $20,000 (67%), more likely than those earning $50,000 or more (45%).

It is reasonable to expect that from such a large pool of people for whom religion is important there are going to be clients who would welcome counselors' sensitivity toward and respect for their religious and spiritual beliefs. This expectation is directly supported by a 1992 Gallup survey showing that two-thirds of the respondents, when faced with a serious problem, would prefer to see a counselor who personally holds spiritual values and beliefs (Lehman, 1993). Similar to findings with respect to the importance of religion generally, women and lower-income individuals indicated a generally higher preference for counselors with spiritual values and beliefs than did men and individuals with higher incomes; also, people with less formal education also reported a generally higher preference for such counselors. A related finding in the same survey shows that 81% of the respondents would prefer a counselor who integrates their values and beliefs into the counseling process. These data parallel those of Quackenbos, Privette, and Klentz (1985) who found that for many potential clients the religious dimension of their lives is considered a legitimate aspect of counseling, especially in marriage and family issues.

Some caution must be exercised in interpreting persons' stated opinions about the importance of religion and their preference for religious and spiritual values in counseling. Gallup (as cited in Kinsolving, 1992), for example, has found a knowledge and behavior gap in American spirituality, noting that whereas 8 of 10 Americans profess to be Christians, only 4 of 10 know who delivered the Sermon on the Mount (Jesus did). Furthermore, whereas regular survey reports spanning many years show that 70% of Americans claim church membership and 40% attend religious services weekly (Warner, 1993), other counts of actual attendance are about half that of reported attendance (Hadaway, Marler, & Chaves, 1993). Social desirability (attendance at religious service is what is socially expected), personal desirability (I value going to religious service), and cognitive mixing of *events* stored in short-term memory (what I actually did last weekend) with *rules* in long-term memory (I go to church on Sunday) all may play a part in the significant discrepancies between perceived, self-reported behavior and actual behavior with regard to recent attendance at religious services.

Differences between individuals' reported values or preferences and their actual behavior are a well-known phenomenon in research and ordinary experience, not only in religion but also in other life areas such as marital, family, and relationship behavior. For counselors, differences between stated values or preferences and actual behavior spotlight the need for a careful and balanced weighing of client values, including spiritual and religious, and how values with varying personal potency can be used effectively in counseling. Chapter 4 will examine in more detail how counselors can assess the presence, power, and relevance of spiritual and religious values and beliefs for clients' developmental and therapeutic welfare.

The point to be emphasized here is that the widely stated valuing of religion and spirituality should be viewed in light of people's actual knowledge and practice; taken together they provide a balanced perspective for neither neglecting nor overestimating the importance of these values in counseling. In this perspective spiritual and religious beliefs and values are seen as potentially relevant to counseling as any other set of personal attitudes that influence a client's thoughts, feelings, and behavior. Counselors need a knowledgeable openness to the developmental and therapeutic relevance of spiritual and religious issues comparable to what they are expected to have for any other set of client beliefs.

Spirituality, Religion, and Critical Life Issues

In addition to quantitative data pointing to the potential significance of spirituality and religion, qualitative connections of the

35

spiritual/religious dimension with other critical areas of human development and behavior especially underscore the potential relevance of the spiritual/religion dimension to counseling. Schumaker (1992) recently brought together a series of reviews examining the consequential connections between spirituality and religion on the one hand and critical life areas like sexual adjustment, depression and suicide, anxiety and fear of death, self-esteem, rationality, self-actualization, meaning in life, and psychological well-being on the other. In addition to these life issues, other areas in which spirituality and religion may play an important role include, for example, issues of aging (Idler & Kasl, 1992; Owens, Berg, & Rhone, 1993; B. P. Payne, 1990), stress and coping (Maton, 1989), AIDS and death anxiety (Franks, Templer, Cappelletty, & Kauffman, 1990), community service work (Serow & Dreyden, 1990), alcoholism (R. A. Johnson, Sandler, & Griffin-Shelley, 1987), and attitudes toward work (Chusmir & Koberg, 1988; Iwata, 1993). Counselors can expect that at least for some clients spirituality and religion play a part in how the client feels and thinks about these issues and problems. As counselors explore the cognitive, affective, and unconscious elements of issues such as these, they can help clients by an alert openness to how spiritual and religious threads may be woven into such concerns and used in their resolution.

The spiritual/religious values of counselors and other mental health professionals

Counseling is clearly not a value-free enterprise (Jensen & Bergin, 1988; E. W. Kelly, in press; Norcross & Wogan, 1987), and there is a subtle, complex, and influential interplay between the values of the counselor and those of the client (Beutler & Bergan, 1991). Various patterns of similarity and dissimilarity between counselor and client values indicate that client values sometimes shift in the direction of counselor values. With respect to spirituality and religion, the interaction of client-counselor values raises several questions: What in general are the spiritual/religious values of counselors? How in general do counselors' own spiritual/religious values affect the counseling process? What are counselors' ethical obligations with regard to the inclusion of spiritual and religious values in counseling? What methods can counselors ethically use to integrate spiritual and religious values in counseling for the benefit of the client? The first three of these questions will be addressed here, and assessment and treatment methods will be discussed in chapters 4 and 5.

Counselors' Spiritual and Religious Values

A recent survey of counselor values, based on a nationally representative sample of counselor members of the American Counseling Association, showed that almost 64% of the respondents believe in a personal God while another 25% believe in a transcendent or spiritual dimension to reality (E. W. Kelly, in press). Approximately 70% expressed some degree of affiliation with organized religion, with almost 45% indicating that they were highly active or regularly participate in religion. Those who identified themselves as religious also expressed a substantially greater intrinsic than extrinsic religious orientation, that is, they value religion more for its importance as a guide in life than for its socially beneficial or personally comforting aspects. This last finding suggests that counselors who are religious tend to have a religiousness grounded in a spiritual orientation toward life.

With respect to spirituality as distinguished from religion in its more external manifestations, the survey showed that counselors affirm spirituality more extensively than religion expressed as an affiliation with organized religions. For example, 85% of the counselors agreed with the statement, "Seek a spiritual understanding of the universe and one's place in it," with 69% highly agreeing. Eighty percent agreed with the statement, "Seek inner wholeness and strength through communion with a higher power," with 62% highly agreeing. Fewer than 5% of the counselors expressed an opinion that the notions of transcendence or spirituality are illusions, while another 7% expressed no opinion regarding their religious or spiritual ideology. The difference between the combined percentage of counselors who affirmed a spiritual or spiritually grounded religious orientation and the percentage who indicated a specific religious affiliation suggests that many counselors make a distinction between spirituality and religion and that more counselors value spirituality in its broad understanding than religion understood in its institutional sense.

Surveys of other mental health professionals have shown that the spiritual and religious values and beliefs of clinical psychologists, social workers, and psychiatrists are, in some respects, similar to those of counselors (Haughen, Tyler, & J. A. Clark, 1991; Bergin & Jensen, 1990; Shafranske & Malony, 1990b), while in other respects are somewhat dissimilar. For example, other mental health professionals indicate rates of religious affiliation (approximately 70%) and participation (approximately 40%) similar to those of counselors (Jensen & Bergin, 1988; Shafranske & Malony, 1990b), and rate their religious commitment relatively high on an 8-factor scale of mental health values (Haughen et al., 1991). On the other hand, 68% of these mental health professionals agree that seeking a spiritual understanding of one's place in the universe is an important mental health value (Jensen & Bergin, 1988), compared with 85% of counselors who agree with the same statement. Also, 70% of clinical psychologists express a belief in some transcendent or divine dimension in reality and 30% believe these notions are illusory products of human imagination (Shafranske & Malony, 1990b), compared with 89% of counselors who believe in a personal God or transcendent dimension, with less than 5% believing that these are illusory. Although counselors and other mental health professionals differ to some extent in their spiritual and religious beliefs, all groups show a high to moderately high valuing of spiritual and religious belief and practice in general.

In contrast to this generally high valuing of spirituality and religion, counselors and other mental health professionals manifest substantial differences about specific, traditional religious beliefs. Indeed, while counselors and other mental health professionals indicate high levels of agreement on a wide range of mental health values such as self-determination, personal responsibility, and human relatedness, they differ significantly in their opinions regarding specific kinds of religious belief—for example, in the nature of humans' relationship to God or the transcendent and in religiously associated morality in the area of sexuality (E. W. Kelly, in press; Jensen & Bergin, 1988).

When the spiritual and religious beliefs of counselors are compared with those of the general population, we find that counselors' overall beliefs and rates of affiliation and participation are similar, although not identical, to those of the general population. For example, about 90% of the general population report that they never doubted the existence of God (Gallup & Castelli, 1989), while 89% of counselors indicate a belief in a personal God or a transcendent dimension to reality. Both professional counselors and the general population, as well as other mental health professionals, report about a 70% level of some affiliation with organized religion, with 40% reporting a high to moderate level of participation; however, these self-reports may be subjective overestimations of actual participation (Hadaway et al., 1993). On the other hand, the almost 30% of clinical psychologists who believe that God or the divine are illusory notions contrasts with the 90% of the general population who report a belief in God. These data suggest that a substantial minority of clinical psychologists share the nontheistic, nontranscendental perspective that has prevailed for many years in much of psychology and Freudian-influenced psychotherapy (Beit-Hallahmi, 1989). These discrepancies have led a number of authors to highlight a historical tension or even animosity between religion and the mental health professions, especially psychiatry and psychology (Bergin, 1980a; Giglio, 1993). Nonetheless, the accumulation of recent evidence indicates that a substantial majority of major mental health professionals appear to believe in the validity and value of a spiritual dimension to reality (Bergin & Jensen, 1990; E. W. Kelly, in press), with moderate numbers of these reporting affiliation with organized religion in percentages not much different from the general population. Counselors specifically report a valuing of spirituality and religion in percentages very close to the general population.

Counselors' Spiritual and Religious Values in the Counseling Process

That so many counselors on average report a valuing of spirituality and religion quite similar to the general population creates a reasonable probability that clients who bring spiritual and religious issues to counseling will be met by a counselor who personally values these issues. Counseling, however, does not occur on the "average." Specific clients with their own particular beliefs and values meet with specific counselors who have distinctive beliefs and values. This raises the question of how counselor-client dissimilarities and similarities in religious values and beliefs may affect the counselor's relationship with the client and the counseling process. A good deal of evidence suggests that nonreligious counselors do not in general assess or treat spiritual/religious clients differently from counselors with a spiritual/religious orientation.

For example, religious and nonreligious clinicians have been found to make very similar clinical judgments about religious, moderately religious, and nonreligious clients (Houts & Graham, 1986), not to differ in their diagnoses according to clients' religious affiliation (Wadsworth & Checketts, 1980) or their religious beliefs (Hillowe, 1985), or to differ in their perception of the therapy process (Gibson & Herron, 1990). Christian and secular counselors, despite some differences in attention to clients' spiritual issues, have been found not to differ in their rating of the pathology of clients, in their degree of "liking" of religious clients, or in their expectations of clinical success with religious clients (Worthington & Scott, 1983). In a study of cognitive-behavioral treatments with and without religious content, nonreligious therapists were found to be as effective in religiously oriented treatment of clinical depression of religious individuals as were religious therapists in a nonreligiously oriented treatment (Propst, Ostrom, Watkins, Dean, & Mashburn, 1992). Potential clients who were asked to rate several counselors who differed only in terms of religious values have reported a willingness to see all rated counselors and a belief in their helpfulness (Wyatt & Johnson, 1990). Based on their thorough review of research on the effects of client-counselor similarity and dissimilarity on values, including religious values, Beutler and Bergan (1991) concluded:

> Given the social importance of views about one's relationship to God and nature, we emphasize that there is currently little evidence that counseling outcome is substantially affected by the degree of client-counselor similarity of such views. This not to say that research should not proceed on the effects of client-counselor differences of religious belief. However, the lack of evidence indicating that the differences that exist between counselor and client groups on this dimension exert either a positive or a negative effect on counseling processes and outcome suggests the concerns that [have been] raised may not be as serious as proposed. (p. 23)

One possible exception to this general finding about the nonsignificance of counselor and client similarity on religion is that of *highly religious* clients, who might be expected to do better in counseling and be less likely to drop out of counseling when matched with a counselor with similar religious values (McCullough & Worthington, 1994; Weisbord, Sherman, & Hodinko, 1988; Worthington, 1991). Another area in which a counselor's religiousness or nonreligiousness may have an effect is the extent to which the counselor shows concern about spiritual values as relevant to counseling and includes spiritual goals as important to counseling (Worthington & Scott, 1983). Although evidence indicates that a counselor's personal nonreligiousness does not generally affect his or her assessment and professional treatment of religious clients or the process or outcome of counseling, a counselor's personal religiousness or spirituality may prompt the religious counselor to be more sensitive to the explicitly spiritual aspects of a client's issues. If this is the case, survey findings showing that a substantial majority of counselors themselves value spirituality and that many counselors are religiously affiliated mean that religious clients who wish to incorporate their spirituality into counseling have a reasonably good chance of matching their spiritual interests with those of a counselor. Such matching is relatively easy in counseling settings associated with religious institutions or explicitly offering spiritually oriented counseling. Furthermore, the large numbers of counselors who value spirituality and religion irrespective of their work setting (E. W. Kelly, in press) further increases the likelihood that spiritual/religious clients might receive counseling that is explicitly attuned to the spiritual/religious dimension.

Influence of the Counseling Setting

A counselor's work setting, however, may affect how a counselor responds to the spiritual/religious dimension (Worthington & Scott, 1983). Not only are religiously and spiritually associated counseling settings likely to employ religiously oriented counselors, but such settings also provide an atmosphere and expectation conducive to the raising of spiritual and religious issues.

But what about religiously sensitive counseling in secular settings? Most professional counseling and psychotherapy takes place in the secular domain, in public schools and colleges, human service agencies, clinics, workplaces, and nonaffiliated private settings. Moreover, the prevalence of spiritual and religious beliefs among the general population, the preference of so many individuals for counselors who value spirituality, and the connection of spirituality and religion to many critical life issues certainly suggest that the spiritual/religious dimension is pertinent to counseling in secular settings. Because many counselors and other mental health professionals, regardless of their work setting, hold the spiritual dimension as important in their personal life and relevant to counseling, we can reasonably assume that clients will encounter spiritually/religiously oriented counselors working in secular as well as religious settings.

It does not necessarily follow, however, that even religiously believing counselors will be actively responsive to the spiritual/religious dimension in secular settings. Secular counseling settings, like other secular settings, are likely to be characterized by what might be called a passive neutrality with respect to persons' spiritual and religious beliefs. This stance is often unarticulated, a mark of American society in which the typical cultural norm is that individuals' religion and spirituality are private matters, usually confined to specifically religious settings and activities and separated from the day-to-day affairs of the secular world. This passive neutrality toward religion and spirituality in the secular counseling setting is mirrored in the widespread omission of religious and spiritual issues in the training of counselors and other mental health professionals (E. W. Kelly, 1994b; Sansone, Khatain, & Rodenhauser, 1990; Shafranske & Malony, 1990b). Given this atmosphere of passive neutrality toward the spiritual/religious dimension and the effect it has on typically suppressing discussion of spirituality and religion, counselors in secular settings, including those who value spirituality and religion, need to be particularly sensitive that they do not inadvertently miss or sidestep clients' religious and spiritual concerns when these are relevant to the counseling process and outcome. Nor should counselors work only with religious issues that appear to have a negative effect on a client's development and mental health.

Counselors' Openness to the Spiritual/Religious Dimension in All Settings

Counselors' alert openness to spiritual and religious issues in secular settings, although it may go against the grain of how these issues are ordinarily ignored in secular settings, is justified by the nature of counseling itself. The very purposes of counseling for enhancing personal development, facilitating personal problem solving, and overcoming emotional and mental distress provide a clear rationale for incorporating the cognitive, affective, attitudinal, and behavioral aspects of individuals' religious beliefs and values as these bear on client improvement. How is it that a counselor would have clients explore all life aspects germane to their improvement yet omit exploration of pertinent spiritual and religious factors? Seen in this light, a carryover of the general cultural tendency to separate the spiritual/religion dimension from secular activities is contrary to the purposes of counseling. The point here, of course, is not to elevate religious values and attitudes to a special place in counseling nor should counselors' own personal spirituality intrude into the counseling process. Rather, in line with counseling's concern for all psychosocial factors pertinent to clients' development and improvement, it is to encourage counselors in the many secular settings in which most professional counseling and psychotherapy occur to be as alert to spiritual and religious concerns as they are to other counseling-relevant issues in clients' lives.

A counselor's personal spirituality/religiousness may provide a value base for being especially attuned to clients' spiritual and religious issues; however, it is not necessary for being sensitive to and dealing effectively with these issues in counseling. We have already seen that nonreligious counselors and therapists have been found to be little different from religious counselors in their assessment and effective clinical treatment of religious clients. Furthermore, nonreligious therapists trained specifically to provide treatment with religious content to religious clients have been found to be as effective as religious therapists (Propst et al., 1992). Sensitivity and skill in working with spiritual and religious clients do not require counselors to be personally spiritual or religious. Counselors' authentic respect for others, their relationship abilities, and their technical competence, not their personal religiousness or nonreligiousness, constitute the fundamental base for sensitive and effective counseling with religious as well as nonreligious clients. An attentive openness to spiritual and religious issues in secular counseling settings depends on counselors' knowledgeable sensitivity to the potential pertinence of the spiritual/religious dimension for clients, despite the inattention typically given to this dimension in secular settings. This is not to say that a counselor's special interest and expertise in spiritual and religious issues are unimportant in particular cases involving these issues (which will be addressed later in this book), but that proficient counselors, irrespective of their personal spiritual/religious orientation, can and should incorporate clients' spirituality or religiousness when appropriate.

43

Spirituality and Religion in Life Development and Personal and Social Well-Being

As we saw in Chapter 1, spirituality and religion are widespread and influential in the personal and social spheres. Equally clear is their great diversity, representing a variety of personal beliefs and experiences, creedal affirmations, institutional structures, and life philosophies as well as evoking widely varying personal reactions and evaluations. Spirituality and religion, across all their disparate meanings and expressions, are widely perceived as influencing life development and personal well-being for good or ill (or both), in ways that are significant and trivial. Because they are so pervasively influential in human attitudes and behavior, spirituality and religion invite close scrutiny into their particular effects. Questions, then, must be asked about how and to what extent spirituality and religion affect individuals' personal development, mental and emotional health, behavioral competence and responsibility, and sense of well-being—and, by extension, how they affect individuals' social environment. The answers to these questions have considerable bearing on how counselors work with the spiritual/religious dimension in counseling.

The diversity of spirituality and religion complicates the exploration and clarification of relationships between human development and personal functioning on the one hand and spirituality and religion on the other. There is no avenue to easy or unqualified generalizations. On the contrary, the human and conceptual complexities of spirituality and religion require a high tolerance for nuances among sometimes complementary and sometimes competing definitions, explanations, interpretations, and lived experiences. However, despite the difficulties that the diversity of spirituality and religion present in examining their effects on human functioning, an extensive and still expanding body of knowledge has developed that sheds light from many different, and sometimes contrasting, perspectives on the multiple effects of spirituality and religion on human development and behavior. Given the predominant concern of counselors to foster positive human development and change, knowledge that illuminates the dynamic and influential relationship of the spiritual/religious dimension with human functioning has a significant claim on counselors' attention.

The purpose of this chapter is (a) to elucidate the role and influence of spirituality and religion in human development and human functioning, especially as these are relevant to counseling theory and practice, and (b) to use this information as the basis for suggesting a guiding perspective for counselors. To this end, the chapter presents major lines of theory and significant research findings that attempt to examine, interpret, and explain the meaning and impact of spirituality and religion on psychosocial development and functioning. A brief introductory section is devoted to the generally positive estimation that early and influential founders of modern counseling had regarding spirituality and religion in personal development and counseling. This is followed by a discussion of major psychological theories about spirituality and religion vis-à-vis human functioning. The third section looks at theory and research on spiritual and religious development across the life span, and the last section presents and analyzes empirical research on the relationship between the spiritual/religious dimension and various aspects of mental health. The chapter concludes with principles for practice based on this review of theory and research.

Spirituality and religion in the origins of counseling

Contemporary professional counseling has important historical roots in turn-of-the-century efforts to develop organized, well-founded procedures of "expert counsel and guidance" (Parsons, 1909, p. 4) designed to help individuals, especially young people, choose a vocation in line with a clear and detailed understanding of themselves. Although focused primarily on vocational development and choice, these early writings detailed the nature and scope of individual counseling and guidance as vitally connected with the whole of a person's life development. While drawing on knowledge in closely related fields (e.g., psychology and the study of human development), the progressive extension, in knowledge and practice, of this ground-breaking work in individual vocational counseling and guidance represents a core, distinctive strand of thought and practice influencing the development of modern-day counseling.

The early work of Frank Parsons (1909, 1911) and Jesse Davis (1914) in vocational counseling and guidance was the starting point of contemporary professional counseling. Their thinking on spirituality and religion is important because it constitutes an important orienting perspective in the formative period of counseling. In the case of spirituality and religion, this perspective, as illustrated below, was largely positive and quite different from the predominantly negative perspectives on spirituality and religion in the origins of scientific psychology and the work of Freud. Although the spiritually/religiously affirmative perspective of Parsons and Davis cannot be considered normative for professional counseling today, it deserves thoughtful consideration, on its own merits and as a serious, integral component in original conceptualizations of counseling.

Frank Parsons

Parsons's (1909, 1911) attitude toward spirituality and religion, mostly implicit in his major writings, affirms their potentially positive value for personal development. For example, in describing vocational counseling with a prospective minister, Parsons (1909) wrote approvingly of "religion [that] invades the week, stays with the people seven days instead of one, and goes with them into market, factory, street, court room and legislative hall; religion becomes part of life instead of a thing more or less apart from life. . . ." (p. 127). For Parsons this kind of active religion was clearly associated with character traits that made individuals personally industrious, socially responsible, and tolerant of religious

47

differences. It is in the context of Parsons's (1909, 1911) stress on tolerance, open-mindedness, concern for others, and social responsibility that we understand his comment to a potential minister that "the world is hungry for ministers of a high type," persons "who can help the people solve the problems of daily life," and "apply ethical ideas and inspirations to life in all its phases, so that religion invades the week . . . ." (p. 127). Parsons's perspectives here bear a striking parallel to later conceptualizations of "mature" religion (Allport, 1950).

Parsons does not offer a direct analysis or critique of spirituality and religion. Furthermore, in line with a method of personal investigation that is conducted almost exclusively according to conscious processes, we do not find probings about spiritual and religious issues rooted in unconscious dynamics. However, it would certainly be incorrect to consider Parsons's views as unexamined or naive. Although his primary purpose in writing about vocational counseling is to offer a practical guide in the realm of conscious processes rather than a theoretical or psychodynamic treatise, he nonetheless begins his particular work on vocational counseling with an introductory chapter on "the importance of the scientific method" (pp. 3–4). Moreover, his probing approach, implicit recognition of superficial religiousness that does not satisfy people's "hunger," and sharp criticism of the social and economic conditions of his day (Parsons, 1911) provide a presumption that he did not view religion with a blind eye.

Jesse Davis

Davis (1914) was even more explicitly affirmative of spirituality and religion in his discussion of vocational guidance in the schools. Davis clearly saw a causal connection between vocational success and the moral qualities of workers and between moral qualities and positive religious influence. He conceived of guidance as directed toward the "pupil's better understanding of his own character . . . an awakening of the moral consciousness" (p. 18). For Davis, vocational guidance was, in the first instance, a matter "not . . . of finding vocational tendencies," (p. 47) but of counseling young people to "seek out those elements of character—habits, virtues, and faith—which stand out prominently as the very foundation of . . . success" (p. 49).

No doubt some will object, and with good reason, to Davis's explicit and strong connection of morality with religion (although he does not assert that the former necessarily requires the latter). From this position, it is all too easy, as history clearly shows, to slide from religion *for* morality to religion *as* morality, with all the dreadful consequences of dogmatism, intolerance, oppression, persecution, and deadly conflict. Although Davis's view of the role of religion in the public sphere does not preclude such consequences, this is clearly not Davis's intention. Quite the contrary. He writes critically of "religious thought . . . dominated by self motives," and likewise of "religious dogmas . . . dominating the actions of men," and, along with barriers of blood and caste, limiting social interest (p. 99). Religion in modern times, according to Davis, purports to impress people with their responsibilities for others and stir them "to actions in behalf of human society as never before in the history of the world . . . to promote the social welfare of those less fortunate . . . to serve the masses rather than the favored few. . . ." (pp. 99–100). These are hardly the words of some unenlightened religionist.

Both Parsons and Davis place their understanding of religion as a viable human possibility squarely in the context of enlightened self-knowledge and personally clarified decision making, deep and active concern for the good of others, and a forthright and energetic sense of social interest and social reform. By so conceiving religion, they have bequeathed to modern professional counseling a heritage in which spirituality and religion are afforded the opportunity to act as personally and socially humanizing forces, and, to the extent that they fail to do so, are to be criticized as contrary to human well-being and resisted as antagonistic to human enlightenment, freedom, and justice.

Spirituality, religion, and human functioning

Theory and Research

Spirituality and religion have been the subject of considerable theoretical speculation and research in the behavioral sciences. Especially relevant to counseling are research and theory in the overlapping fields of psychology, human development, and psy-

49

chiatry, which for the purposes of this book will be considered as representing a basically common body of psychological knowledge. From the beginnings of modern psychology, the spiritual/religious dimension has been an object of psychological inquiry (Beit-Hallahmi, 1989). Although scholarly interest in the psychological study of religion has waxed and waned over the years, an important—but still fragmentary—body of knowledge has continued to build (Wulff, 1991). However, the data and theory that constitute this particular field are diverse and sometimes conflicting, leading to divergent conclusions, depending in part on the data available and the philosophical and theoretical assumptions that are brought to the interpretation of the data. This heterogeneity of data, inferences, and theory means that different organizations of the material are possible. The one used here is to review the whole field from two complementary perspectives: first, to take a look at psychologically based *theories* regarding the role of spirituality and religion in human functioning; and second, to review *research* findings that bear on one or more aspects of the relationship of spirituality and religion to human well-being.

This form of organization is not meant to suggest that theory and research are categories of discrete information. Certainly they overlap in several important ways. Nonetheless, the organization has heuristic value. Prominent theoretical positions represent substantive, organized interpretations of major psychological effects of spirituality and religion, and they exercise considerable influence in shaping research and clinical practice. Theories also provide assumptions that behavioral scientists, clinicians, and counselors can incorporate into their own perspectives toward spirituality and religion. Empirical data are likewise critical to a view of spirituality and religion that accords with human reason. Such data are necessary for testing and rethinking assumptions and theoretical positions and for informing clinical judgments and decisions. Empirical research findings also provide concrete information about specific aspects of the relationship between the spiritual/religious dimension and human behavior and human development.

The Great Analysts: Freud and Jung

The theoretical positions of Freud and Jung on religion are important because they represent comprehensive, systematic interpretations of the psychology of spirituality and religion, and because they have had and continue to have a pervasive influence in psychology, psychotherapy, and counseling. The point is not that their positions, especially that of Freud, represent how most people regard spirituality and religion. On the contrary, the data on religious belief in the United States clearly indicate that a large majority of Americans hold positive views of religion, which are quite different from those of Freud in particular.

Even among major counseling authorities examining spiritual and religious issues in counseling and human development, some pay scant attention to Freud and Jung (see, e.g., Worthington, 1989). However, the extensive analyses that continue to appear on their work (see, e.g., Aziz, 1990; Jones, 1991) indicate that within the wider field of counseling and psychotherapy, their ideas continue to receive serious study and exercise considerable influence. Their respective contributions are important because they purport to explain, with scholarly authority, how spirituality and religion function psychologically and how, regardless of majority opinions, they affect human development and well-being.

Freud. Freud (1913/1950, 1927/1964, 1930/1962, 1939/1958) formulated a comprehensive explanation of religion in line with his psychoanalytical theories of development, unconscious behavior, and defense mechanisms. His psychological explanations of religion reflect his detailed theories of human behavior and the mechanisms of therapeutic change, as well as his study of ethnographic investigations into the origins of religion. The main thrust of Freud's conclusion is that religion is an illusion. God is a projection of humans' infantile wishes rooted in the father-complex; religion is an obsessional neurosis with neurotic wishes expressed in ritualistic compulsions. Religion is contrary to human progress, and the moral aspects of religion should be replaced with science and nontheistic humanism. Religious ideas are "not precipitates of experiences or end-results of our thinking," but "illusions, fulfillments of the oldest, strongest and most urgent wishes of mankind. The secret of their strength lies in the strength of those wishes" (Freud, 1927/1964, p. 47). These wishes are rooted in "conflicts of childhood arising from the father-complex" and are "never wholly overcome" (p. 48). Although many ordinary, nonpsychologically oriented persons find these ideas alien and shocking, and although noted scholars have critiqued them from

51

a variety of perspectives, they nonetheless retain value and exercise influence that call for counselors' attention.

In terms of critical responses, Freud's views on religion were countered early by Jung and Adler. Modern anthropological investigations highlight the limitations of the ethnographic studies on which Freud relied. Historical evidence strongly suggests that Freud's atheism, which was in line with the scientific materialism of key mentors, preceded, rather than evolved from, his major psychoanalytic studies. These critiques point clearly to a nonconclusive link between Freud's major psychoanalytical principles (e.g., sexually based developmental crises, unconscious motivation, repression, projection, and wish fulfillment) and his explanations of religion (Kung, 1981). On the other hand, Freud's thinking on religion continues to be substantively influential not only because he holds a historically preeminent position in psychology and psychotherapy and his religious skepticism is consistent with that of many psychologists (Gorsuch, 1988; Starbuck, 1899), but also because his work continues "to be capable of positive and creative contributions" (Spinks, 1963, p. xiii).

Freud's arguments cannot demonstrate his conclusion of atheism, and his critiques incorrectly paint all spirituality and religion with the same dark brush. Nonetheless his critique of religion has positive aspects that are important to counselors' understanding of potentially negative and detrimental effects of religion. Kung (1979) summarizes these as follows. Freud rightly criticizes defective forms of religion and their psychological effects: self-deception, escapism, satisfaction of personal needs through wish fulfillment, and religious legalism and ritualism that narrows one's range of thinking and behaving. Freud exposes how the traditional image of God as father figure, sometimes benevolent, sometimes authoritarian and even vindicative, represents a culturally determined concept and a wish-fulfilling projection associated with what should be a passing stage of childhood development. And at the societal level, Freud's critical analysis of religion highlights institutional religion's misuse of power and influence, its history of intolerance and abusiveness of those who are different or deviant, its violent crusades, its inquisitions, its suppression of open inquiry and research, its attempts to dominate or intimidate the human spirit in the name of God and to exploit the dependence and immaturity of those who are psychologically or spiritually vulnerable, and its continual negative obsession with, not to mention suppression of, human sexuality.

Freud by no means is the sole critic in these matters. But his powerfully penetrating psychological analyses, especially emphasizing the unconscious forces at work in religious belief and practice, carry special cogency in understanding the potentially negative effects of religion on mental health and human functioning. Indeed, even for proponents of the positive potential of spirituality and religion, Freud's contributions are regarded as important. The Swiss pastor, Oskar Pfister (1923; Meng & E. L. Freud, 1963), early noted that Freud's work was helpful in guiding persons from fear and hate to love. J. W. Jones (1991) has recently written of Freud's ideas being transformed "toward a psychoanalysis of the sacred" (p. 111), open to "acknowledging a connection to a self-sustaining universal matrix" (p. 135).

Jung. Jung's view of religion is very different from that of Freud. Jung, as well as Adler, broke with Freud (and with one another) because of differences regarding their understanding of human psychodynamics (Clarke, 1992). They also disagreed with him about religion. As Kung (1981) notes, "Freud uncompromisingly rejects religion as such . . . Adler benevolently tolerates it, [and] Jung's attitude is in principle friendly toward it" (pp. 292–293). Jung in particular continues to have great influence on how the spiritual/religious dimension is important to the understanding of human development and the practice of counseling and psychotherapy.

Jung's theories of personal development and therapeutic change include a fairly specific and essentially affirmative psychology of religion, and they also weave the spiritual/religious dimension into his more comprehensive theories of individuation (Aziz, 1990). Illustrative of this point is Jung's statement that "many neuroses are caused primarily by the fact that people blind themselves to their own religious promptings because of childish passion for rational enlightenment. It is high time the psychologist of today recognized that we are no longer dealing with dogmas and creeds but with the religious attitude *per se*, whose importance as a psychic function can hardly be overrated" (Jung, 1954/1977). This view of spirituality and religion, reflected in many of Jung's works, has contributed significantly to counseling and psychotherapeutic approaches in which spirituality and religion are accepted and used as positive elements in personal development and human well-being (see, e.g., Caprio & Hedberg, 1986; Daniels, 1992; Jacoby, 1991).

Jung's thinking on religion is generally akin to the concept of spirituality as presented in Chapter 1 and is not to be confused with creeds as these have been codified and institutionalized in denominational religions (Jung, 1938/1966). At one point Jung (1938/1966) wrote that "religion appears to me to be a peculiar attitude of the human mind, which could be formulated in accordance with the original use of the [Latin word] 'religio,' that is, a careful consideration and observation of certain dynamic factors, understood to be 'powers,' . . . such factors as [humans have] found in [their] world powerful, dangerous or helpful enough to be taken into careful consideration, or grand, beautiful and meaningful enough to be devoutly adored and loved. . . . Religion, it might be said, is the term that designated the attitude peculiar to a consciousness which has been altered by the experience of the numinosum" (pp. 5, 6). Numinosum is a term that Jung subsequently equated to the "divine" (Heisig, 1979, p. 91).

For Jung religion is an understandable and legitimate expression of deep and important psychological movements in people toward individuation, that is, the gradual emergence or development of the true self through the authentic integration of unconscious and conscious factors. Religion gives legitimate expression to archetypal images lodged in persons' collective unconscious (i.e., unconscious material not from an individual's personal history but from the collective history of the whole human race). Religion, especially insofar as it authentically symbolizes spiritual meaningfulness, has the potential for helping people understand and express a psychological and spiritual movement of resolving and unifying the interplay of various intrapersonal dynamic forces (e.g., the ego, persona, personal unconscious, anima/animus, collective unconscious) around the self (Jung, 1933). For Jung, the self in the process of individuation, harmonizes these various intrapersonal forces for the individual and this self is an inner spiritual reality, an inner psychological expression of God. Religion, when adequate, gives outward expression to this inner spiritual search and objectifies the inner God of the self into the outer world.

Jung's views on religion, as positive as they are, should not be stretched to conclusions beyond his own *psychological* purposes. In several works, Jung indicated that he regarded religion and God as important and positive *psychological* realities, but that he was not, *as a scientist and psychologist*, addressing their objective reality. Jung posited the psychological desirability, even necessity, of spirituality and religion, but he resisted others' efforts to have him unequivocally affirm the actual truth of a God or the objective value of religion. For example, Jung wrote on various occasions:

> It is not for psychology, as a science, to demand a hypostatization [i.e., make an actual real person] of the God-image. But, the facts being what they are, it does have to reckon with the existence of a God-image. (1960/ 1981, p. 278)

> There are unfortunately many feeble minds who thoughtlessly imagine [the problem of God] is a question of truth, whereas it is really a question of psychological necessity. (1968, p. 3)

> A new *Weltanschauung* [philosophy of life] will have to abandon the superstitious belief of its [the self in its likeness to God] objective validity and admit that it is only a picture that we paint to please our minds, and not a magical name with which we can conjure up real things. (1960/1981, p. 379)

The position reflected in statements such as these led Martin Buber (1952) to challenge Jung on his psychologizing of religion, which Buber argued was not neutrality but an implicit rejection of the objective truth of God on psychological terms. In an interview late in his life, when asked if he believed in God, Jung responded that he did not have to believe, he knew. He later expanded on this remark: "I do not know a certain God (Zeus, Yahweh, Allah, the Trinitarian God, etc.) but rather: I do know that I am obviously confronted with a factor unknown in itself, which I call "God" in *consensus omnium* [the general agreement of all persons]. . . . Since I *know* of my collision with a superior will in my own psychical system, *I know of God* [italics in original]" (quoted in Heisig, 1979, p. 90). Clearly, care must be taken not to confuse Jung's positive *psychological* understanding of spirituality and religion as equivalent to an affirmation, much less a demonstration, of an objective reality with *ontological* validity, no matter how personally beneficial that might be.

Religion's objective validity. As illustrated in Jung's dispute with Buber, the issue of the psychological validity of the spiritual/ religious dimension vis-à-vis its objective validity (that is, ontological existence, independent of human ideation) involves a perplexing question for counselors. Although the direct argumentation of this issue is beyond the scope of this book, it involves factors that call for reasonable clarity on the part of the counselor, if not complete resolution. One way of putting the issue is to ask if, and how, counselors might affirm for others the psychological value of others' belief in the objective validity of the spiritual/religious dimension and spiritual domain, while themselves remaining personally and intellectually neutral, skeptical, or repudiatory with regard to such spiritual or religious "realities." If, according to Freud, religion and a belief in "God" are representative of some degree of mental aberration or distortion, then it follows that religious belief *in itself* is a psychological deficit, a problem, if you will, to be worked through, on the way to greater self or ego integrity. Among the early psychologists of religion, J. H. Leuba, writing prior to Freud, stands out for his position that "religion deals with an illusory reality" (Pruyser, 1968, p. 5). This is essentially the position of Albert Ellis (1980, 1986, 1989a), who maintains that atheism, although not absolutely demonstrable, is nonetheless about 99% probable, thereby overwhelmingly representing a more rational, more truly human, basis for living one's life. According to this perspective, belief in spiritual and religious entities is irrational and constitutes a psychological deficit for the individual and, in its institutional forms, an obstruction to social well-being.

On the other hand, it can be argued cogently that the atheistic preference is itself a choice of illusion. The atheistic position does not represent a conclusion from evidence but a *choice*—a choice to reject the theistic or spiritual implications of psychological experience and physical evidence pointing to an objective reality corresponding to ultimate transcendent meaning. Repression, wishful thinking, and projection can be at work in atheism as well as in theism. Atheism may represent a repression of trust and affirmation that the universe is really and ultimately meaningful, wishful thinking that ultimate meaning is limited by the limits of human capacities and human experience, and projection of this *dis*affirmation onto reality. As to the question of probabilities regarding theism and atheism, the probabilities are, at least, closer to 50-50, in contrast to Ellis's assertion. According to the British physicist Paul Davies (1992), the universe is not a "purposeless accident," a position held by "a surprisingly large minority of scientists" (Suplee, 1992). "The universe is put together with an ingenuity so astonishing that I cannot accept it merely as brute fact" (Davies, 1992, p. 21).

If one fixes on anthropomorphic *symbols* of God and institutional elaborations of religion, atheism is an easy, if unsophisticated, step. However, when one is able to separate the function of symbols from that which is being transiently symbolized, then the question of God, spirituality, and religion is open and free. Considering, for example, serious arguments made for an innate sense of the sacred ("drive to find God") in human knowing (Liddon, 1989), the meta-empirical outreaches of scientific probings of the universe (Davies, 1992), and the extensively positive compatibility of the spiritual/religious worldview with the subject matter and practice of psychology (S. L. Jones, 1994), the believer's affirmation of ultimate transcendence (variously named God, the divine, spirituality, and other terms) shows itself at least as reasonable as the unbeliever's denial.

With respect to counseling, an explicit, not to say hostile, repudiation of the validity of spirituality may be problematic— open only to a tentative tolerance of spiritual and religious belief. This is not to say that such tentative toleration is without *respect for the client as a person* (see Chapter 1). However, a potential limitation of spiritually and religiously skeptical counselors with spiritually and religiously believing clients is that this aspect of the client's life may not be allowed to yield its positive potential for the client's development and problem resolution. Pruyser's (1968) comment is apropos here: "Though it is true that the reality of God cannot be asserted or denied by psychology, it is also true that a miserly and unimaginative attitude on the part of the scientist (read: counselor) cannot do full justice to the nature of the experience of God in believing subjects. . . . To know what aspects of experience have religious significance for a person presupposes some familiarity with the possibilities and perplexities of religion in the investigator (read: counselor)" (p. 18).

Returning to Jung's line of thought on this matter, Jung's refusal to claim that his psychological affirmation of the spiritual/religious dimension equates to its objective validity carries an important intellectual and practical caution for spiritually or religiously believing counselors. Counselors who experience a personal congruence between their knowledge of human psychology and their own personal affirmation of a transcendent reality, may improperly treat such congruence as proof of their spiritual beliefs. A believing counselor may allow this spiritual/religious conviction to intrude improperly, consciously or unconsciously, into the counseling relationship. In this case the potential limitation of a spiritually and religiously believing counselor is that client problems involving beliefs (e.g., an agnostic outlook in bereavement) discordant with the counselor's own spiritual and religious beliefs may not receive empathically therapeutic attention. In the intersection of their spiritual/religious belief or disbelief and their *distinctively psychological* point of view, counselors need sufficient conceptual clarity and counseling-process flexibility to accommodate clients with a diversity of positive and negative spiritual/religious beliefs.

Psychology of Religion

The psychology of religion is made up of a diverse array of systematic and scholarly efforts to understand the specifically human elements—cognitions, affects, attitudes, behaviors—associated with religious belief and practice. It includes many prominent theorists and researchers who have sought to explain the role of religion in the personal and social life of humankind (Wulff, 1991). From a global perspective all the authorities mentioned in this chapter may be considered as contributors to the psychology of religion. However, for purposes of this book, we may identify prominent psychologists whose work represents an especially focused attention to the psychological study of religion. From among many prominent scholars and investigators, William James, Gordon Allport, and Paul Pruyser are chosen as leading examples of how the psychology of religion contributes to our understanding of the relationship of religion and spirituality to human development and human functioning.

William James. General agreement exists that William James's (1902/1961) *The Varieties of Religious Experience* was, in the words of Beit-Hallahmi (1989), "epoch-making" (p. 20), "probably [what] still constitutes the most important single psychological work on religion" (Pruyser, 1968, p. 3). James, similar to Jung, focused his attention on what we might call the personal psychology of religion, as distinguished from theologies, creeds, structures, and institutions. With an understanding quite close to what we earlier identified as spirituality (as distinct from our definition of religion), James (1902/1961) defined religion as "the feelings, acts, and experiences of individual men in their solitude, so far as they apprehend themselves to stand in relation to whatever they may consider the divine" (p. 42). Within this framework, which forms a kind of micropsychology of religion, James analyzed the various ways that personal "religious life," although subject to considerable distortion and perversity, represents a set of belief experiences linking individual humans to "a more spiritual universe" from which they draw significance. Understood in this way, religious life, James concluded, enriches the believer through prayer, which is a source of "spiritual energy . . . a zest which adds itself like a gift to life," "a temper of peace," and "loving affections" toward others (p. 377).

It must be acknowledged that these optimistic conclusions, no matter how carefully derived from James's analyses, appear in stark contrast with our ordinary observations of other religiously affiliated behavior: petty disputes among individuals and fanatical conflicts among groups; psyches twisted and grieved by rigid and dehumanizing rules and prohibitions; oppression and violence in the name of one's god; literal, dogmatic, and mind-closing interpretations of religious writings. James certainly knew all of this. He accounted for it in part with his distinction between the "healthy-minded" and the "sick soul," that is the morbid-minded. In the latter case, religious sentiment is colored by an attention to evil and negation, with a resulting need to control and limit and with experiences of joylessness. And when this religious morbid-mindedness is reinforced in religious creeds, structures, and institutions, the stage is set for such religion to wreak personal and social havoc.

Healthy-mindedness and morbid-mindedness, of course, are found not only in religion but also in other major areas of life such as politics, economics, and art. A major contribution of James to the specifically psychological understanding of spirituality and religion was to carefully identify essential characteristics of spirituality and religion, which, when joined with a nonsuperficial healthy-mindedness, have the potential for contributing to or positive humanizing of personal and social life. James's analysis offered a simple but important psychological typology for understanding religious experience and for relating religion to mental hygiene (Pruyser, 1968). It would be for Freud, Jung, and those who followed to uncover more fully the unconscious dynamics of religion. Nonetheless, counselors will find in James a set of careful distinctions that are valuable in understanding and counseling those whose religious beliefs, for better or worse, significantly affect their personal and social adjustment.

Gordon Allport. According to Beit-Hallahmi (1989), "Allport's *The Individual and His Religion* (1950) is a masterpiece in the James tradition, and it deserves a place among the classics of the psychology of religion" (p. 51). Like James, and in contrast to Freud, Allport's psychology of religion is optimistic. In certain important respects, it is especially congenial to professional counseling's developmental focus and characteristic emphasis on understanding human functioning and facilitating human change primarily in the light of intrapersonal strengths rather than psychopathology. Allport (1950) wrote: "I am seeking to trace the full course of religious development in the normally mature and productive personality. I am dealing with the psychology, not the psychopathology, of religion" (p. viii). Allport was aware of the "commonly encountered . . . neurotic function of religious belief, its aid as an 'escape from freedom' " (p. viii), but he disagreed with those who see this as the only or dominating function of everyone with religious sentiment.

Allport offers a developmental view of religious sentiment, understood in the Jamesian sense, that is diverse in its origins and expressions. In line with his purpose and analysis, Allport, while recognizing the possibility (but unprovability) of unconscious factors in religion, devotes his inquiry to the "large array of conscious causal forces . . . at hand" (p. 8). Allport locates the origin of religion in a complex of human desires for companionship, value, and especially intelligibility and meaning. Contrary to the proposition that religion is associated with the desire to *escape* reality, Allport views religion (remembering that religion has the Jamesian sense of personal spirituality) as a desire *toward* reality. As Allport notes: "It is true that religion tends to define reality as congenial to the powers and aspirations of the individual, but so too does any working principle that sustains human endeavor. Those who find the religious principle of life illusory would do well not to scrutinize their own working principles too closely" (p. 23). Tracing the development of religious sentiment through the vicissitudes of doubt, experimentation, and a critical testing of institutions and traditions, Allport comes to describe what he calls the "religion of maturity" (pp. 52–53). Because "in probably no region of personality do we find so many residues of childhood as in the religious attitudes of adults" (p. 52), Allport explains the concept of religious maturity in detail.

According to Allport, religious maturity is based, not primarily on a specific type of religious content, but rather on its psychological components, that is, characteristics that are "drawn from a defensible theory of the nature of human personality" (p. 53). With this general understanding, Allport describes six characteristics of religious maturity:

1. The mature religious sentiment is *differentiated*, that is, it is the evolving product of critically cognitive discriminations based on accumulating knowledge and experience toward an organized pattern of religious understanding and living.

2. It is *functionally autonomous* and dynamic, that is, it does not derive its motivating force from fear, self-justification, self-fulfilling wishes, guilt, or similar secondary motives, but acts as an autonomous (albeit interdependent) motivating force for humanizing personal and social development.

3. Religious maturity is productive of a *consistent morality*, that is, it is characterized by a congruence between one's religious beliefs and practices and one's active social concern and the well-being of others.

4. The mature religious sentiment is *comprehensive*, that is, it is concerned especially with addressing the larger questions of meaning in formulating a philosophy of life.

5. Religious maturity is *integrally related* with a receptivity to scientific knowledge and an honest confrontation with the many harsh and dehumanizing outrages against humanity.

6. Religious maturity is essentially *heuristic*, that is, it is held as a kind of tentative hypothesis, a way of religious belief and practice that is open to reformulation and development as one gains new knowledge and experience.

In subsequent writings, Allport (Allport & Ross, 1967) developed the concept of religious maturity along the lines of intrinsic religiousness and contrasted it with extrinsic religiousness, a distinction that continues to prevail in current studies (Donahue, 1985; Gorsuch & McPherson, 1989; Kirkpatrick & R. W. Hood, 1990). Although the notions of intrinsic and extrinsic religiousness are not beyond debate (Kirkpatrick & Hood, 1990), accumulating theory and research converge on an understanding of intrinsic religiousness as the commitment (Donahue, 1985) and importance (Gorsuch & McPherson, 1989) that a person attaches to religion as a guide in life, while extrinsic religiousness signifies a valuing of religion for personal and social purposes unconnected to the inherent spiritual and altruistic purposes of religion. Beit-Hallahmi (1989) rightly cautions about the probable ethnocentric, largely Western-liberal orientation of this understanding of religious maturity. Nevertheless, Allport's formulation is a usefully heuristic understanding of religious maturity or intrinsic religiousness—a well-grounded formulation of humanizing psychological characteristics against which particular spiritual and religious beliefs and practices can be tested.

Such testing, however, is not done solely in the light of a theory of religious maturity. Culture (including culturally oriented religious differences) and science, to mention just two of the more prominent domains of life, provide complementary sets of knowledge and experience for understanding and testing the humanizing or dehumanizing effects of particular spiritual and religious beliefs and practices. Allport himself reports that he consulted with experts outside his own background to avoid undue psychocentrism and ethnocentrism in his psychological studies of religion.

Paul Pruyser. A further elaboration and deepening of the psychology of religion is represented in the extensive scholarly and clinical work of Paul Pruyser—work that has "assured his place among the best known of this century's psychologists of religion" (Malony & Spilka, 1991, p. i). In some respects, Pruyser (1968) follows in the tradition of James and Allport, but his psychodynamic orientation and extensive clinical involvement, as well as his considerable knowledge of theology, led him to an especially rich explication of religion in human functioning. He extends James's focused study on the subjective experiences of religion, predominantly expressed in feelings, to understand personal religion as an ongoing process of cumulative, hypothesis-testing experiences that engage all aspects of the person, including perceptual, intellectual, linguistic, emotional, physical, and, especially, relational.

Pruyser did not share Freud's antipathy to religion and objected to his positivism. However, he made use of Freud's concept of religion as illusion, that is, religion as a fulfillment of deep and strong wishes. But Pruyser did not consider that illusion necessarily corresponds to nonreality. Rather an illusion, according to Pruyser (1968)

> is like Columbus thinking he had discovered a new seaway to India, while he had actually discovered America! An illusion is not necessarily false, that is, incapable of realization or contradictory to reality. The great question is: If illusions are needed, how can we have those that are capable of correction, and how can we have those that will not deteriorate into delusions? (pp. 7–8).

Illusion, in this sense, thus becomes the psychological-religious meeting place, the place of personal spiritual/religious imaging, in which peoples' profoundest wishes, or hopes, as Pruyser (1985/1991) preferred to call them, are linked with the religious domain that believers affirm as real. And this personal religious domain, the psychological domain of personal religious significance, is not limited to some psychological compartment (although this is sometimes the case—an important clinical issue that will be considered elsewhere); "rather *all* data—events, processes, actions, objects, and object relations—may have . . . a religious . . . significance for the patient, or for the [therapist], or for both" (p. 15).

Given Pruyser's analysis of the psychological or intrapsychic pervasiveness of spirituality and religion, rather than its compartmentalization, it can be expected that spiritually or religiously oriented factors may occur, if they occur at all, in almost any aspect of a client's life: family and relationship concerns, sex, career issues, guilt, self-esteem, disabilities, sickness, depression, failure, acting out, grief, and the like. Counselors certainly do not want to read spirituality and religion into concerns where they have no relevance, just as they would not want to read in sex inappropriately; on the other hand, just as they would not ignore sex as a potential factor in a problem, so also spirituality and religion should not be ignored.

In what might be considered as the reverse side of Allport's religious maturity, Pruyser (1977/1991) describes what he terms neurotic religion. Although not entirely free of what Beit-Hallahmi (1989) saw as a Western-liberal ethnocentrism in Allport, Pruyser's analysis of neurotic religion uncovers the psychologically oppressive, mind-closing, and narcissistic side of spirituality and religion. With special attention to how neurotic religious beliefs, attitudes, and institutions can constrict the freedom and development of thought and emotion, Pruyser points to several negative consequences of neurotic religiosity. These include dissociation and denial, for example, in shutting out information that might conflict with one's religious beliefs or ignoring social miseries while maintaining a Pollyanna or detached religious attitude. Also included is the displacing of conflict-laden urges onto the body, for example, with religiously motivated physical severity toward presumably offensive or offending body parts; crass forms of magic, ritual, and symbolism, as expressed, for example, in Satanism, occultism; and obsessive-compulsive religiosity. Neurotic religiosity is also manifest in the manipulative use of religiously arrogated or invested power, for example, in the fraudulence and dishonesty of religious leaders who stimulate and reinforce personally and socially debilitating behavior in religious adherents.

Contemporary Humanistic Traditions

The humanistic tradition in psychology is understood here to comprise humanistic psychology and the existential perspective. Transpersonal psychology is also included as a special outgrowth of the humanistic movement. This tradition has included spirituality and religion as significant aspects of understanding human development and human functioning. Wulff (1991) notes:

> The humanists ascribe to religion—broadly defined—a major role in the dynamics of the self-actualization process. Only certain forms of religion are thought to support the realization of human potential, and thus a major feature of [humanistic] literature is the distinguishing of religious types . . . .: intrinsic versus extrinsic (Allport), humanistic versus authoritarian (Fromm), peakers versus nonpeakers (Maslow). Although May and Frankl are apparently less given to typology, they, too, have a vision of genuine religiousness. It must arise anew from within, they say, free of sectarian dogma, if it is to be a source of purpose and meaning. (p. 622)

Erich Fromm. The humanistic tradition generally approaches a psychological understanding of religion from the point of view of how the religious sentiment contributes to an expansion of human potential, self-actualization, and the ennobling of the human person and human society. For example, noting how the human situation is characterized by a number of existential dichotomies (e.g., the aspiration toward continuing existence and the fact of death) that threaten peoples' mental health, Fromm (1947) describes peoples' religious need for a frame of orientation and object of devotion. For Fromm, this need is authentically realized in humanistic religion that focuses on human self-realization and the development of human potential in relation to a world approached with loving care. Humanistic religion is contrasted with authoritarian religion in which human power and potential are surrendered to an outside entity (e.g., God, a political leader, a guru), thereby alienating individuals from their own inner resources for reasoned and compassionate growth and development. Although Fromm was a nontheist, he maintained that humanistic and authoritarian religion may be associated with either theistic or atheistic traditions. The key distinguishing factor of positive religion in either case is not a belief in God or the supernatural but the extent to which one's basic frame of orientation and one's basic object of devotion enhance human development toward love, the assertion of one's own powers, and a humanized society, rather than lead people toward fear and submission (Fromm, 1950, 1992).

Abraham Maslow. In Maslow's (1968/1980) humanistic psychology, the phenomena of the "peak experience" and "the plateau experience" (a more cognitively aware and enduring state of being than the passing, highly affective peak experiences) express authentic religiousness. Such religiousness has essentially nothing to do with God, the supernatural, or traditional religious practices. However, "what is surprising is that this resolute atheist [Maslow] developed a psychology so close to what we are already familiar with from many of the world's mystics" (M. Friedman, 1992, p. 105). The peak experience, in its ideal form, is an ecstatic, "godlike" experience of transcending the limits of one's ego and experiencing with wonder and peacefulness a sense of universal connectedness as well as personal integration (Maslow, 1968). Peak and plateau experiences are important as spiritual or religious (but in no sense supernatural) phenomena because they are characteristic of highly self-actualized individuals (Maslow, 1970), who have fully matured in their personal and social human potential. They represent a deeply personal, naturalistic core of religious experience that cuts across all institutionalized and ritualistic expressions of religion. Thus authentic spirituality/religion understood in its humanistic (nontheistic, noninstitutional) sense represents a focus on self-actualizing human development, in contrast to a focus on human deficits, pathologies, or humanly debilitating forms of religiosity.

Transpersonal psychology. Maslow's work in humanistic psychology was a major influence in the development of transpersonal psychology (Wulff, 1991). The defining perspective of transpersonal psychology is the application of scientific methods to those areas of human experience beyond the strictly empirical, such as unitive consciousness, mystical experience, transcendence of self, spirit and spiritual practices, meditation, and compassion based in a cosmic consciousness.

We can highlight only a few of the many contributors to transpersonal psychology. Roberto Assagioli's (1965/1971, 1993) seminal work in psychosynthesis and recent work in transpersonal development lay out an influential transpersonal model for the integration of spirituality and psychotherapy. Stansilav Grof's (S. Grof & C. Grof, 1989) early experiences with psychedelic drugs began several decades of developing transpersonal counseling applications that explore theoretical and clinical distinctions between beneficially transformative spiritual experiences and pseudo-spiritual experiences rooted in mental disorders. Transpersonal psychology has come to give particular attention to Eastern religious experience and Eastern psychology. Prominent among transpersonalist theorists who have integrated Eastern thought with Western psychology is Ken Wilber. Wilber (Wilber, Engler, & Brown, 1986) has presented "a full-spectrum model of human growth and development" (p. 65) that incorporates hierarchically ordered prepersonal, personal, and transpersonal levels of development (with corresponding levels of pathology and therapeutic treatment) with transpersonal levels comprising "contemplative or spiritual realms of development" (p. 105). The transpersonal realm involves levels of spiritual experiences—described primarily in terms of Eastern religious/psychological thought—moving toward enlightened oneness with ultimate reality.

Viktor Frankl. Of special importance in the broad humanistic tradition is the existential perspective of Viktor Frankl. Frankl's (1946/1984) emphasis on a person's will to meaning as the most fundamental ground of human motivation involves a self-transcendence in which meaning is achieved through commitment to and responsibility for an important humanizing task, a significant human relationship, or the choice of personal dignity in the face of dehumanizing conditions. The realization of meaning in this sense is the primary source of ennobling human development. The failure to seek and choose such meaning responsibly and freely (substituting instead direct efforts at pleasure, self-gratification, and utilitarian control) lies at the root of human deterioration in neurosis and antisocial behavior.

Closely associated with the will to meaning are Frankl's (1948/1975) notions of (a) the spiritual unconscious, the human in-depth locus of human freedom (in contrast to the instinctual unconscious of Freud), (b) the religious unconscious, which is a "latent relation to transcendence inherent in man" (p. 61), and (c) the unconscious God, referring to "man's hidden relation to a God who himself is hidden," (p. 62) but is nonetheless the personal referent for realizing ultimate meaning in a self-transcending I-Thou relationship. Religion in this sense is the expression of a free personal choice toward ultimate meaning congruent with the most authentic ground of human existence. Frankl (1948/1975) clearly ties positive human development and therapeutic/counseling practice (logotherapy) to a search for meaning that is inherently associated with a spiritual self-transcendence and with the unconscious God touched by the religious unconscious. He nonetheless strongly cautions against confusing counseling and psychotherapy with pastoral activity. In religious matters, the therapist is bound to "unconditional tolerance," and "least of all is a [therapist] who personally is religious released from this obligation. . . . He will only be interested in a spontaneous breakthrough of religiousness on the part of the patient" (p. 71).

Theory and practice in the humanistic tradition have special relevance for understanding the role of spirituality and religion in secular counseling settings. The humanists' emphasis on human potential and on the practical realization of humanizing values is very much in line with counselors' predominant value set, which might be summarized as a strong core valuing of holistic-humanistic empowerment related to personal development and interpersonal/social concern (E. W. Kelly, in press). This value set provides a positive context in which counselors' sensitivity to clients' spiritual depth (expressed either theistically or nontheistically, in religious forms or in secular/naturalistic forms) can be part of the overall therapeutic effort to help clients realize their developmental potential and resolve their problems.

Spirituality, religion, and human development

The previous section summarized contributions of major theorists to understanding key psychological dynamics of spirituality and religion in a largely nondevelopmental perspective. Now we turn our attention to the developmental perspective, examining theories of spiritual and religious development across the life span and noting the relationship of general developmental theories (e.g., cognitive, psychosocial, moral) to spiritual and religious development.

Human Development and the Spiritual/Religious Dimension

One approach to understanding spiritual/religious development over the life span is to recognize how major domains of human development (e.g., cognitive, psychosocial, moral) undergird and find expression in specifically spiritual/religious experience and content. For example, with respect to cognitive development, Piagetian theory forms a basis for understanding how object permanence, symbolic representation, logical thinking, and formal operational thought are involved in increasingly advanced cognitive abilities for representing the presence of an unseen God, symbolizing objects of faith, thinking about religious questions, and conceptualizing the complex interactions between religious faith and life experiences (Elkind, 1970, 1978). In his review of research and theory connecting general developmental theories to religious development, Worthington (1989) summarizes other connections, including, for example, how the generic processes of Erikson's stages of psychosocial development can help us recognize religious content woven into major life processes such as identity formation and interpersonal intimacy, how transition theories of development can be applied to spiritual growth or decline, and how concepts of moral development may be affected by the religious context in which they arise. Although specific connections between the major processes of life development and the spiritual/religious dimension have different results for different individuals, it is clear that spirituality and religion play a significant part, in casual and consequential ways, in the lives of many people, sometimes with developmentally beneficial repercussions, sometimes negative, and often mixed.

The counselor who is alert to the potential of the spiritual/ religious dimension in counseling recognizes that developmental issues may carry therapeutically significant spiritual/religious content and dynamics. This is illustrated, for example, by Robert Coles (1990) in his moving accounts of children's descriptions of spiritual/religious beliefs and issues. He writes in lively detail about children's cognitive formulations and emotional struggles to understand the sometimes obscure connection between a belief in God's goodness and their trust in the face of adversity, and between a belief in God's power and their own autonomous initiatives to grow and achieve.

Erikson's (1968, 1964) discussion of authentic religion highlights religion's potentially important roles in human development. These roles include:

1. Fostering a faith that supports a child's sense of trust and hope, in contrast to religious faith that instills fear.

2. Building up a system (ideology) of values, sometimes manifested in religious tradition, that adolescents may relate to in their expanding search for personal identity.

3. Promoting a sense of universalism to undergird the generative care of adulthood.

4. Contributing to older adults' formulation of a mature sense of the meaningful and integral wholeness of life.

The influence of religion, as Erikson notes, is not always benign in life development tasks—indeed it may play a role in an individual's misdevelopment. In any case, however, the counselor's responsibility as a developmental specialist implies an informed recognition and knowledgeable readiness to consider how spirituality and religion may be influentially woven into clients' overall development, as a direct influence in the developing lives of their clients as well as through the influence of parents and other significant individuals.

Spiritual and Religious Development

Theory and research dealing directly with spiritual and religious development across the life span includes the work of Jung, Allport, and Wilber (Worthington, 1989), all of whom were discussed above. In addition, in the psychoanalytic/object-relations perspective, Rizzuto (1979, 1991) has presented a theory of religious development that emphasizes developing representations of God, and Spero (1992) has described a developmental theory that correlates peoples' religious transformations in the quality of their relationships with a religious community and their God concept with their passages through the separation-individuation phases in object-relations development. Genia (1990) has proposed a five-stage model (egocentric, dogmatic, transitional, reconstructed internalized, and transcendent [mature] faith), which she applies in a developmental approach to counseling religious clients (Genia, in press). Two other well-formalized and researched theories are those of James Fowler (1981, 1991) and Fritz Oser (1991).

James Fowler: Faith development. For Fowler faith is directed toward a person's object(s) of ultimate concern, irrespective of the specific content of faith. Fowler (1981) construes faith *structurally*, aside from content, but recognizes that lived faith expresses itself in certain content. In this sense, faith represents how we develop cognitively, affectively, and spiritually in our handling of ultimate, transcendental reality and meaning. "Faith, at all levels, [is] the search for an overarching, integrating and grounding trust in a center of value and power sufficiently worthy to give our lives unity and meaning" (p. 5). Portrayed in this way, faith is clearly relevant to the spiritual/religious dimension in counseling because it represents peoples' inner or psychodynamic orientation to questions of meaning and value, that is, to questions that for many people are associated predominantly with spirituality and religion.

Fowler (1981; 1991) describes faith development in six stages, with a prefaith stage (ages 1–3) representing an emergent stage in which a fund of trust and mutuality is built up. The six stages are:

1. *Intuitive-projective* faith (ages 3–7), which is a fantasy-filled, imitative phase in which the child can be powerfully and permanently influenced by the visible faith of primally related adults. Imagination predominates in this stage. For example, a child may imagine a world of kind angels and feel trusting toward reality, or a child may imagine a punitive God and develop guilt and fear.

2. *Mythic-literal* faith: (ages 7 to puberty) in which individuals begin to take on for themselves the stories, beliefs, and observances that symbolize belonging to their community. Beliefs and symbols

are understood literally, and anthropomorphic stories are the major way of understanding faith content.

3. *Synthetic-conventional* faith: (puberty to adulthood) in which faith is structured in interpersonal but mostly conformist terms, with authority as important. Beliefs and values (ideology of clustering values) are felt deeply but are largely unexamined. Fowler maintains that this stage is typical of adolescents and normative for adults.

4. *Individuative-reflective* faith (emerging in young adulthood) in which the self and one's beliefs begin to take on a personalized system of explicit meanings to which one is personally committed. Symbols are translated into concepts for self-examination and critical reflection, although there is still much unconscious material.

5. *Conjunctive* faith, which involves the integration into self of much that was suppressed or unrecognized in the interest of stage 4's self-certainty and conscious adaptation to reality. Sensitive to paradox and ready for closeness to that which is different, one strives to establish syntheses of opposites and sees the possibility of an inclusive community of being. People in this stage are ready to exert themselves energetically for their beliefs.

6. *Universalizing* faith involves looking beyond the constraining paradoxes and the specific content of one's particular faith to seek a future order of relating justly and lovingly to others. People at stage 6 exhibit qualities that shake our usual criteria of normalcy: heedless to self-preservation; vivid attention to transcendent moral and religious actuality; devotion to universalizing compassion; enlarged vision of universal community. The rare person in stage 6 resembles in many respects Erikson's (1958) *homo religiosus*, including such people as Martin Luther, Soren Kierkegaard, Mohandas Ghandi, and Mother Teresa, "for whom the final challenge of integrity is a lifelong crisis" (Wulff, 1991, p. 384).

Fowler's developmental scheme has several implications for the spiritual/religious dimension in counseling. By outlining cognitive, affective, and behavioral elements of religious development at different life stages, Fowler provides the counselor with a way of understanding typical and problematic spiritual/religious development. Spiritual/religious belief is a process of growth in the multiple dimensions of faith, of transforming religious meaning, not clinging to a particular symbolization or formulation of content. Thus, faced with issues involving the spiritual/religious dimension, the developmentally aware counselor may help a client examine and transform literal and symbolic formulations of religious meanings and at the same time retain the essential reality of religious meaning behind the words and symbols. In this way, the counselor helps the client personalize and individualize faith meanings without breaking from the authentic core of one's religious roots. For clients who are concerned about remaining faithful to their religious tradition and overcoming the restraints and problems associated with specific symbols or formulations of earlier stages of believing, the counselor who understands the developmental dynamics of faith may be able to help the client to consider alternative perspectives that are still essentially congruent with the client's core spirituality/religiousness. For example, for a client whose disturbance involves a connection between the power of God and the symbol of a stern father, the counselor may help the client rethink and feel God's power as a supporting, transforming care linked to people who symbolize human care irrespective of gender.

Fritz Oser: Development of religious judgment. Oser's (1991) theory of religious development centers on the "development of religious judgment and what underlies that development, namely, transformations in the way individuals define their relationships to God or some Ultimate Being in concrete situations" (p. 5). Clearly, this perspective is close to that of Fowler, dealing with "deep structures" for "balancing different value elements" in the individual's "struggling for faith" (p. 6). With an emphasis on the cognitive domains in the total meaning-making process of religious development, Oser writes that religious judgment means "reasoning that relates reality as experienced to something beyond reality and that serves to provide meaning and direction beyond learned content." He adds that "such reasoning may occur at any time but is especially likely in times of crisis" (p. 6). This is a theory of religious *development* because it recognizes that "an individual relates his or her experience to an Ultimate Being (God), and that this is done *in qualitatively different ways during the life cycle, depending on the developmental stage* [italics in the original]" (p. 7).

Based on research interviews with individuals at different ages, Oser and his colleagues identified seven polar dimensions constituting major domains in which individuals seek to make religious sense of particular life situations. These seven dimensions are freedom versus dependence, transcendence versus immanence, hope versus absurdity, transparency versus opacity (quality of understanding God's will), faith (trust) versus fear (mistrust), the holy versus the profane, and eternity versus ephemerality. Examining these polar dimensions in religious dilemmas presented in extensive interviewing, Oser and his colleagues identified five qualitatively different forms of religious judgment displaying a sequence of five invariant, hierarchically and epigenetically structured stages of how the person conceives his or her relationship with the Ultimate Being. The five stages are conceptualized as follows:

1. The Ultimate Being is seen as powerfully active and effective and the person reactive.

2. The Ultimate Being is still seen as external and all-powerful but also subject to restricted influence via good deeds and rituals.

3. The Ultimate Being (if acknowledged as existing) is consciously assigned a transcendent realm of hidden influence separate from the immanent autonomy and responsibility of the human person.

4. The Ultimate Being is drawn back into the humanly immanent realm where the human person is now seen to have autonomy in responsible concert with an ultimate meaning or plan tied to the Ultimate Being. "Social engagement becomes a religious form of life" (p. 10).

5. As in Fowler's stage 6, a stage of rarely found individuals whose deeply coordinated religious reasoning harmonizes all polar opposites in a way of being in which the "Ultimate Being informs and inhabits each moment and commitment, however profane and insignificant" (p. 12).

The movement of people through these stages is a "process of disequilibration and subsequent restructuring" (p. 13), similar to that described by Wilber (1986) as a need for the person to "accept 'death,' negation, or release of the lower level . . . [the need] to dis-identify with or detach from an exclusive involvement with that level—in order to ascend to the greater unity, differentiation, and integration of the next higher level" (p. 81).

A sense of "disequilibration"—the feeling of being more or less painfully off balance, blocked, or not right in some aspect of one's life—is an apt general description of many clients' particular experiences. When this disequilibration involves, consciously or unconsciously, the spiritual/religious dimension, the counselor's developmental understanding can inform counseling approaches that may help the client find a way to turn loose and/or transform the reasoning of lower, more disintegrated (polarized) stages of religious judgment. The counselor can help the client work through literalisms and polarizations toward a more cognitively flexible and balanced stage of reasoning in which the client is better able to integrate personally and socially the disharmonies and tensions that he or she is experiencing. For example, to the client who is fearfully anxious and de-energized by a literal understanding of hell under the unfailing scrutiny of a punishing God, the counselor may conceptualize this struggle not as a need for the client to throw off all religiousness in general but as an invitation for the client to explore his or her religiousness beyond its current constricting forms and to find ways to express this religiousness with transformed integrity and a more hopeful and less anxious sense of self.

Ana-Maria Rizzuto and Moshe Spero: Development of the God representation. Rizzuto's (1979, 1991) theory of religious development focuses on "God representations" within psychoanalytically oriented object relations theory, in which the concept of "object relations" or "object representations" signifies the child's internalization of significant individuals and the relational dynamics with such individuals, and the continuing psychic influence of these internalized object relations. Rizzuto (1979) does not deal with the question of God's actual existence, although she clearly respects such belief. A person's God representation is a "special type of object representation created by the child" (p. 177), beginning "the psychic process of creating and finding God—this personalized representational transitional object—[a process that] never ceases in the course of the human life" (p. 179). God is a special object representation because, unlike other early representations, "instead of losing meaning, God's meaning becomes heightened" (p. 178) through the developmental phases of childhood, and remains throughout life "always available for further acceptance or further rejection" (p. 179). Rizzuto (1991) notes the potential therapeutic value of counselors' understanding the developmental transformations of a client's God representation:

> Careful exploration of the subjective description of an individual's God may reveal precious information about the type of psychic and interpersonal events that led to the particular characteristics attributed to God. . . . An understanding of an individual's God representation may provide, in turn, information about his or her psychic history and the types of obstacles that

interfere with potential belief, or with the updating of the God representation. I am referring now to [intrapsychic] processes . . . that may obstruct the transformation of the God representation and of religious behavior to a level more compatible with the individual's developmental moment. (pp. 56–57)

Spero's (1992) highly elaborated correlation of interpersonal object-relations development with ongoing religious transformations in the quality of one's God concept specifically comes to grips with the issue of God as objectively real and not just an intrapsychic construct. On the one hand Spero relates the development of the God concept (an "anthropocentric" God) to the separation/individuation processes of internalizing significant early others (especially one's mother) and progressively differentiating one's self from the internalized other. At the same time Spero extends this developmental process toward a "deocentric" affirmation of an "objective God object," in which an "individual is on the road to experiencing a relationship with God not based wholly in anthropocentric experiences" (p. 69).

Summary. The developmental perspective in understanding spirituality and religion prepares the counselor to approach a client's religiousness not as a static set of internalized beliefs but as an ongoing transformational process with potential significance for the person's overall development. Whether viewed primarily as development in faith (Fowler), religious judgment (Oser), or God representation (Rizzuto, Spero), the counselor can enter the client's spiritual/religious world ready to learn from the client his or her present understanding and experience of the spiritual/religious dimension. Having this developmental understanding and respecting the client's particular spirituality or religiousness, the counselor may carefully invite clients to open a door to transformations in faith, religious judgment, and God representations that will make their religiousness or spirituality a positive rather than a debilitating force in their total development and functioning.

Empirical studies of religion, spirituality, and mental health

As we have seen, spirituality and religion play important roles, for good or ill, in psychological development and human well-being. Through the years, since the early formulations by James, Freud, and Jung, the effect of religion on human functioning has been examined empirically. Research findings regarding the psychological effects of religion are clearly relevant to the professional work of counselors. A central question that runs through much of the empirical research is whether spirituality and religion are by their very nature detrimental to emotional and mental well-being. Ellis (1980) states explicitly the position against religion: "Religiosity is in many respects equivalent to irrational thinking and emotional disturbance. . . [and] the elegant therapeutic solution to emotional problems is to be quite unreligious . . . the less religious they are, the more emotionally healthy they will be" (p. 637).

Review of Representative Empirical Findings

The research summarized here addresses this central question of the link between religion and mental health from several different aspects. The picture that emerges in these findings is complex and still evolving. On the one hand, evidence indicates that some forms of religion are linked with emotionally and mentally unhealthy characteristics and behaviors. On the other hand, substantial evidence also exists indicating that there is no necessary connection between religion and emotional disturbance and that in fact many highly religious people are mentally healthy, competently functioning human beings. In a number of empirical studies, religious and nonreligious individuals are found to have similar normal psychological and developmental characteristics.

In an article that has had considerable influence on the recent renewal of the study of the psychological effects of spirituality and religion, Bergin (1980a) described what was for many years not only the relative paucity of the study of religion in mainstream psychology but also a general perspective in empirical and theoretical studies that took a predominantly dim view of spirituality and religion. Furthermore, as Bergin (1980a, 1980b, 1983) has shown in the case of spiritual and religious values vis-à-vis human functioning, the value assumptions that researchers bring to their work have potentially biasing effects—a point with which Ellis (1980), who takes a dim view of religion, has generally agreed. In a review of empirical studies of religion through the 1950s—studies that presented a generally negative view of religion's effect on human functioning—Bergin (1983) made a strong case that these findings, although not without merit, are often "conditioned by ideological bias, stereotyping, or empirical artifacts," resulting in a generally " 'sick' portrait" of the religious believer. This negative portrayal was reflected in Martin and Nichols's (1962) review of almost a dozen studies in the 1950s suggesting that religious be-lievers tended to be emotionally distressed, conforming, rigid, prejudiced, unintelligent, and defensive—a portrayal that coin-cided with Rokeach's (1960) conclusion that religious believers tended to be more tense, anxious, and symptomatic than nonbe-lievers. However, in their attempt to replicate the negative cor-relations between personality and religious variables that they found in their 1962 review, Martin and Nichols obtained *no* sig-nificant correlations.

To bring some organization into the continuing contradictory findings regarding religion and human functioning, Bergin (1983) performed a meta-analytical reexamination of 24 usable empirical studies from 1955 through 1979, with a total subject population of 9,799, and was able to tabulate 30 effects. Given the generally dismal picture of religion presented in the behavioral sciences, the results are, as Bergin notes, "surprising":

> Of 30 effects tabulated, only 7, or 23%, manifested the negative relation-ship between religion and mental health assumed by Ellis and others. Forty-seven percent indicated a positive relationship and 30% a zero relationship. Although most of the results were not statistically significant, the overall pattern was interesting. Considering statistical significance of results, 23 outcomes showed no significant relationship, 5 showed a positive relation-ship, and 2 showed a negative relationship. Although the findings provide no support for an Ellis-type theory, they also do not provide much more than marginal support for a positive effect of religion. (p. 176)

A sampling of recent research from among many studies pro-vides an expanded picture of this link between psychological well-being and the spiritual/religious dimension. Of particular note is C. G. Ellison's (1991) comprehensive analysis of survey data of 997 respondents from the 1988 General Social Survey, a national cross-sectional sample of American households. Using a special set of survey items on religious organization, belief, and practice in relation to other items having to do with social integration, recent life crises, and subjective assessments of life quality, Ellison found considerable evidence for a direct and substantial positive influence of strong religious faith on self-reports of life satisfaction, personal happiness, and fewer psychosocial consequences of traumatic life events. Several findings of this large and sophisticated study are especially noteworthy, namely: (a) firm religious beliefs significantly enhance cognitive and affective perceptions of life quality; (b) religious practices such as church attendance and private devotions appear to contribute to well-being indirectly, for the most part, by strengthening religious beliefs and worldviews; (c) religious faith appears to buffer the negative effects of trauma on well-being; (d) persons with liberal, nontraditional, and nondenominational Protestant ties report significantly greater life satisfaction than unaffiliated individuals.

A more focused study of 60 undergraduate students who were practicing members of the Mormon church showed that the total sample scored in the normal range on all scales of the MMPI, the Eysenck Personality Inventory, the California Psychological Inventory, and the Tennessee Self-Concept Scale (Bergin, Stinchfield, Gaskin, Masters, & Sullivan, 1988). Relevant to the issue of religious development and human functioning, the findings indicated that those who underwent continuous development of their religion and mild religious experiences tended to be more mentally healthy than those who had discontinuous religious development and intense religious experiences—though both groups scored in the normal range on all measures. Interview data of the students indicated that some subjects who deviated from their religious and moral beliefs appeared as a more disturbed subgroup, engaging in denials and rationalizations, rather than honest self-confrontation, to resolve their internal conflicts. A three-year follow-up study of all subjects showed that they gave evidence of no changes indicating any link between measures of psychopathology and religiousness.

These several findings, indicating some negative relationships in the context of an overwhelmingly positive relationship between religiousness and mental health, underline the diverse effects of spirituality and religion. This diversity is reflected in Parker's (1990) findings of a high correlation between orthodox (i.e., fundamentalist) Christian belief and dogmatism in a nonrandom sample of 50 beginning graduate students in counseling. This is congruent with earlier findings (Rokeach, 1960) and suggests that certain forms of religiousness are related to mental characteristics generally taken to be detrimental in human development and functioning. Some research also points to connections between prejudice and religiousness, particularly extrinsic religiousness (All-port, 1966), although prejudice among religious individuals may also reflect a strong mediating factor of non-religiously based cultural prejudice (Griffin, Gorsuch, & A-L. Davis, 1987).

On the more positive side, a study of religiousness and attribution of causality found that highly religious subjects, including fundamentalists, although attributing some causality to God, also considered themselves to be in control, thereby assuming an internal locus of control (Gorsuch & C. G. Smith, 1983). These religious subjects considered themselves to be active agents in achieving desired outcomes, at the same time acting with the help of God, thereby allowing for a cooperating external locus of control. Indeed, religious subjects in this study exhibited more "optimism" about achieving results than less religious people. This religiously "collaborative" view of life has been operationalized as "collaborative religious problem solving," which contrasts with "deferred religious problem solving" in which the individual is seen as passively deferring problems to God (Pargament et al., 1988). The collaboratively religious perspective has been shown to be a positive link between intrinsic religiousness and measures of psychosocial competence (Hathaway & Pargament, 1990). The religiously collaborative coping style may also be associated with belief in "A Helpful God," which, in combination with an active religiousness and rejection of a wrathful God, has been shown to be negatively associated with feelings of loneliness and manifestations of neuroticism (Schwab & Petersen, 1990). Collaborative religious problem solving, which appears to run counter to neuroticism and loneliness in intrinsic and actively religious people, lends itself to interactive counseling techniques that may be therapeutically valuable for religious clients.

In another study of the relationship of intrinsic/extrinsic religiousness of 119 college students of committed religious belief and practice (Mormon), results indicated that more than 95% of the sample were religious "intrinsics." Furthermore, when their personality scores (including measures of anxiety, self-control, irrational beliefs, depression, and various other psychological measures) were compared with those of other normal populations, there were trends slightly favoring the "intrinsics" of this study (Bergin, Masters, & Richards, 1987). These results are congruent with earlier findings indicating that, even when religion is measured simply according to denominational association and church attendance, those who are psychiatrically impaired are significantly less religious than community control subjects (Lindenthal, J. K. Myers, Pepper, & M. S. Stern, 1970; Stark, 1971). In a similar vein, considerable evidence shows that actively religious young persons, although reporting significant involvement in at-risk behavior, nonetheless are involved in such behaviors (e.g., alcohol abuse, drug use, sexual activity, police trouble, theft) at substantially lower levels than nonreligious young persons (P. L. Benson & Eklin's study as cited in Eklin & Roehlkepartain, 1992).

In a study examining the religiousness of clients within the counseling/psychotherapy process, a sample of religious clients scored higher on measures of shame and lower on existential well-being than religious nonclients, but they were *not* significantly different from religious nonclients on several measures of religiousness (intrinsic/extrinsic religiousness and religious well-being), moral reasoning, and guilt (Richards, S. A. Smith, & L. F. Davis, 1989). Although, as the authors suggest, this study does not cancel clinical evidence of relationships between certain religious beliefs and emotional disturbance, it does clearly indicate that such connections are not necessarily and always the case. Indeed, clients' healthy religiousness could well prove to be an asset during counseling with counselors who can enter with sensitivity into the clients' religious world.

In a related study with a college population, Richards (1991) found that the depression, shame, and existential well-being scores of religiously devout intrinsic students were within normal range and did not differ from less religiously devout extrinsic students. Religiously devout students did obtain higher guilt scores and lower parent-separation scores than less religious students, although, again, all were within normal range. The latter differences suggest that counselors need to understand the potential, complex function (sometimes negative, sometimes helpful) of guilt and close parental ties in some religious individuals.

We can complete this survey of empirical research by citing Schumaker's (1992) comprehensive review of previous reviews (1958–1991) summarizing the relationship between religion and mental health. Noting that there are many ways to define and measure religion and mental health, Schumaker's review of reviews highlights the complex diversity of findings regarding the relationship of the two. For example, on the positive side, previous reviews offer the following conclusions and suggestions:

1. In adult populations (especially the elderly) religiosity is positively associated with measures of personal adjustment, appears overall to be marginally helpful in times of crisis, and plays a role in the control of compulsive behavior (Argyle & Beit-Hallahmi, 1975/1958; Lea, 1982).

2. Psychiatric patients are far more likely than so-called normal people to be nonreligious, and people with high psychic inadequacy and neurotic trust are less likely to score high on measures of religiousness (Stark, 1971).

3. Religion tends to have a positive effect on mental health, defined as the absence of psychological symptoms (Batson & Ventis, 1982).

4. Intrinsic religiousness is positively correlated with the seven mental health criteria of absence of mental illness syptoms, appropriate social behavior, freedom from worry and guilt, personal competence and control, self-acceptance and self-actualization, unification and organization, and openmindedness and flexibility (Batson & Ventis, 1982) and is a generally positive force in the three broad areas of psychological adjustment, social conduct, and mental health (I. R. Payne, Bergin, Bielema, & Jenkins, 1991), whereas extrinsic religiousness is negatively associated with these seven mental health criteria and acts as an impediment in the three general areas.

5. Religiousness has a beneficial association with suicide risk, drug use, alcohol abuse, delinquent behavior, divorce and marital satisfaction, psychological well-being, depression, and physical health and longevity (Gartner, Larson, & Allen, 1991).

Examples of possible negative relationships between religion and mental health as presented in various reviews include:

1. In student populations religiosity is related to personal inadequacy (Argyle & Beit-Hallahmi, 1958/1975; Lea, 1982).

2. There is a trend for religion to be associated with unhealthy levels of dependency, pathological levels of suggestibility, and a relatively defensive, constricted personality (Dittes, 1969).

3. No compelling evidence exists that religion is correlated with mental health or moral behavior or that it acts to deter deviancy or social pathology (Lea, 1982; Sanua, 1969).

4. Religion is related negatively to authoritarianism, self-actualization, suggestibility/dependency, temporal lobe epilepsy, and dogmatism/tolerance of ambiguity/rigidity (Gartner et al., 1991).

These discrepant and at times contradictory findings again reflect the variety of ways of defining and measuring religion and mental health. A pattern noted by some researchers is that negative relationships between religion and mental health tend to occur when "soft" or intrapsychic measures of mental health (e.g., paper-and-pencil instruments with authoritarianism) are used, whereas positive relationships tend to occur when "hard" or behavioral variables are used (e.g., measures of drug use, rates of delinquency) (Bergin, 1983; Donahue, 1985; Gartner et al., 1991; Schumaker, 1992). In light of these divergent findings, Schumaker (1992) notes:

> It seems unrealistic to expect that definitive conclusions will ever be possible concerning religion and all-encompassing conceptions of mental health. A more reasonable approach assumes that mental health is, in fact, a constellation of variables that have differing relationships to religion. . . . Religion (and the different types of religion) has a much different effect on some areas of functioning than others. (p. 11)

Among the many areas or dimensions of behavior that Schumaker and his colleagues discuss as being affected positively and/or negatively by religion (depending on how religion is conceptualized) are: the mental health of women; sexual expression/adjustment; depression and suicide; anxiety and fear of death; guilt, shame, and self-esteem; rationality; self-actualization, psychological well-being, and meaning in life; neuroticism and psychoticism; development in various life stages (e.g., children and the elderly); marital adjustment; crime and delinquency; and alcohol and drug use. There are substantial connections between religion and positive functioning in every area, especially when religion is defined as intrinsic or mature—as well as detrimental connections.

These findings again highlight the complex and diverse connection between spirituality and religion and human functioning—sometimes positive and sometimes negative. These diverse links in turn reflect the diversity of religion itself. In this light, spirituality and religion represent for the counselor complex, dynamic intrapersonal and interpersonal domains with potential for positive and negative effects on clients. At the very least, therefore, a therapeutically beneficial mindset of counselors toward the potential spirituality/religiousness of clients would be one that holds open the possibility of a type of spirituality and religiousness (e.g., healthy-minded, mature, intrinsic) that may be beneficial to clients' personal development and well-being as well as a type of spirituality/religiosity (e.g., morbid-minded, immature, extrinsic) that contributes to mental, emotional, and developmental difficulties.

Conclusions Regarding Empirical Findings

The question of how and to what extent religiousness and spirituality are related to psychological well-being and human functioning clearly receives a mixed response in empirical research. Evidence suggests that people understand, internalize, and express spirituality/religion in divergent, even contradictory, ways—some apparently helpful to good mental and emotional health and some harmful. Earlier studies indicating a connection between religiousness and such conditions as emotional distress, dogmatism, conformism, rigidity, defensiveness, and anxiety are now being re-evaluated in light of studies that measure different expressions of religion, for example, intrinsic and extrinsic. Recent studies have found that religious believers, including conservative believers and especially those whose beliefs are held as intrinsic, display normal personality and developmental patterns and characteristics similar to those of religious nonbelievers. Research data disconfirm the assertion that religiousness *per se* is associated with some degree of emotional unhealthiness.

Although the data do not permit drawing a *causal* link between religiousness and good emotional health, nonetheless some evidence suggests that in certain cases clients' spirituality and religiousness offer a set of personal characteristics and dynamics that may be useful in the clients' development and problem solving. The obvious practical implication for counselors is that they need to be alert and sensitive to their clients' divergent spiritual/religious beliefs and practices. Counselors need to be ready not only to work with those religious elements that are detrimental to clients' good mental and emotional health but also to incorporate those positive elements of clients' religiousness that hold promise for clients' counseling progress.

Guiding principles

The theory and research surveyed in this chapter provide a detailed, complex, and in-depth picture of how religion and spirituality play a major influential role in personal and social development across the life span of many individuals. No single comprehensive theory emerges from this wealth of information and speculation, but it is certainly possible, on the basis of this cumulative knowledge, to formulate several general principles for guiding counselors in cases when the spiritual/religious dimension is important.

1. *Regardless of a counselor's own religious or spiritual beliefs in relation to those of clients, the counselor can call on a substantial body of knowledge to work with clients who bring to counseling personally relevant elements from the spiritual/religious dimension.* A counselor may be personally unreligious, or the counselor's own spiritual/religious beliefs may differ substantially in content or intensity from those of the client. Spiritual/religious differences between the counselor and client can have an effect on counseling process and outcome, *especially if the counselor is unaware or negligent about these differences.* However, such differences by no means preclude effective counseling with spiritual/religious issues. Because the spiritual/religious dimension is interwoven into peoples' intrapsychic, behavioral, and interpersonal worlds, the counselor's relational and technical competence in working with clients serves as a substantially adequate *foundation* for incorporating the spiritual/religious dimension in counseling. This is especially true as the counselor becomes better informed about the client's religiousness from the client and from pertinent study.

2. *Counselors can be prepared to assess the **therapeutic** relevance of clients' spiritual and religious issues, just as they would any issue or topic of interest that a client introduces into counseling.* Clients for whom the spiritual/religious dimension is important may bring, explicitly or implicitly, tentatively or straightforwardly, spiritual/religious beliefs, symbols, language, or practice into their discussion of counseling issues. In addition to being sensitively attentive to these aspects of the client's self-presentation, counselors need to explore and assess the relevance of these spiritual/religious elements to the client's primary developmental and therapeutic issues and problems. In making this assessment counselors need to dis-

tinguish between the general importance that a client attaches to the spiritual/religious dimension and the specific significance of the client's spirituality/religiousness to the therapeutic purposes of the counseling process.

3. *Counselors can be prepared to appreciate that with different clients religiousness and spirituality have either positive or negative effects on their development and functioning or a combination of positive and negative consequences.* Looked at from the point of view of their impact on human development and human functioning, theory and research indicate that spirituality and religion have diverse meanings and consequences in peoples' lives and that consequences may be beneficial and detrimental. Indeed, it is not uncommon for the spiritually/religiously oriented client to manifest therapeutic and developmental problems that are negatively influenced in part by some element of spiritual/religious belief *and at the same time* present a latent, undeveloped, or unclarified spirituality and religiousness that may be beneficial to positive development and problem resolution.

4. *To understand the therapeutically relevant impact of the spiritual/religion dimension in peoples' lives, counselors can be prepared to explore (a) the personal meaning(s) that a client gives to the spiritual/religious dimension; (b) the cultural, traditional, and/or institutional context with which this meaning is associated; (c) the particular formulations and symbolizations in which spiritual/religious meaning is clothed; (d) the developmental process in which this meaning has evolved; and (e) the connections of the spiritual/religious elements to other areas of the client's development and functioning.*

The large body of knowledge that has been reviewed in this and the previous chapter provides a substantive conceptual foundation for counselors to refine their work with spiritually and religiously oriented clients. In the following chapters we will examine more closely specific ways in which counselors can apply this knowledge in the relational and technical components of counseling.

CHAPTER THREE

The Counseling/Therapeutic Relationship: Spiritual and Religious Implications

Counseling may be viewed as consisting of two major interwoven domains: (a) the counseling/ therapeutic *relationship*, and (b) the *technical tools* for shaping and extending the relationship in ways specifically helpful for each client (E. W. Kelly, 1994a). There is considerable diversity of opinion with respect to the content and relative importance of the relational and technical components of counseling (e.g., varying degrees of emphasis on the real and transference aspects of the therapeutic alliance, and differing degrees of accent on the cognitive and behavioral elements in technical interventions). Nevertheless, across most counseling approaches, relationship and technique represent the two most fundamentally comprehensive dimensions of conceptualizing and organizing the total counseling process. As such, the relationship and technical dimensions provide reasonable and useful categories for organizing our understanding of how spirituality and religion can be ethically and effectively incorporated into the counseling process.

This chapter discusses spirituality and religion from the perspective of the relationship dimension of counseling. The next two chapters discuss them from the technical aspect, including approaches and techniques of assessment and treatment.

The relationship dimension of counseling

Research and integrative theory have clearly established the far-reaching importance of the counseling/therapeutic relationship (Beutler, Crago, & Arizmendi, 1986; Gelso & Carter, 1985, 1994; Luborsky, Crits-Christoph, Mintz, & Auerbach, 1988; Marziali & Alexander, 1991; Orlinsky & Howard, 1986; Sexton & Whiston, 1994; Wolfe & Goldfried, 1988). Based on accumulating research and scholarship from several related disciplines on the significance of relationality in human development and personality formation, I have argued extensively elsewhere (E. W. Kelly, 1994a) that the counseling relationship constitutes a comprehensive, in-depth therapeutic field with two substantive purposes. First, the counseling relationship itself forms a human and humanizing bond between the counselor and client, and second, it serves as the interpersonal, psychosocial ground for the integration of technical expertise within the totality of the counseling art. In this sense, counseling is relationship-*centered*. The counseling relationship in itself does not make up the whole of counseling. Rather, the counseling relationship functions as the vitalizing, in-depth center and unifying framework of counseling. It is pertinent, especially with respect to spirituality and religion, to note that this integrative relationship-centered counseling is based on a comprehensive epistemology, that is, a way of knowing that embraces the empirical/scientific and meta-empirical/in-depth aspects of reality. This epistemology encompasses the qualitative depth and the empirically observable aspects of the counseling relationship as well as the empirical sphere of counseling techniques and strategies.

In light of this comprehensive epistemology, the counseling relationship is itself made up of two major aspects or dimensions: (a) an in-depth, qualitatively human center and (b) a repertoire of expressive, interaction skills. Although these two components are inextricably connected in the full expression of the human (and counseling) relationship, each makes a distinctive contribution to human relationality. The in-depth center of the human relationship is a personal-relational sphere of *spiritual depth*. This center is the dynamic, existential ground of qualities and potentialities that are uniquely integral to humanness in its personal depth and interpersonal connectedness: reflective self-awareness,

intrinsic freedom, intentional purposefulness, inherent relationality, ethical responsibility, and transcendent meaningfulness.
This *in-depth* humanness of personal creativity and relational connectedness is extended and expressed in the complex interpersonal
field of interactional behaviors and skills. The counseling relationship is a bondedness grounded in human depth and expressed in
behavioral interaction.

This twofold aspect of the counseling relationship—human
depth and expressive interaction—provides an initial framework
for understanding how spirituality and religion may be woven into
the counseling relationship for the benefit of the client. We will
consider first the potentially beneficial contributions of a spiritual
perspective to the in-depth dimension and qualities of the counseling relationship. We will then look at how the expressive skills
of the counseling relationship may be used to work effectively with
spiritual and religious issues in counseling.

Spirituality in the counseling relationship

Based on current definitions as described in Chapter 1, spirituality
most significantly involves an inner awareness of and trust in a
deep sense of wholeness and connectedness along with an openness to a transcendent, infinite dimension associated with the
meaning and purpose of life in light of what one considers the
Ultimate (Elkins, Hedstrom, Hughes, Leaf, & Saunders, 1988;
Shafranske & Gorsuch, 1984). Spirituality thus represents an especially keen, active, and affirmative attention to the in-depth
center of personal and relational humanness. Spirituality entails
not only an awareness of human potential and creativity in personal depth, but also a sense of fundamental human relatedness
within a larger sphere of universal connectedness and transcendental meaning. Spirituality is a hopeful and participatory opening to all reality, bright and dark, and to an open-ended course
of life development, in which the evolution of the individual person—the "I"—is inextricably grounded in relation reality—the
"I-Thou" of human relationship and the "I-Thou-He/She" of human community (Buber, 1937; Jacques, 1982/1991; E. W. Kelly,
1994a). Spirituality's hopeful awareness of personal and relational
potentiality encompasses not only the bright and positive side of

89

reality—a movement toward the full realization of human potential—but also the dark and destructive side—the dehumanizing choices and forces that block human development.

A counselor's personal affirmation of spirituality as described above clearly coincides with—indeed, enhances—the in-depth humanness of the counseling relationship. This reinforcing congruence of spirituality with the humanly in-depth quality of the counseling relationship occurs along four significant dimensions— personal and relational awareness, benevolent connectedness, unconditional and hopeful openness, and transcendent meaningfulness. It is further expressed in the field of interpersonal behavior between the counselor and client—an interactional field characterized by what are frequently called the counselor-offered, facilitative conditions (and skills) of the counseling relationship, namely congruence, empathy, and unconditional positive regard or respect (C. R. Rogers, 1957, 1989; Carkhuff, 1969, 1987; Egan, 1994; Gelso & Carter, 1985; Sexton & Whiston, 1994)—as well as in the more challenging relational conditions of confrontation and immediacy (Egan, 1994; Ivey, 1986). We will first consider the interconnection of spirituality and in-depth relational humanness according to the four dimensions noted above and then examine spirituality and religion in light of the facilitative and challenging conditions and skills of the counseling relationship.

Spirituality and In-depth Relationality

Awareness. The integrity of the counseling relationship depends first on the counselor's sensitive and multidirectional awareness. This awareness involves an intrapsychic component, extending toward the ideal of a clear, nondefensive knowledge of self and an undistorted, clarified experiencing of one's feelings. The counselor's self-awareness puts him or her in the position of being personally self-possessed. This is the critical first step toward inner congruence, of being insightfully honest with oneself and undistortedly oriented toward the reality of oneself and others. Awareness establishes the ground for the integrity of the "I" and signifies a receptive readiness to enter into the client's world and to see, hear, and experience that world from the client's point of view. In its clarifying embrace of the client, counselor awareness establishes the client as an authentic "Thou." Given the interconnectedness of all reality, this awareness also constitutes a sensitive appreciation of the deep human relationality of "I-Thou"—the fundamental relational ground in which personal development occurs.

Authentic spirituality is inherently a movement toward a keener awareness of the in-depth existential ground of self-reflective freedom in which positive human development occurs. Highlighting the prime significance of awareness in spirituality, particularly in the context of counseling, Verge (1992) points out that "spiritually oriented psychotherapies are defined by the presence of spiritual awareness in the therapist, and the set of inner actions that correspond to the presence of this awareness" (p. 42). This spiritual awareness is a faith (or trust) in or experience of some greater consciousness, which across diverse conceptualizations (e.g., God, Spirit, the Divine, the Ultimate) establishes an openness to all reality as it is and a willingness to engage this reality courageously and without constricting judgments. Spirituality involves a movement toward expanded awareness, "the [personally] noticed, recognized, appreciated, or otherwise *sensed* [italics in the original]" (May, 1982b, p. 46) experience of consciousness, in contrast with a dulled, vague, or distracted sense of consciousness.

Spiritual awareness, especially in the Eastern tradition (Brown & Engler, 1986), involves a focus on the *processes* of conscious experience rather than the contents. In this sense it is a mindfulness that progressively opens, deepens, and expands one's perception of reality. Because the development of spiritual awareness involves a sharpened alertness of *reality*, it is a process of growing willingness to give active attention to the very real demands and responsibilities of life as these come to us in their nitty-gritty ways. Thus, the development of spiritual awareness in its active fullness, reflecting especially Western tradition, is an open-minded, deepened-minded engagement in reality, in its depth (or transcendental openness) and in its concreteness.

Spirituality in this light is for the spiritually oriented counselor an expansive, in-depth reality base that enhances the counselor's nonjudgmental openness toward the client. Spirituality infuses the counselor-client relationship with an augmented awareness of an in-depth bond grounded in a fundamental human connectedness that has the potential for healing power in the concrete, contextual expressions of individual personness. A counselor's *spiritually* oriented awareness enlarges the alert and comprehensive openness of the counseling relationship, and it expands the reality-orientation essential for the counselor to work through the unaware-ness, distortions, and discrepancies that block the client's positive development.

Benevolent connectedness. A major component of the counsel-ing relationship is the emotional bondedness (Bordin, 1975) be-tween the counselor and client—a bondedness that plays a signif-icant role in an emotional alignment of the working alliance between the counselor and client (Gelso & Carter, 1985). A primary characteristic of this client-counselor alignment and bondedness is the respect with which the counselor engages the client. The bondedness of respect is rooted in the counselor's taking the client seriously at the very core of the client's person-ness and caring about the client in his or her distinctive devel-opment. This respect conveys the counselor's goodwill, which penetrates behavioral, cognitive, and affective distortions that impede the client's distinctive personal development of the client and uncovers the potential at the vital core of the client's unique humanness. Respect endows the counseling relationship with a benevolent care that guides the whole counseling endeavor—the relational and technical components—according to the client's uniquely personal humanness.

Writing about spirituality in counseling and psychotherapy, Propst (1988) describes the counseling relationship as a "healing partnership." In this healing partnership, authentic spirituality/religion lead toward a full humanness that includes emotions join-ing us in compassionate solidarity with other people. It is a rela-tionship that allows clients to display ideas, feelings, and passions "without fear that such displays will be trampled beneath others' judgments, or quenched by others' disregard, or their indifference" (p. 30). In describing the healing spirit, Fleischman (1989) describes "affirming acceptance" as a process of entering peo-ples' human depths with unblinking and affirmative clarity. The sense of benevolent connectedness that is integral to the healing spirit and expressed in the healing partnership undergirds the spiritually oriented counselor's respect for the client's core, unique personness.

Because spirituality carries within it a deep sense of benevolent connectedness with others, it has the inherent potential for mag-nifying the counselor's respectful bonding with the client. In the spiritual perspective, respect as manifested in the counseling relationship is rooted in and enriched by a belief that all reality is not only inherently interconnected, it is also built up by our active concern for one another and the universe. In the spiritual perspective, respect in the human and counseling relationship is an in-depth attitude, a qualitative orientation toward human mutuality and serious care for positive human development. A spiritually imbued respect on the part of the counselor acts to enlarge the sphere of caring safety for the client within the demands of the counseling effort and to help the counselor and client believe in, search for, call forth, and activate the positive life energies that will enliven the client's growth and improvement.

Unconditional and hopeful openness. The relational bond between the counselor and client is built largely on the condition of *hope*, an "expectation of or trust in the satisfactory value of future experience" (Mahoney, 1985, p. 37). Citing research on the significance of positive client expectations, Yalom (1985) notes the bonding-holding effect of hope as well as its direct therapeutic power:

> The instillation and maintenance of hope is crucial in all of the psycho-
> therapies: not only is hope required to keep the patient in therapy so that
> other therapeutic factors may take effect, but faith in a treatment mode can
> in itself be therapeutically effective. (p. 6)

The need for change that motivates clients to come for counseling (or impels a parent, teacher, or other third party to send someone for counseling) implies some degree of hopefulness, or at least a readiness to be hopeful, to expect a change for the better. This nascent hope on the part of the client may be fairly robust as with clients who are looking to change their life with a career move, or it may be quite fragile as with clients who are experiencing the breakup of a long and cherished relationship, or it may be almost nonexistent as with clients deeply demoralized (Frank, 1985) by repeated failure or abuse. In every case, however, the counselor's own deep and lively hopefulness acts to catalyze the client's more or less active sense of hope.

Therapeutic hope is conveyed to the client by three major counselor characteristics: a conviction about the potential for improvement, the expectation of a legitimately helpful process, and confidence in a positive outcome. Although all three of these characteristics are integral to the full counseling/therapeutic endeavor, it is the counselor's attitudinal conviction about improvement that infuses the counseling relationship and the counseling process with the human vitality to carry forward the demanding tasks of personal development and healing change. This optimistic conviction is not a vacuous cheeriness or a Pollyanna view that shuts out the limitations and sufferings of life. On the contrary, it is a way of being toward all reality that is ready to look clearly and responsibly at things the way they are with a confident openness to the possibility of positive human development and transformation.

The quality of unconditional openness inherent in spirituality has the power to enrich and strengthen the counselor's responsible conviction about positive change. Spirituality in the counselor is a trust that is open to transcendence and infinity. It bears a trust that incorporates, but is not limited by, reductionistic or positivistic empiricism. Based on a comprehensive epistemology that is reasonable without being rationalistic, it is a trust that is expansively open to transformations toward ultimate meaning. Spirituality in this light can act as a deep motivating force to sustain the counselor and client through the often difficult work of counseling, pain of change, and sometimes slow healing of deep hurt and sorrow. When infused with the spirituality of trustful openness, therapeutic hope becomes an expectation filled with determined confidence, not in blindness or insensibility to limitations and pain but with persistence toward the promise of a "satisfactory value of future experience."

Transcendent meaningfulness. The in-depth humanness of the counseling relationship—a relational humanness that is the vitalizing ground and context of personal development—is characterized by effectively directional purpose. The working relationship between the counselor and client is built not only on the positive emotional bond linking them, but also on the valid, mutually developed expectation of an effective helping process leading to client improvement. In other words, the relationship is inherently meaningful, reflecting the powerful meaning-making orientation in personal development. Frankl (1946/1984) refers to this fundamental human orientation as the "will to meaning," a "striving to find meaning in one's life [that] is the primary motivational force in man" (pp. 104–105). Discussing the motivation toward meaning in the context of culture and anthropological evidence,

Jerome Bruner (1990) notes that the "quest for meaning within culture" constitutes, with culture itself, "the proper causes of human behavior" (p. 20).

An active orientation toward meaning is distinctively human and represents a twofold striving: (a) to discern or make sense of one's reality in its parts and as an interrelated whole, and (b) to achieve a sense of direction with significance. In part, this is a cognitive endeavor, the constructing of cognitive "patterns or templates" by which persons make sense of their world (G. A. Kelly, 1955/1963, p. 8). Human meaning-making, however, is more than a cognitive process. It is an in-depth orientation of the whole person, engaging the affective domain (see, e.g., Kegan, 1982; Guidano, 1991) as a part of the full human experience of movement toward meaning. Meaning-making in the counseling process occurs as a "movement from meaninglessness to meaning" (Carlsen, 1988, p. 4).

In spirituality human meaningfulness finds full expression in an orientation toward ultimate purpose, based on an awareness of and trust in a transcendent connectedness open to the infinite. A spiritual orientation in the counselor represents a profound orientation toward the meaningfulness of reality. By grounding a counselor's meaning orientation in a transcendently inclusive sense of reality, spirituality infuses the meaning-making direction of the counseling relationship with a distinctive perspective and energy. A spiritually rooted orientation to meaning involves a sense of an inherent patternness in reality, of a significance that transcends and indeed evokes peoples' particular meaning-making efforts. Thus a counselor's spirituality has the potential to augment, at least implicitly, the meaning-making motivation of the counseling relationship with a special invitational as well as driving energy. This special energy derives from a reasonable trust that the client's counselor-assisted striving toward meaning is not simply an individual construction and manipulation to squeeze sense from an absurd universe but a personally and socially enhancing collaboration with a larger reality that is itself fundamentally and ultimately meaningful.

Spirituality: Implicit Force, Not Imposed Belief

The argument that a counselor's spirituality has the potential to enhance the counseling relationship is most certainly *not* an argument that the counselor seek to unethically influence a client in the realm of spiritual beliefs. The point made here is that a counselor's authentic spirituality acts as a personal belief/attitudinal system that is highly congruent with the positive relationality that undergirds an effective counseling relationship. This congruence, however, occurs primarily as an intrapersonal reinforcement in the counselor, not as a vehicle for the counselor to convey spiritual beliefs through the counseling relationship.

With respect to the counseling relationship, the beneficial effect of a counselor's spirituality resides in its power to strengthen the positive therapeutic bond between the counselor and client. The therapeutic effect of authentic spirituality might be seen as analogous to the indirect benefit that a counselor's intellectual or physical condition can have in the counseling relationship. For example, the counselor's knowledge about relational skills, ability to think complexly, and physical energy level may make important contributions to the development of an effective counseling relationship, usually without the counselor conveying any personally specific ideas about his or her intellectual or physical condition. So, too, in the spiritual domain, the contribution of a counselor's spirituality is fundamentally indirect, achieving its effect through the relational elements of the counselor-client bond, without the counselor conveying any personally specific beliefs about his or her spirituality. "Spirituality in the counseling art above all means an honoring of the unique human integrity of the client and never, in its authentic expression, takes a form or force contrary to the clients' voluntary participation" (E. W. Kelly, 1994a, p. 50).

Although the counselor's spirituality works indirectly as an intrapersonal enhancement of the counselor's therapeutic bonding efforts with the client, it must be recognized that counselor beliefs and values may have more direct influence on the client. Research indicates that certain counselor beliefs (e.g., about the positive worth of other persons) may be significantly related to effective counseling (Combs, 1989) and that certain counselor values (e.g., responsible self-direction) may be taken on by a client over the course of effective counseling (Beutler & Bergan, 1991; T. A. Kelly & Strupp, 1992). In view of the now almost universal agreement that counseling is a value-laden enterprise (Bergin, 1991), and in view of evidence that client values in some respects tend to converge toward those of the counselor over the course of effective counseling (T. A. Kelly, 1990), counselors with a spiritual orientation need to pay particular attention to avoiding any unethical attempts, explicit or implicit, to improperly influence clients toward specific spiritual beliefs. At the same time, counselor beliefs, *if* relevant to the client's unique developmental and therapeutic needs, may be expressed explicitly in the course of counseling as part of a client's aware and willing consideration of multiple perspectives pertinent to the client's improvement. In this case, the client has the opportunity to consider spiritual beliefs along with other perspectives that the client may adopt and/or adapt as a fresh cognitive framework for improved self-direction and decision making. In this process the counselor needs to be clearly aware of his or her own beliefs and values and to ensure that these beliefs are brought forward in a way that respects the client's rights and ability to consider freely and clearly alternative beliefs as these have therapeutic relevance for the client.

Case illustration. This indirect infusion of spirituality in the counseling relationship and tentative exposing of spiritual beliefs is illustrated in my work with Jason, whose case I have described elsewhere (E. W. Kelly, 1994a). Jason was a 55-year-old physician, who was married and had one adult daughter. Jason had been active in a mainline Protestant church until about the age of 35, at which time he left the church as an agnostic, a perspective that he maintained at the time of our counseling. Jason spoke of a growing, deepening sense of loneliness and disconnection. Although not clinically depressed, Jason did talk of a kind of inner void, an absence of meaning that previously had given his life a feeling of direction and vitality. Even his clinical work did not dispel his empty feeling. In my efforts to empathically join Jason in his inner world and journey, I noted within myself (but did not articulate to Jason) an awareness of my own trust in the ultimate connectedness and meaning of reality. Jason talked about the uncertainty of human meaning but was reluctant to find meaning in any kind of transcendence or spirituality. As counselor, I responsively joined Jason in his disheartened and perplexed searching for what he hoped would be a renewal of meaning and inner vitality. While doing this, I felt with a special awareness a spiritual depth in my relationship with Jason, at the same time refraining from mentioning or alluding to my own spiritual beliefs. As he looked to the future, Jason wondered aloud about his old beliefs, his struggles with faith, and the effects of his agnosticism.

As our relationship grew in mutual respect and understanding, my responses to Jason gradually began to reflect not only his own perspectives but a relational region of shared exchanges comprising some of my beliefs as well as his. At the end of our time together, Jason did not come to affirm an explicitly spiritual perspective. However, he displayed a renewed sense of vigor and direction from our intensely bonded exploration of meaning in terms of his own life. Although Jason did not close the door to the possibility of spirituality, he did not assume my spiritual stance, nor was it my intention that Jason should assume any perspective other than that which was consistent with his own authentic development. With Jason, I would argue that my spirituality enhanced the therapeutic effect, not as a perspective that I sought to impose on Jason, but rather as an "existential field of new possibilities and hope—a field in which Jason had both the freedom and scope to discover his own meanings" (E. W. Kelly, 1994a, p. 91).

The counselor's sensitive understanding of the creative connectedness inherent in spirituality constitutes an experiential base for the counselor to form a counseling relationship in which the counselor is alert to the client's in-depth creative potential as this emerges within the transformative context of the counselor's relational participation in the client's development. Framed in terms of Buddhist spirituality, Rosenthal (1990) has described a process of the "meditative therapist," whose alert attentiveness in the counseling relationship (nurtured in the practice of mindfulness meditation) moves sensitively in the moment-by-moment "walk" of the counselor with the client. This is a deeply connected walk in which the actively aware spiritual counselor resonates with the client at all levels of experience (e.g., affective, cognitive, physical) and at the same time is alert to corresponding reactions within himself or herself. It is important to recognize that this spiritually in-depth relationship is not a counselor's muddled or uninformed meandering with the client. It is deeply informed with the counselor's knowledgeable and skillful expertise. This expertise, however, is an extension of the counselor's being in an in-depth relationship *with* the client—a vitally open relationality whose spiritual depths (or "creative void" in Rosenthal's [1990] words) "accommodate the emergence of an infinite variety of spontaneous and creative responses" (p. 41) that give therapeutic power to the counselor's expert knowledge and skills.

Counselor Spirituality:
An Enhancement, Not a Requirement

A substantial majority of counselors affirm spirituality understood in its broad sense (E. W. Kelly, in press). For these counselors their spiritual beliefs offer, as I have proposed, a perspective that can enhance their relationship with clients. However, certainly not all counselors have a spiritual belief, affirming instead a humane rationality informed by a scientific, pan-materialistic empiricism. This is the view of positivism, "a theory that theology and metaphysics are earlier imperfect modes of knowledge and that positive knowledge is based on natural phenomena and their properties and relations as verified by the empirical sciences" (*Merriam Webster's Collegiate Dictionary*, 1993, p. 909). Wolpe (1990) gives a cogent articulation of this perspective in his rejection of any "ghost in the machine" of the universe and his position that all phenomena, including mental and affective, "obey the same mechanistic laws as other behavior" (p. 18). Wolpe's positivistic position is significant with respect to the counseling relationship because it is representative of a decidedly nonspiritual view that at the same time affirms the importance of the counselor-client relationship, as reflected in empirical research in counseling and psychotherapy. In this case, the counseling relationship is made up of "nonspecific effects" most likely associated with the "emotional impact on the patient of the therapist, a trusted and supposedly wise and competent person to whom the patient has entrusted himself" (Wolpe, 1990, p. 333).

I cite the example of Wolpe's positivistic (i.e., nonspiritual) interpretation of the importance of the counseling relationship to highlight that spirituality is presented here as a *potential enhancement*, not a requirement, of an effective counseling relationship. The facilitating conditions of the counseling relationship (e.g., the empathy, genuineness, and respect that establish the counselor as "a trusted and supposedly wise and competent person") may be defined in behavioral, mechanistically interactional terms (see, e.g., Derlega, Hendrick, Winstead, & Berg, 1991) and may be effectively implemented by counselors with a nonspiritual orientation. Thus the point being made about spirituality in the counseling relationship is *not* that counselors with a positivistic perspective cannot form effective counseling relationships; indeed, evidence and experience show that they most certainly can and do. The point rather is that spirituality—based on a comprehensive epistemology made up of empirical and meta-empirical modes of knowing—represents an authentic dimension of reality that provides a reasonable elucidation of the in-depth aspects of the counseling relationship and an expanded knowledge base for an aware and enhancing infusion of these spiritual aspects into the relationship.

Conditions and skills of the counseling process: spiritual and religious aspects

The inclusion of spirituality and religion in the relationship component of counseling can be made more concrete by examining them in light of the major facilitative and challenging conditions and skills of the counseling relationship and related process dimensions of counseling. The term "condition" refers primarily to the attitudinal or personally in-depth quality of a counselor's interpersonal responses but also includes the skillfully expressive aspects of the counselor's responsiveness. The term "skill" conveys principally the behaviorally expressive aspect of the attitude. Humanly in-depth attitudes ("way of being" [C. R. Rogers, 1986/1989]) and expressive skills together constitute the facilitative/challenging conditions of the fully human responsiveness of the counseling relationship (E. W. Kelly, 1994a).

The considerable diversity across various approaches to counseling (e.g., analytic-psychodynamic, humanistic, cognitive, behavioral) precludes a single formulation of facilitative conditions and process dimensions that would precisely satisfy all points of view. To specify significant ways in which spirituality and religion come to play in the counseling process, I will use the well-known and widely accepted facilitative conditions as formulated primarily in the Rogerian tradition, specifically empathy, congruence, and respect (unconditional positive regard) (Gelso & Carter, 1985; Sexton & Whiston, 1994), as well as two widely regarded challenging conditions and skills—constructive confrontation and immediacy (Carkhuff, 1969; Egan, 1994; Ivey, 1986). I will discuss these conditions and skills in the context of a counseling process made up of three major process dimensions (sometimes viewed as process stages) involving (a) initial engagement in alliance building and early self-exploration, (b) understanding and perspective shifting, and (c) consolidation, generalization, and action planning (see, e.g., Carkhuff, 1969, 1987; Egan, 1994; Steenbarger 1992, 1993).

Facilitative and Challenging Responsiveness to Spirituality and Religion

Spiritual/religious dimension. The facilitative and challenging conditions and skills of the counseling relationship are as therapeutically relevant to the spiritual/religious dimension of clients' lives as they are to the nonspiritual/nonreligious dimensions. The perspective here is that the spiritual/religious dimension involves a complex and dynamic set of spiritual/religious beliefs (cognitions), affects, values, choices, and related behaviors. Personal spirituality or religiousness in this sense represents a specific psychological set or dimension organized around spiritual/religious meanings or beliefs, as well as intrapersonal factors that have the potential for influencing and coloring other dimensions of human functioning. That is to say, spiritually or religiously oriented people typically identify in themselves a specific sphere of spiritual and religious meanings—the more or less organized elements that distinctively constitute their spirituality or religiousness. Furthermore, this specific spiritual/religious dimension interacts with other intrapersonal dimensions, including, for example, the rational/intellectual, physical/biological, affective and artistic, and interpersonal dimensions, as well as various life-role domains such as spouse and family member, student, worker, and citizen. This is in line with Pruyser's (1968) notion that the psychological dimension of personal religious significance is not limited to some psychological compartment, but "rather *all* data—events, processes, actions, objects, and object relations—may have . . . a religious . . . significance for the patient, or for the [therapist], or for both" (p. 15).

Spirituality/religion across the counseling process. In broad outline, what the counselor needs to accomplish with respect to clients' spiritual/religious dimension during the relationship-building/exploratory, understanding/perspective-shifting, and consolidation/action-planning phases of the counseling process may be summarized as follows.

1. Establish a counselor-client relationship that is respectfully open to the spiritual/religious dimension, and in clients' self-exploration, facilitate the inclusion of spiritual/religious elements that are significantly and therapeutically relevant, positively and negatively, to clients' issues and problems.

2. Help clients integrate personally beneficial spiritual/religious material into an expanding and perspective-shifting clarification of the various elements of their issues and problems, and/or clarify and eliminate (or at least positively recast) negative spiritual/religious elements.

3. Use positive spiritual/religious resources, as appropriate, for clients to plan and carry out a course of action that will implement their new understandings and/or will effectively overcome any negative impact of religion or spirituality in their steps toward developmental, problem-solving action.

The concrete implementation of this overall process of responding to the spiritual/religious dimension of clients' lives depends on several factors, including the setting in which counseling takes place, an assessment of the quality and degree of clients' religiousness/spirituality, and the relevance of religion to the kinds of issues and problems presented by clients (the last two are discussed more fully in Chapter 4). These factors are important in determining how and when counselors may appropriately use facilitative and challenging skills in responding to spiritual/religious material.

Settings. With respect to counseling settings, especially non-religious settings, which are the focus of this book, the response of the counselor to the spiritual/religious dimension will depend to some extent on the particular nature and requirements of the setting and perhaps on various cultural and community expectations that bear on how personal religion is to be expressed. For example, the general sensitivity about religion in the public schools, not to mention specific regulations that may exist in particular schools or school systems, may lead public school counselors to pass over or respond only broadly to the spiritual/religious dimension of a client's issue. Even in this case, however, unless the counselor is tightly bound by specific regulations or restrained by rigid community standards, leeway often exists for sensitive and appropriate responses to religiously tinged issues. The point here is that the counselor's facilitative and challenging responsiveness to spiritual/religious issues must be tempered (although not necessarily cancelled) according to the setting in which the counseling occurs.

In many nonreligious settings, however, such as colleges, human service agencies, and corporate and private settings, therapeutically relevant responses to the spiritual/religious dimension can often be both proper and germane. The impediment to such responses in these settings is not so much the requirements of the settings as it is the counselor's own lack of alertness to spiritual/religious concerns, lack of skill or experience in responding to this dimension, a sense of discomfort (or even distaste) in discussing spiritual and religious issues, or a fear of unethically trespassing in value-sensitive areas of the client's life. When one or more of these concerns impede relevant responses to clients' spiritual/religious issues, the counselor can break through these impediments initially by using facilitative responses to tap the spiritual/religious dimension. These facilitative conditions (e.g., attentive listening, respectfully empathic responsiveness), which are usually well developed in most counselors, provide an important set of responses for spiritual/religious issues and a ready repertoire of skills for initially formulating responses to the clients' spiritual and religious issues.

A Case of Spirituality and Religion in the Counseling Process

An extended example, adapted from actual case materials, illustrates how a client's spirituality and religion can be integrated into the major components of the counseling process. Philip, a 35-year-old journalist, came to the counselor in intense distress, triggered by his wife's recent decision to seek a divorce, their actual separation, and his move from their home. On the intake form he noted that he had never been in counseling before and had no other pressing problems or issues. For the intake form item, "Religious or spiritual heritage," he wrote "Agnostic (formerly Lutheran)." He indicated on the intake form that he and his wife had three young sons, ages ten, seven, and three. He said that his wife was adamant about getting a divorce and refused to come to counseling. During the first three sessions held over a two-week period, Philip expressed great emotional pain, often crying while describing what he called the breakup of his family and the loss of his children.

Alternately expressing anger at his wife and his love for her, he readily ascribed much of the blame for the breakup to himself. He said that he had been sexually unfaithful to his wife on several occasions, first about two years after the birth of their second son, and then again during his wife's third pregnancy and continuing thereafter. His wife had found out about a recent affair, confirming her long-standing suspicions; it was shortly after that she confronted him with his unfaithfulness, told him that she had contacted a divorce lawyer, and demanded that he move out. Struck by what he experienced then as a sudden discovery of his wrong-doing, his pangs of guilt and embarrassment, the impending collapse of his family life, and his wife's angry determination, he moved to a nearby apartment.

In the first three sessions, while Philip was mostly venting his anguish, regret, and anger, the counselor responded with non-judgmental understanding, while beginning to help him explore and gradually focus on the events, thoughts, feelings, and behavior that were most relevant to his problem and pain. In the next three sessions, Philip's mood shifted somewhat and his field of concern expanded to include his loneliness and his sexual needs. Part of what the counselor did during these three sessions was to help Philip clarify for himself a difference between friendly, nonsexual contacts as a way to alleviate loneliness and interest in sexual relationships. Philip was receptive to this distinction, and he began to take some steps toward framing solutions to his loneliness, at least in part, with friendly, nonsexual relationships.

In the seventh session, he said that he was resigned to the eventuality of his divorce. He said he felt more in control of himself. He spoke briefly of a couple of sexual encounters but did not see them as a problem. The counselor responded to this last aspect of Philip's self-presentation by contrasting for him his current sexual behavior and the problems, as he himself had stated them, that led in large part to the breakup of his family. He did not object to this confrontation, but he would not explore it further during this session.

At no time during the first seven sessions did Philip mention anything remotely related to spirituality or religion, and these formed no part of the counselor's responses to Philip. In the eighth session, however, Philip's field of exploration shifted. Near the beginning of the eighth session, Philip mentioned with hesitation and embarrassment that since last week, he had had a kind of religious experience that had started him thinking. He seemed unsure about whether this should be a part of counseling. The counselor responded to Philip's remark with a respectful empathy, "Something has touched you deeply, something that you experience as religious. As a result of this experience—this religious experience—you've seen and felt some significant shift in your thinking." Philip still had some mixed feelings about discussing his experience: he said it might seem a little crazy and kind of strange, but he thought it did have a positive effect on him. The counselor responded empathically not only to Philip's sense of strangeness about his experience but also to what appeared to be his even stronger sense that the experience was authentic and positive for him.

With similar respectfully empathic responses, the counselor helped Philip to talk about the details of his religious experience and explore its potential meaning for him. As Philip became more assured that the counselor was understanding and respecting his religious experience, he spoke of how he had flipped on the TV early one Saturday morning after a sleepless night and heard a preacher talking about God's love. The message was that God's love sometimes shatters a life built on lies so that a person's life can then be rebuilt in genuine love and truth—a process that can be terribly painful but also an act of God's saving love. Philip said that he had the feeling that these words were being spoken directly to him and for him. He felt in himself a reconnection with his Lutheran religious heritage, which, as the counselor learned later, had been very important in Philip's life until about 10 years earlier when he had dropped all religion. Philip said that the next day (Sunday) he attended services at a nearby Methodist church. He sat in the back and, as he said, was flooded with thoughts and feelings that he could hardly describe and "felt kind of funny talking about." He said he felt a mixture of inner release, a freeing, a peace, and a kind of acceptance into "a clean and rich" reality. He said he had to fight back tears and try to keep people from seeing the tears that did come. With occasional remarks like, "I guess this sounds pretty funny to you" and "It even sounds kind of strange to me," Philip said that he was now feeling strongly reconnected with his religious past in a new and deeper way.

In this session, with the respectful empathy of the counselor, Philip moved from the initial exploration and understanding of his problem and his responsibility for hurting his family to an expanded exploration of his life in light of the religious beliefs and new spiritual experience. This session ended in what might be called a mixture of peace and anticipation. Had the counselor not responded with understanding and respect to the client's initially tentative statement about religion and his increasing sense of the importance of this spiritual experience, we can hypothesize that a potentially beneficial area of the client's life may have been cut out of the counseling process. On the other hand, the counselor did not have to directly encourage the client's talk of religion or expand on his own spiritual understanding of his experience. With responses of genuine and accurately empathic respect for the client's own understanding of his spiritual/religious experience, the counselor offered a therapeutic opportunity for the client to reflect on and integrate this experience into his expanding self-understanding and changing sense of direction.

During the next several sessions the counselor helped Philip to use his revitalized spiritual and religious experiences as part of his continuing reflection on his life. He spoke of his responsibility for what his behavior had done to his wife and children. The counselor sensitively responded to an unspoken note of guilt. With the counselor's clarifying empathy, Philip began to discuss his guilt, but not in a crippling or self-denigrating way. Rather, his guilt feelings led him to realize that he had chosen and then been emotionally caught in sexually irresponsible behavior that betrayed his wife, deceived himself, and set in motion the consequences leading to his divorce and family breakup. The counselor also helped Philip examine these perceptions in the broader context of his relationship with his wife and to sort out his own irresponsible behavior from what he said were his wife's faults. He accepted now that his divorce was inevitable and, painful as it would be, he would not have custody of his children. Although his marriage was over, he thought he had a responsibility to finally be honest with his wife. At this point, the counselor helped Philip formulate a simple interim action plan to have an honest talk with his wife. As it turned out, this became an important piece in what eventually was a mostly civil and cooperative divorce.

Throughout this process the counselor was aware of the spiritual/religious motivation that was now part of Philip's movement toward change. When relevant, the counselor responded empathically to Philip's occasional, but often deeply serious, references to religion in his life. Philip did not put everything in a spiritual or religious context. However, he did think that the loss of "a religious sense of life" set the stage for choices leading to a slide into infidelity and irresponsibility that played such a large part in the breakdown of his marriage and life. He also believed that his renewed religious life would be a source of personal strength to help establish honest relationships. While responding respectfully to this perspective, the counselor continued to help the client use this spiritual/religious perspective to achieve a broader understanding of himself. For example, over several sessions, with the counselor's sensitive responsiveness to the religious and sexual elements of his life, Philip easily mixed in discussions of his increasing spirituality (e.g., periods of prayer each day and participation in the Methodist church) with telling the counselor about new female relationships, some of which were sexual.

As Philip's self-understanding deepened and perspectives shifted, the counselor was able to use Philip's spirituality as one of the ways that Philip could confront himself and reevaluate his behavior. As this dimension of Philip's life assumed more importance, the counselor, who herself valued spirituality, was able, at therapeutically appropriate times, to occasionally and briefly self-disclose religious elements in her own life—for example, how some Biblical psalms were meaningful to her. The counselor also worked collaboratively with Philip to help him think through personally and socially enhancing activities, including spiritual and religious activities such as daily short periods of meditative prayer and religiously based human service projects.

Philip discontinued counseling at the end of about a year. But the case did not end there. About 18 months later, Philip saw the counselor again. He was doing well in most areas of his life, including a new marriage and his relationship with his children. He then told the counselor that about three months earlier he had begun to participate in a charismatic prayer group connected with a local fundamentalist church. He said that he found the group to be spiritually uplifting. The counselor, although inwardly puzzled by Philip's move from his mainstream religious traditions to a fundamentalist group, responded empathically to Philip's new experiences; she also noted that Philip seemed a bit distracted or unsettled. At this, Philip said that he wanted to talk with her about the group's belief that men should be the head of the household and that women should stay at home and raise their children. Although Philip had some misgivings about this belief (and felt bad telling the counselor this because she was a woman), he was beginning to wonder if it might not have some merit; it seemed to have some justification in the Bible, and it might be a good way to maintain a religious home.

As Philip talked about these ideas, the counselor felt her initial puzzlement change to aversion. Philip's religious journey had now taken a twist that the counselor was very reluctant to follow. However, she believed that she could not let her values interfere with Philip's particular life development. She had to bracket her own values and strong negative reaction and make a genuine effort to enter Philip's puzzling world without prejudgment. Her first efforts might be described as a kind of "bending over backward" to respond with respectful empathy to Philip's religiously based notion of the relative place and role of men and women. In taking this neutral stand and distancing herself somewhat from her own reaction to Philip's notions, the counselor became better able to hear a note of tentativeness in Philip's own voice. She was able then to respond to Philip's affirmation of this unequal man-woman relationship and to the unspoken questions and disquiet he seemed to be having with this new belief.

With the clarifying empathy, Philip began to speak about his doubts and the vague but nagging discomfort surrounding his doubts. He mentioned again his desire to have a religious family and not to fall away from religion. At this the counselor responded with empathy to Philip's serious spiritual quest and noted how this quest was at the moment tied up with his charismatic group and the group's particular ideas about religion. This opened the door for Philip to explore his religiousness *in contrast* to the group's without feeling that he was moving away from religion itself. The counselor helped Philip revisit the connections that he had made in their earlier sessions between spirituality and self-possessed freedom and caring human service. As Philip spoke about how this would affect his wife, the counselor wondered along with him about the links between his own spirituality and his commitment to the wholeness and integrity of his wife. When the counselor raised the possibility of his bringing this up with the charismatic group, Philip seemed reluctant. The counselor helped him to explore this reluctance and noted how, paradoxically, this reluctance was a possible indicator of Philip's uncertainty about the group's helpfulness to him in his particular spiritual journey. Despite his reluctance, Philip, already beginning to give some weight to his doubts, agreed to bring this up to the group.

The following week, Philip came back for his last session with the counselor. He said that he now saw how he had been on the verge of giving up his spiritual freedom and growth for somebody else's idea of what religion requires. He said that he did tell the group's members about his doubts, and, although they were friendly, they were adamant about the importance of male primacy in marriage. He said he couldn't go along with that; in fact, his religiousness led him to affirm the essential equality and freedom of all people. He thanked the counselor for helping him to see what he said he should have been able to see all along for himself.

Counselor Responsiveness in the Counseling Process: Reflections on Philip's Case

Philip's case illustrates how the counselor's sensitive and skillful responsiveness can ethically and beneficially weave the positive and negative aspects of spirituality and religion into the relational, exploratory, understanding, and action-planning dimensions of the counseling process. We do not know, of course, what would have happened had the counselor not responded to Philip's first tentative statements about a religious experience or not used Philip's developing spirituality to help him gain a new perspective and find more effective ways of living. From that point of view, case material is not a proof, nor is it intended to be one. However, Philip's case, as with any similar situation, points to two important realities.

First, it points to the personal validity of Philip's reality. This reality does not constitute a demonstration for anyone else, but, as we can best determine, it was true and right for Philip (intrapersonally) and in the wider circle of Philip's life (interpersonally). This is no small matter. Although counseling and the behavioral sciences rely in large part on the reasonableness and predictability that are the hallmarks of scientific generalizations, nonetheless a fundamental criterion for assessing counseling's value is its humanizing effectiveness with *individual* clients. When we observe, with a reasonable degree of confidence, that counseling achieves this effectiveness with a client, we are justified not only in affirming the positive significance of a humanizing development in one person's life but also in looking more closely at the counseling elements associated with that change. This brings us to the second reality to which Philip's case points.

Our observation of Philip's case makes it very difficult to avoid the key role that spirituality and religion played in Philip's change. There can be no doubt that other factors (e.g., Philip's early life experiences, the cognitive and behavioral patterns that he formed over many years of social interaction and intrapersonal reaction, the relationship dynamics with his first wife) also greatly influenced Philip's life and his change during the course of counseling. Nonetheless, spirituality and religion came to the fore as influential factors; to ignore these factors or completely transmute them into nonreligious factors would require considerable diffidence, inattention, negligence, bias, or philosophical assumptions antithetical to the spiritual and religious domain. Philip's case and others like it (see, e.g., Benner, 1988; Lovinger, 1984; M. E. Stern, 1985) highlight the potential importance of spirituality and religion for achieving positive therapeutic effects. In terms of major process elements, the spiritual and religious elements of Philip's case suggest the following points.

Spiritual/religious dimension in the relationship-building/exploratory phase of counseling. The counselor's facilitative responsiveness helps to bond the counselor to clients in the spiritual/religious dimension. It also helps clients to explore pieces of their spirituality and religion insofar as these are significantly and therapeutically relevant, positively and negatively, to the issues and problems they present in counseling. One can expect that the counselor's facilitation of client self-exploration usually will predominate early in the counseling process; but it is also a process component that weaves in and out of the total counseling process. Philip's case illustrates how important it is, in the case of spiritual and religious material, for the counselor to be alert for facilitatively expanding or revisiting the client's self-exploration at any point in the total counseling process. Clients may be hesitant about bringing up the spiritual/religious dimension. It may remain implicit in clients' issues and unnoticed by the counselor. It may, as in the case of Philip, occur unexpectedly later in the counseling process, calling for the counselor to have a more refined empathy with the client.

Counselors can work with typical client problems with little thought, much less expectation, that these problems have a religious or spiritual dimension. To counter the possibility—indeed, in many cases the probability—of neglecting or missing therapeutically relevant religious or spiritual material, counselors need to include this dimension explicitly in their conceptualization of the clients' total world. That is to say, counselors need a framework of humanness that accommodates and taps into all major dimensions of clients' lives, including the *spiritual/religious* as well as physical/biological, intellectual/cognitive, affective, unconscious, behavioral, interpersonal/social, and cultural. Without a comprehensive conceptualization that explicitly includes the spiritual/religious dimension, counselors will tend to hear clients with limited attentiveness for their spiritual/religious concerns and with shallow empathic and nonspecific responsiveness to these concerns. In this case, the counselor does not necessarily lack respect for clients in their spiritual/religious dimension. Rather, the counselor can find little room within his or her own cognitive set to explore and expand on the spiritual/religious elements of clients' lives, either as a distinctive concern, or, as is more often the case, as these elements relate to other therapeutically relevant areas of the clients' lives.

The relationship-building/exploratory component of counseling, therefore, places three demands on the counselor: first, to acquire an explicit conceptualization of the spiritual/religious dimension within the totality of humanness; second, to maintain a readiness to respond to that dimension in its positive, negative, and ambiguous aspects; and, third, to use exploratory-facilitating conditions that explicitly incorporate concrete terminology specifically congruent with clients' religiousness and spirituality. In Philip's case, the counselor's concept of humanness explicitly included the spiritual/religious dimension. When Philip unexpectedly brought up religious material, the counselor could accommodate this material easily in Philip's expanding and deepening exploration of himself. The counselor's respectful openness to this dimension in her own thinking established her readiness to hear and respond to this material.

In the case of Philip, this readiness was first activated along a positive line by the way he used his spirituality and religion to deepen his understanding of himself and make positive changes in his life. This readiness was tested later in the process when

Philip returned, with potentially debilitating results, to his religious concerns. At this point, the counselor did not fall back on her *own negative reaction* to Philip's new religious belief but sustained her readiness to hear Philip bring out negative pieces of his religiousness. Finally, the counselor effectively facilitated Philip's exploration of his spiritual/religious dimension with her careful and client-focused listening, respectful and empathic responding to the elements of that dimension as the client himself experienced them, and skill in having the client particularize his distinctive spiritual/religious experiences and their effects on his personal and social life.

Spiritual/religious dimension in the understanding/perspective-shifting phase.
Within the context of a strong and deepening therapeutic relationship, the counselor uses challenging and facilitative conditions to help clients to integrate relevant spiritual/religious elements into new, life-improving perspectives. With the counselor's help, clients evaluate how spirituality and religion can contribute to their new or altered conceptualization of themselves and their world. These spiritual/religious elements become an integral part of clients' revised understanding of themselves, part of a shift in perspective that constitutes a cognitive, experiential, and motivational base for making positive changes.

As illustrated in Philip's case, integration of a spiritual/religious dimension is based on (a) how well the counselor has facilitated the exploration and clarification of this dimension, (b) the meanings and influences that this dimension has in the client's life, and (c) the relevance of these meanings and influences to the issues and concerns that the client presents in counseling. Assuming that the counselor attends effectively to the spiritual/religious dimension in the exploratory components of the counseling process, what will emerge are the distinctive, personalized spiritual/religious attitudes and beliefs of the client. This individually personalized system of spirituality/religion will vary in meaning and influence for each client. Thus, in the understanding, perspective-shifting phase of the counseling process, the counselor helps clients to clarify how their unique spiritual/religious beliefs can be integrated beneficially into a more personally effective perspective in line with their developmental and therapeutic needs.

In the case of Philip, the counselor, during an early understanding phase in the counseling process, used depth empathy and mild challenges to help the client through a process of rediscovering and clarifying for himself spiritual/religious sentiments that apparently had been dormant for several years. By responding with empathic respect and constructive confrontation to the client's reemerging religious values in contrast to his behavior, the counselor helped the client validate for himself a set of spiritual/religious experiences and relate these experiences to his needs for coming to terms with his self-defeating and irresponsible behavior, sorting out and reframing the cognitions and emotions associated with that behavior, and identifying new, beneficial patterns of thinking, feeling, and behaving.

In this process the counselor's concrete empathy and understanding helped the client to *explicitly* discuss and reflect on his spirituality/religiousness. Had the counselor not concretely facilitated Philip's explicit consideration of his spirituality/religiousness, Philip would have been left to sort out the meaning and impact of these powerful factors himself while talking with the counselor about other pieces of his life. He may have come to disregard their potential benefit to his improvement, or he may have left counseling because it did not come to grips with a significant area of his life. However, because the counselor responded with respectful specificity to his spiritual/religious experiences, she became a trusted and expert partner in his efforts to understand and use his spirituality/religion to shape new, more personally advantageous life perspectives.

Later in the client's self-understanding processing, the counselor was again explicitly helpful with regard to Philip's spirituality/religion by responding with nonjudgmental empathy to his tentativeness about a particular religious belief. In the context of understanding and respecting the basic value of Philip's overall spirituality, the counselor was able to help him contrast the value of a particular, potentially self-defeating religious belief in the light of his larger, basically positive religious belief system. With the counselor's focused help, Philip was able to retain a religiously oriented life perspective and to do so without muddying that overall perspective with negative influences from a specific religious belief out of sync with his own well-being and the integrity of his relationship with his wife.

The perspective-shifting component of counseling, therefore, makes a threefold demand on the counselor. First, the counselor explicitly *includes*, often with deepening empathy, therapeutically relevant spiritual/religious material into the client's acquisition of new self-understandings and new beneficial self-perspectives. Second, the counselor uses empathy-based challenges to help the client *clarify* the meaning and influence of the client's own spirituality/religiousness. Third, the counselor uses cumulative summarizations to help clients *apply* clarifications of the spiritual/religious dimension to their developmental and therapeutic concerns.

As Philip's case illustrates, the counselor's concretely empathic attention to the evolving nuances of Philip's several religious experiences enabled him to clarify these experiences and apply their meaning toward new perspectives and shifts in personality dynamics. The counselor was able to facilitate Philip's beneficial perspective-shifting with: (a) empathic responses that helped Philip to clarify implicit meanings in his spiritual/religious dimension; (b) expressively genuine and relevantly self-disclosing responses that helped Philip reflect on and refine his own spiritual/religious sentiments and resources in relation to those of the counselor; (c) several open-ended questions and probes that encouraged Philip to expand on and clarify specifics of his spirituality/religion; (d) constructive confrontations that helped Philip to get in touch with discrepancies not only between elements of the spiritual/religious dimension and his broader developmental and problem-solving needs but also between particular, potentially debilitating religious beliefs and his overall, basically positive spirituality; and (e) immediacy responses that helped the client to examine his behavior in light of its effects on the counselor in the context of the client-counselor relationship. Later in this chapter we will look at additional examples of how such responsively challenging conditions and skills can foster growing client understanding and perspective shifting in the spiritual/religious dimension.

Spiritual/religious dimension in the action-planning phase. The action-planning component in counseling includes an extensive array of primarily cognitive, behavioral, and systemic-environmental problem-solving, decision-making, and action-motivating strategies that extend and refine the therapeutic effects of the counseling relationship. These strategies flow from and build on the counselor-client relationship and the client's self-exploration, new understandings, and new perspectives. With respect to spirituality and religion, this means that the spiritual/religious elements that have been clarified as part of each client's new understandings of self will also form a piece of the goals, objectives, and varied action steps that clients formulate and take to implement new understandings. In Philip's case, the counselor helped him to integrate mature religious sentiments and behavior into a changed, positive way of thinking and living and to think through and actively exclude from his life what for him was a potentially debilitating religious belief.

The action-planning component of counseling, as it relates to the spiritual/religious dimension, makes use of many techniques and methods that are found in various approaches to counseling. In Chapter 5 we will consider a number of these action-oriented methods and techniques in detail.

Examples of responsive skills with spiritual and religious issues

Counselors can use facilitative and challenging counseling skills to respond to any content area in clients' lives (e.g., work, family, and school), any internal or behavioral process (e.g., cognitions, feelings, unconscious motivations, behaviors), and any developmental or problem area in which particular content and processes are involved (e.g., distress and confusion about work and career direction, anger and perplexity about a troubled marital relationship, discouragement and misdirection in school progress). The purpose here is to emphasize the importance and relevance of the *spiritual/religious* dimension of clients' issues and problems as a significant focus for responsive (facilitative and challenging) counseling skills. The examples presented below illustrate how the counselor can use responsive skills to respond to the spiritual/religious dimension of various client problems. These examples concretely highlight the relative ease with which a skilled counselor, who is sensitive to and knowledgeable about the therapeutic potential of clients' spiritual/religious dimension, can use familiar counseling skills to integrate this dimension into the counseling process. These examples, which portray only a very small set of responses, point to an extensive universe of spiritually and religiously oriented responses that counselors can elaborate on as relevant for clients' development and problem solving.

Representative responses are presented here according to a typology categorizing several ways in which clients' issues and problems may be connected with the spiritual/religious dimension (see Chapter 4). Examples of five types of responses—simple (initial) empathy, open-ended questioning, depth (advanced) empathy, self-disclosure, and confrontation—are presented for each of three categories of problems and issues with potential spiritual/religious implications. These three categories, which are described at greater length in Chapter 4, include: (a) issues or problems that are predominantly or specifically religious, for example, a fear of losing one's faith; (b) issues or problems that are not directly religious but are directly or significantly affected by some religious factor, for example, converting from one religious faith to another to marry or to make peace in the family; and (c) life issues or problems with high potential for connections with the spiritual/ religious dimension, for example, the death of a loved one or serious illness. The problem examples presented below are based on actual cases. The sample responses, although not verbatim from actual counseling in these cases, nonetheless are closely representative of the types of responses that were actually used.

Responsive Skills with Predominantly or Specifically Spiritual/Religious Issue/Problem

Problems or issues that are primarily spiritual or religious in nature (category one) are less likely to occur in secular counseling settings than the issues presented below in the second and third categories. However, they are by no means unheard of and call for a conceptual framework and set of skills that help counselors to be responsive to this category of issues and problems. Counselor competence in dealing with these issues may help clients distinguish the spiritual/religious aspects of their problems from more purely psychological or behavioral aspects. This sorting may result in referrals to specifically religious counselors or to consultations with clergy. Counselors with adequate knowledge and skills in spiritual and religious issues may be able to help the client resolve concerns in this specifically spiritual/religious category.

For purposes of illustrating facilitative and challenging responses in this problem category, consider a male client, near the end of high school or in the first year of college, with a a fear of losing his religious faith. In this case the client is experiencing an inner turmoil that leads him to talk to a high school or college counselor. Early in the course of his discussion with the counselor, he talks explicitly about how discussions with his friends and certain classroom lectures are upsetting and confusing him, even provoking doubts about his religious beliefs. He mentions that he thought about talking to his minister, but he is afraid that the minister might be upset with him. This is why he is bringing it up to his school or college counselor.

A counselor who understands and respects the client's religious dimension is prepared to enter that part of the client's world. At this point the counselor does not need an expert knowledge of the client's particular spiritual or religious belief but rather an alert sensitivity to this dimension of the client's life. By responding with respectful understanding to the spiritual/religious aspect of the client's problem, the counselor in effect is journeying with the client, ready to learn from the client and to help the client clarify how his or her spirituality or religiousness may be understood and folded into fresh perspectives and new decisions for positive growth and change. The sample responses given here are intentionally simple and straightforward (but nonetheless important pieces of the overall counseling process); they indicate how counselors who are seeking to implement an understanding and helpful respect for a client's spirituality and religiousness may begin to do so with responsive skills that are likely to be a familiar part of their counseling repertoire.

The first two sample responses are forms of empathic responding. Empathy represents and expresses the counselor's understanding and appreciative way of being with the client in the client's world. The responses presented here are presumed to arise from the counselor's empathic way of being with the client and are presented not as a method but as the simple yet skillful expression of the counselor's entering into the client's world.

The first response example—simple or initial empathy—represents the counselor's early effort to communicate empathic understanding of the young man's experience; it is a response that conveys what the counselor first understands about the client as he presents himself. The second type of empathic response assumes ongoing, deepening interaction between the counselor and client, so that the counselor is able to read between the lines of the client's surface presentation of himself. Based on the expanding sphere of understanding between the counselor and client, the counselor is able to respond to elements of the client's experience that the client may not be aware or only dimly aware of. In depth empathy the counselor may articulate client ideas or feelings that the client does not clearly perceive, put together the meaning of the client's experience more clearly than the client can at the moment, or point to consequences of the client's behavior that the client cannot see. The following are examples of simple and depth empathic responses to the client's expression of losing his faith.

Simple (initial) empathic response. "It feels like your religious faith is slipping away from you and that's scary for you." This simple response verbally conveys a deep respect for the young man's religious predicament and a sensitive understanding of his core experience as he has communicated it. The counselor has taken a first step into the client's religious world and respectfully articulated the content and feeling of his disturbing experience. The client is given a safe and supporting place to talk about what he feels is most troubling to him.

Depth (advanced) empathy. "You feel your religious faith is fading. This frightens you, and you'd like to find your way to an enlivened faith and peace." Or "You feel your religious faith fading. Although this frightens you, you're beginning to sense that you need to find another way to understand your religion in relation to your friends and what you're learning in class."

These responses assume different directions in the client's exploration of himself. Both point in the direction of mature development, but along somewhat different routes. The first takes the route of the client's primarily affirming his religious faith while dealing with intellectual and life-style conflicts that test his faith. The second reflects that the client is probably ready to reexamine his religious beliefs in the light of learnings that appear to be in conflict with his beliefs. With these responses the counselor has reached a culturally and religiously sensitive area. For a public high school counselor in particular, movement beyond this point, especially in the case of the second response, would be ethically dubious and perhaps contrary to school system guidelines, not to mention professionally perilous if parents or community members should raise objections to the schools' intruding on students' religious beliefs. In Chapter 5 I will discuss consultation with and referral to religious counselors and clergy—a course of action that in this case could be therapeutically valuable and deserves the counselor's serious consideration for the client's total welfare.

Open-ended questions. Questions do not in themselves constitute a facilitative or challenging responsive condition as do empathy and confrontation. Questions, however, are used for various purposes in counseling such as obtaining initial intake information or implementing specific techniques (e.g., constructing a family genogram). With respect to the responsive conditions and skills particularly associated with the relationship dimension of counseling, questions are one way of articulating such conditions as empathy or confrontation. When used carefully in connection with building and expanding a counseling relationship that is focused on the client and counselor's expanding understanding of the client's world, relevant questions may help to implement and expand the therapeutic effect of facilitative and challenging responses. Full descriptions of the effective formulation and use of questions in counseling, a topic beyond the scope of this book, are described in detail by several authors (see, e.g., Corey & Corey, 1992; Cormier & Cormier, 1991; Egan, 1994; Ivey, 1994).

Types of questions that might be asked as part of counseling with the young man who is discussing his loss of faith are: "When did you feel your faith beginning to slip?" Or "What was happening in your life at the time?" These questions, especially the second, encourage the client to give details about his life that are relevant to the issue of religious doubts. They are not understood to be part of a series of questions, but rather part of the counselor's empathic effort to enter more fully into the client's world by becoming more informed about that world. With relevant specifics, they have the potential for expanding what the client perceives as influencing his religious doubts. The connections that are made as a result of following this line could be beneficial in facilitating a client's self-understanding that integrates his religiousness and other aspects of his life and in taking specific action in accord with shifts in his religious perspective.

Self-disclosure. Self-disclosure, like the use of questions, is a way of implementing the major facilitative conditions of counseling. It is understood here as a special expression of counselor genuineness. In self-disclosure the counselor speaks of personal events and experiences that are relevant to the client's needs and will help build the client-counselor relationship and facilitate the client's self-exploration and understanding toward positive problem resolution. When used concisely and precisely for the client, self-disclosure can have the effect of expanding the therapeutic bond of understanding between the client and counselor and encouraging the client's own developmental life journey.

The therapeutic value of any self-disclosure, which is a particular type of expressed genuineness, depends on several factors. Most obviously, a counselor cannot disclose an experience that never took place. Self-disclosure is not just storytelling; it is the revealing of some genuine life experience. Therapeutic self-disclosures are not driven by the counselor's interest in relating personal anecdotes based on something that the client has said. They are certainly not lengthy stories of the counselor's experiences. Therapeutic self-disclosure is relevant to the counseling process in relation to the client's needs. For example, particularly as related to the spiritual/religious dimension, it may increase rapport and encourage further clients' exploration of the spiritual/religious aspect of their issues, facilitate clients' consideration of alternative perspectives related to their spirituality/religiousness, or be suggestive of alternative action objectives. Therapeutic self-disclosure is concise and brief, clear as to the aspect of the life event and personal reactions that are disclosed, relevant to the client's needs, and appropriate to the particular phase of counseling in which it is used. On the assumption that the sample self-disclosure presented below meets these requirements, it has the potential to enhance the client's feeling of being with an understanding person and open several reality-based possibilities in which the client may reflect on her own distinctive issues. Furthermore, it suggests to the client several self-enhancing choices and does not have to move in an "either-or" direction.

In the case of the young man with the faith problem, a counselor self-disclosure might take the form of "I remember in my college years how religious realities for a while seemed so unreal and how painful that was to me. I had very real struggles and doubts then and later. For me, confronting these struggles honestly eventually led to deeper convictions." We cannot make a judgment in the abstract about the therapeutic value of this self-disclosure. It would only be therapeutically beneficial to the client if it were truly linked to the client's experience. Its value also depends on how well it focuses and encourages the client's own unique search and how well it provides a sense of hope for coming out of that search a more mature person. If the conditions are right for this to occur at an appropriate place in the counseling process, the self-disclosure suggested here has the potential of offering the client a perspective, or at least a reality-based possibility, for dealing honestly and straightforwardly with religious doubts in the context of total life development.

Confrontation. Therapeutic or constructive confrontation is a major challenging condition that has the potential for deepening and clarifying the client-counselor relationship and for opening the client to consider new perspectives. Although it has slightly different but complementary meanings across different approaches to counseling, it refers essentially to a relational condition and challenging response in which the counselor directly points out to a client a discrepancy in some aspect of the client's experience or behavior. In confrontation the counselor directly and explicitly brings to the client's attention discrepant or resistive ways of thinking, feeling, and acting that are inhibiting the client's change and development and/or blocking the counseling process.

Assuming that the counselor has used facilitative conditions effectively to develop a working relationship with the client struggling with religious faith issues, a constructively confrontive response might be, "You're deriving some satisfaction from what you're currently doing with your friends, but you don't like the effect this is having on your religious faith." Or "You're disturbed in your religious beliefs by some of the things that you're learning in biology and the study sessions that you're having with your friends, but you're also thinking that all of this is making you think more clearly and fully." These two confrontations point in somewhat different directions. They are based, of course, on different assumptions about the line of exploration that has developed in the counseling process. Both confrontations, in their different ways, explicitly highlight discrepancies that are potentially important for the client's behavior in relation to religious beliefs or for the maturity of religious beliefs in relation to intellectual

growth. As was the case with the depth empathy responses suggested above, issues raised in these responses, especially in the
second, may call for consultation and referral to religious counselors or clergy.

Responsive Skills with Nonspiritual/Nonreligious Issues/Problems with a Significant Spiritual/Religious Component

In this second problem category, the client's issue or problem is
not directly religious or spiritual but is significantly affected by
some religious or spiritual factor (see Chapter 4 for a fuller discussion). Examples of such problems might include difficulties
stemming from converting from one religious faith tradition to
another for the sake of marriage, making peace in the family, or
suppressing one's religious practice or spiritual motivations for
career advancement.

For purposes of illustrating facilitative and challenging responses in this problem category, consider a woman who had
converted from one religious tradition to another for the sake of
marriage and several years later comes to counseling with marital
problems. In this case the client presents her marital problems
with overtones of resentment at having left her original religious
tradition for the sake of a spouse who, as it turns out, is not only
difficult to live with but also has little interest in his religion. The
sample of brief and simple responses presented here are crafted to
articulate empathically one or two major elements of the client's
experience of her problem, to stimulate the client to delve into
and expand on her understanding of her experience, and to confront discrepancies in her experience.

Simple (initial) empathic response. "Your marriage was so important to you that you changed your religious faith for your husband, and now you find yourself doubly conflicted: not only is your
marriage in trouble but the change of your religion doesn't seem
to be helping." This response, given relatively early in the counselor-client relationship and the client's exploration of her problem, explicitly responds to the client's vague discomfort about her
change of religion while maintaining a focus on the client's troubled marital relationship. It opens for the client the possibility of
exploring feelings and thoughts that appear to be just below the

surface of her awareness and to make connections between these and the broader issues of her marriage. The point of the response is *not* arbitrarily to introduce a religious factor on the basis of the counselor's interests but to tap into what appears to be an important piece of the client's concern. It may turn out that this religious piece is relatively unimportant either for the marital relationship or the client's own self-clarification. On the other hand, if it is therapeutically relevant, this response or one similar to it allows the client to weave her religiously based concern into the overall exploration of her problem.

Open-ended questions. "How do you feel (or think) the current stresses in your marriage are affected by the experience of your changing to your husband's religious faith?" Or "What role, if any, do your thoughts and feelings about changing your religion play in the problems between you and your husband?" The purpose of these questions, or ones like them, would be to have the client elaborate directly on a previous connection that she herself has already vaguely made. Questions like these may be unnecessary (or even undesirable) if the counselor's empathic responses are eliciting expansive client exploration. However, they do represent a response option that allows the client to reflect on and talk about her current experience of religious change in light of her marital problems. If it turns out that this religious element is significant in her problem, other more specific questions may be appropriate to help the client bring out therapeutically relevant details; for example, "You brought this matter of your religion change up in a recent argument with your husband. How specifically did you do this? What was his response?" These two questions are geared more toward understanding the content and process of unhealthy interchanges with a view toward helping to change them. They are probably appropriate for later, perspective-shifting and action-planning phases of the counseling process.

Depth (advanced) empathy. "You're not only worried about the marriage problems with your husband. You're also troubled that a piece of your own self-identity may be tied in with the change that you made from your original religious tradition to that of your husband's." Responding accurately with empathic depth assumes, of course, that the counselor has facilitated the client's self-exploration sufficiently to accurately perceive implied meanings and

123

feelings that the client herself is not yet aware of. With depth empathy the counselor is not making an interpretation, trying out an unfounded hunch, or pursuing an area of the counselor's interest rather than the client's. Therefore, this sample response assumes that the client's discussion of her marital problems and her change of religion in relation to those problems truly imply a deeper but unarticulated sense of discomfort about her self-concept and her religion. If this is the case, the counselor can help her articulate and reflect on religiously relevant aspects of this self-identity issue, not only as importantly self-clarifying in their own right but also as having potential for helping her resolve broader marital problems.

Self-disclosure. "I once left the religion of my birth and then joined a new religion. I've since shifted back, but my daughters are still in my former church. My own experience has been that there's genuine value in both places and both can be a source of strength." As noted in the previous discussion of self-disclosure, the response given here would be effective only if it is a genuine representation of the counselor's experience and is therapeutically relevant for the client. Assuming this to be the case, this self-disclosure has the potential to strengthen the client's bond of understanding with the counselor specifically in the area of religion as well as provide a universalizing sense for the client, that is, a sense that she is not alone in her feelings and experiences—indeed, that the very counselor she is working with has some firsthand experience of her dilemma.

Confrontation. "You want your marriage to improve and grow, but the new faith that you have in common with your husband is threatening to become part of the problem rather than a solution as you once thought." Constructive confrontation, like depth empathy and self-disclosure, is a challenging responsive condition that assumes that the counselor has established a working rapport with the client and has facilitated exploration to a point where the client can, without undue self-defensiveness, hear and constructively use counselor confrontations. The general conditions that make confrontation therapeutic, as well as the varying degrees and kinds of confrontation (described in extensive literature beyond the scope of this book), apply to confrontation in the spiritual/religious dimension.

In the example here confrontation is given at a point in the counseling process where it has become reasonably clear that the client's change of religion and her current experiences around that change are a significant cause of her marital stress. In this context, the confrontation is mild and has potentially positive and negative elements. The client is directly confronted with the problematic effects of her religious change on her marriage (and implicitly herself), although she had made this change for the sake of her marriage. She is being led—not from the counselor's interest but from the meanings and experiences that she herself has brought out in counseling—to reexamine the meaning of her religious change for her marriage (and implicitly herself), assess the impact of this meaning on her relationship with her husband, and thereby open the door to a beneficial change in direction. If the counselor has been accurate in facilitating the client's movement to this point of self-understanding, the client is now able to deal explicitly with the meaning and impact of her religion on her marriage and her own personal development. If the counselor had not responded to the religious aspects of the client's marital problem, this unresolved issue would likely persist, unclarified and moving in and out of awareness, as an emotionally charged confusion that could continue to undermine the marriage and subvert progress in other areas of the marriage.

Responsive Skills with Nonspiritual/Nonreligious Issues/Problems with a Potential Connection to the Spiritual/Religious Dimension

In this category problems and issues are not necessarily connected to the spiritual/religious dimension but have a plausible potential for raising questions and issues that are frequently related to spirituality and religion. Such issues include questions about the meaning of life and especially tragic life events, the interconnectedness of humans and the universe, the ethical implications of significant decisions, and intense feelings of loneliness and alienation from community. Of course, a theoretical connection between events like these and the spiritual/religious dimension does not mean that this connection actually occurs in every client. In this category of problems and issues the counselor needs to consider the degree of a client's religiousness (see the typology of the degrees of client religiousness discussed in Chapter 4). We can reasonably expect that clients who are spiritually and/or religiously committed or religiously loyal may be especially open to the spiritual/religious dimension. Spiritually and religiously open individuals may also be responsive to the spiritual/religious dimension, but to a lesser extent. (See Chapter 4 for a description of religiously loyal and spiritually/religiously open clients.) The presumption for all other types of nonspiritual, nonreligious clients is that they are not concerned about the potential spiritual/religious dimension of these problems; therefore, it would be nontherapeutic and probably unethical for the counselor to initiate a consideration of the spiritual/religious dimension with these types of clients, regardless of any theoretically possible connection between their problems and spirituality and religion.

To illustrate responses in this problem category, consider a client who is experiencing deep, consuming, and unrelieved grief at the death of his young son. His description of the problem does not contain an explicit reference to spirituality or religion. For the purposes of this example we must assume that the counselor knows that the client has some degree of spirituality or religiousness as explained above. Therefore, the example presupposes that the client has noted regular religious participation on the intake form or has otherwise mentioned it outside the context of his grief problem.

Simple (initial) empathic response. "Your son's sudden death has left you terribly dejected; you feel this pervasive grief, and at the moment can find no consolation in your life or your religious faith." We assume that this response comes at an appropriate point in the counseling process when initial rapport and exploration already have occurred. With this response the counselor sensitively articulates the father's grief. The counselor takes nothing away from the client's deep sadness and the sense of being without consolation or relief from any quarter. However, by explicitly mentioning religion, from which one might stereotypically be supposed to receive relief, the counselor gently opens the door to a dimension that may have therapeutic relevance for the client—or, indeed, an area that may be an additional and unexpected source of disappointment and pain.

It goes without saying that the purpose of the religious element in this response is not to prop up the client artificially (although a client in this state needs a lot of genuine support) or rush the client toward considerations that are not consonant with the client's current experience. The counselor does not pull religion out of a hat of psychoreligious goodies or from the counselor's own field of interest. Rather, the purpose of this response is to gently raise an area of the client's life (his religiousness as he himself previously noted it) that has a potentially significant connection to the client's terrible loss and grief. What the counselor does with this potential connection obviously depends on how the client experiences the connection.

Depth (advanced) empathy. "It's hard to feel anything but sadness because of your son's death, but some part of you would welcome genuine religious consolation." Or "It's hard to feel anything but sadness because of your son's death, and this is made even worse by the feeling that is was terribly unjust, a betrayal by God." Clearly one of these responses is appropriate only if the client has given an indication of a serious regard for his religion, with the positive or negative overtones as divergently reflected in the two responses. Because these are examples of *depth* empathy, the assumption is that the counselor is articulating a religiously based wish, hope, or anger that the client is implying but has not explicitly articulated.

If the counselor is accurate in perceiving the client's implied religious orientation and the direction of that orientation, a door is opened for the client in the first example to explore the positive implications of the client's religion being part of coming to terms with grief; or, in the case of the second example, the client is helped to explore the anger and betrayal that he feels toward God and, if possible, achieve a therapeutic reconciliation of religious beliefs and the experience of being betrayed or punished.

Open-ended questions. "How does your religious faith fit into your feeling and thinking about the loss of your son?" Or "What does your anger stir you to say to God about the loss of your son?" These questions also assume that the client's continued exploration of grief has involved religiously hopeful or angry (or both) overtones. The first question invites the client to reflect in an open-ended way on the potential relevance of religious faith to loss and grief. The second explicitly gives the client permission to express thoughts and feelings that are difficult to put into words. In either case, the question directly helps the client to relate a presumably important aspect of life, namely religious beliefs, to a tragic personal experience that has obvious connections to these beliefs.

Confrontation. "One part of you wants some genuine relief from your deep sorrow, but you still don't feel open to the peace and assurance that your religious faith might give." Or "One part of you is terribly angry at God for taking your son from you, but you are reluctant to express that anger, to tell God how you feel and what you think." These responses continue two possible lines of thoughts and feelings that this grief-stricken father might be moving along. The first—in what might be called a strength confrontation—assumes that the client has been talking about his religion in positive, optimistic ways but that he is finding it difficult to apply these beliefs to his current experience. The second assumes that his anger at God is bottled up and that explicit discussion and venting of his anger will be therapeutically helpful; it may or may not lead to some positive use of his religion. At this point the client needs to come to terms with his religiously based feelings and thoughts of being treated unjustly and being betrayed.

Putting it all together in practice

The case presentation and the sample facilitative and challenging responses presented in this chapter illustrate how counselors can effectively use major responsive conditions and skills to incorporate the spiritual/religious dimension into the relationship-building/exploratory, understanding/perspective-shifting, and action-planning phases of the counseling process. Because these responsive conditions and skills are fundamental in many different theoretical approaches to counseling, counselors with different counseling approaches can use them to open the counseling process to their clients' spiritual/religious dimension. The effectiveness of these responses depends on counselors' sensitivity to the process and content factors at work in real-life situations and on their competence in therapeutically blending religiously oriented responses into the counseling process. The examples in this chapter do point, however, to an unlimited variety of specific responses that spiritually sensitive and responsively creative counselors can formulate to integrate their clients' spiritual/religious dimension with other relevant issues and problems. In the following chapters we will expand and build on these spiritually/religiously oriented responses by describing other more specific approaches to counseling with the spiritual and religious dimension of clients' issues and problems.

CHAPTER FOUR

Assessing the Spiritual/Religious Dimension in Counseling

Assessment methods complement the relationship dimension of counseling with concepts, techniques, and procedures that build on and extend the counselor's relational responsiveness to the client. Whereas facilitative and challenging conditions such as empathy, respect, and confrontation stimulate client self-exploration and understanding within the client-counselor relationship, the assessment component of counseling is made up of particular concepts, procedures, and methods that represent a primarily technical extension of the relationship to increase an understanding of the client.

Assessment in counseling

In the context of the major process components of counseling, assessment is primarily a part of the exploration and understanding process components. Viewed comprehensively, assessment in counseling involves the many ways that the counselor facilitates an increasingly clarified understanding of the client in intrapersonal and interpersonal realms that are relevant to the resolution of issues that the client brings to counseling. A clinical or medical model approach to assessment emphasizes fairly distinct procedures that focus on the counselor's understanding of client functioning for the purposes of the *counselor's* diagnosis and treatment planning. A counseling-oriented approach to assessment, on the other hand, focuses primarily on the *client's* integration into and use of assessment results in the overall process of self-exploration, understanding and perspective shifting, and decision making and action planning (V. L. Campbell, 1990).

While appreciating the important uses of the more discrete clinical/medical approach to assessment, the assessment perspective of this chapter is primarily that of integrative counseling—that is, viewing assessment as a variety of methods that the counselor uses at appropriate places in the counseling process to increase the client's and the counselor's understanding of the client's traits, interests, attitudes, mental and emotional status, aptitudes, values. Assessment methods can also stimulate client self-exploration, suggest different perspectives on problems, and open a discussion of different ways of acting (Goldman, 1990).

The major types of assessment procedures available to counselors include standardized and nonstandardized procedures, nomothetic (group-normed) and idiographic (individually oriented) procedures, quantitative (yielding scores) and qualitative (yielding verbal descriptions) methods, and assessments focused on either the individual or the environment (A. B. Hood & Johnson, 1991). This diverse range of assessment procedures, in conjunction with the responsive relationship conditions that facilitate client understanding, provides the counselor with a wide repertoire of approaches and methods that can be used to throw light on the spiritual and religious dimensions of client issues and problems.

The remainder of this chapter is an expanded discussion of the purposes and methods for making assessments in the spiritual and religious domains. In practice, the actual extent to which a counselor uses formal or informal assessment depends not only on the spiritual or religious aspects of the client and the problem but also on the assessment perspective that a counselor uses in counseling. Some of the methods described below may be used formally, that is, as a kind of clinical assessment procedure discretely preceding or separate from the counseling process. The principal perspective of this chapter, however, is to understand assessment as an integral part of the overall counseling process.

Purposes of spiritual and religious assessment

The purposes of a spiritual and/or religious assessment may be summarized according to three general categories as described by Malony (1985a). The first is diagnostic, pertaining to questions of causation. With respect to spirituality and religion, the diagnostic assessment question asks whether, to what extent, and how does a person's religious faith or spiritual beliefs provoke, cause, or contribute to a client's problem? Put another way, how are a client's spiritual or religious beliefs implicated in the etiology and persistence of a client's problem (Worthington, 1989)? An example of the etiological aspect of assessment was a young adult, female client who described to me her bouts of intense fear, guilt, and severe self-deprecation in the context of an upbringing by a father who hammered away at a literal interpretation of Bible passages focused on sin and punishment.

The second reason for a spiritual/religious assessment is to understand more generally the role of spirituality and religion in a client's basic development and personality. In this case the question is to what extent and how is this client's religious faith or spiritual orientation a basic source of strength or weakness generally, aside from the particular problem at hand? Another way of putting this question is to ask, "How is religion [or spirituality] involved in the life of the client? Is religion [or spirituality] intertwined with daily life or encapsulated apart from daily functioning? Is religion [or spirituality] used primarily as a psychological defense, for life enhancement, or for coping with stress" (Worthington, 1989, p. 590)?

Malony (1985a), writing primarily with respect to religion (and specifically Christianity), has couched this second set of questions in the context of "religious maturity," which in terms of optimal religious functioning (Malony, 1988) refers to the in-depth integrity of a person's religious beliefs and their positive personal and social expression. For counselors in secular settings it is important to expand the context of this second set of questions to include not only spiritual/religious maturity or immaturity but also the closely related but somewhat dissimilar states of spiritual or religious well-being or spiritual distress.

As a prelude to a subsequent discussion of these concepts later in this chapter, it is sufficient to note here that spiritual/religious

maturity versus immaturity generally refers to the integral, qualitative depth and psychosocial effectiveness of one's spirituality/
religion as opposed to a superficial, egocentric, negatively defensive, or fixedly dogmatic belief system. On the other hand, spir-
itual/religious well-being versus spiritual distress generally denotes
a personal, affective/cognitive experience of healthy satisfaction
in the spiritual/religious aspects of one's life in contrast to cognitive and emotional misgivings and anxiety. These categories overlap in concept and life experience; nonetheless, they highlight
that growth toward spiritual/religious maturity may be accompanied from time to time (e.g., in times of crisis or at difficult
stages of personal development) by an *experience* of spiritual distress (an absence of spiritual well-being). Especially in times of
crisis and developmental stress, both may be pertinent to assessing
the general role of spirituality and religion in a client's basic
development and personality.

The third reason for a spiritual/religious assessment is to obtain
information useful for treatment—to help guide the counseling
process for effecting change in clients. The assessment question
in this regard is to what extent can this client's spiritual beliefs or
religious faith be used as a resource in working with this person
or to what extent will they constitute weak points to be overcome
or ignored (Malony, 1985a). This approach to assessment is ex-
emplified in the work done by one of my counselor-trainees, whose
respectful and understanding treatment of her client's spiritual
belief of a father's spirit living on in a son helped the client with
the grieving process.

To achieve these three assessment purposes, the counselor
needs (a) a general conceptual *framework* for initially gauging
whether an assessment of the spiritual/religious dimension is therapeutically appropriate for specific clients and problems, and (b)
general and specific *procedures* for carrying out the assessment. We
will look at both of these in order.

Types of clients and counseling issues: a conceptual context for assessing spirituality and religion

Assessment of the spiritual/religious dimension in counseling is
not only about methods of assessment. It also raises questions

about the relevance and meaning of the spiritual/religious dimension for individual clients and about the potential connections between this dimension and the content of each client's specific issues and problems. As a context for assessing pertinent aspects of clients' spirituality and religion, the counselor in the secular setting needs a frame of reference for initially thinking about how spirituality and religion may or may not be personally important to individual clients and how, if they are important, they are relevant to particular client problems and issues. Such a frame of reference does not answer specific questions about the implication of spirituality and religion in a client's counseling issues, but it does provide an important way of approaching the spiritual/religious aspect of counseling.

The typologies presented below are composed of broad categories by which counselors can organize their understanding of the *personal significance* and *problem/issue relevance* of spirituality and religion in counseling (E. W. Kelly, 1990). These typologies, combined with a counselor's respectful recognition of the potential significance of spirituality and religion in counseling, provide an informed perspective, a *way of thinking* about counseling that is open to a spiritual/religious dimension and that broadly guides counselor decisions about the extent to which this dimension is therapeutically significant for each client.

The extent to which a counselor incorporates the spiritual/religious dimension into counseling depends principally on considerations in two areas: (a) the quality and degree (i.e., personal significance) of the client's religiousness or spirituality and (b) the extent to which religion and spirituality are therapeutically relevant to the client's issues and problems. These two are presented here in typologies that guide the counselor in initially appraising and broadly classifying clients' spirituality/religiousness and the potential connections between clients' issues and problems and their spirituality/religion. These typologies constitute *background* schemas for assessing the spiritual/religious dimension in counseling. They help the counselor approach specific clients and their problems with a conceptual framework for making initial determinations about the ethical propriety and therapeutic relevance of including spirituality and religion in the counseling process.

The categories in each of these two background classifications represent the *general* degree and quality of spirituality and religiousness of clients and their issues; they do not include distinctive religious content, that is, explicit religious beliefs and practices manifested in the various organized forms of spirituality and religion discussed in Chapter 1. The particular content of a client's beliefs is, of course, important to incorporating religion and spirituality in counseling, and we will consider more specific content issues when discussing methods of assessment. At this point, the purpose is to provide broadly organized typologies for initially thinking about whether the religious or spiritual dimension has a legitimate place in counseling with specific clients and specific issues and to discuss the implications of these classifications for the counseling process.

A Typology of Client Spirituality and Religiousness

The extent to which a counselor includes spiritual/religious issues in counseling depends in part on the degree and quality of the client's spirituality or religiousness. The typology presented here contains eight categories for understanding how and to what extent spirituality or religion are part of a client's life. They are not content-specific, that is, they do not include any distinctive beliefs of particular religions or spiritualities. Rather, they represent degrees of religious commitment—differing levels of the personal importance of spiritual and religious belief and practice.

Because degree of commitment here refers to the *personal* significance of spirituality and religion, it has a qualitative aspect made up of both the cognitive/affective explicitness and the attitudinal/behavioral influence that spirituality and religion have on an individual's life. The qualitative dimension of the following typology reflects the notions of intrinsic and extrinsic religiousness, insofar as the former refers to religious belief as an important guide in one's life, and the latter signifies a valuing of religion as a kind of social or cultural accoutrement.

The typology also encompasses the intensity of commitment, that is, the valuing of spiritual/religious expression irrespective of its intrinsic or extrinsic qualities. For example, a Christian may value Baptism, a Jew may value the Passover Seder, and a Muslim may value the Ramadan fast either as filled with life-influencing meaning (i.e., intrinsically important) or primarily as an important expression of one's cultural or social identity (i.e., extrinsically important). Each may value these religious observances with varying degrees of importance, from very important to not so important. Thus, the typology is a classification based on the quality (intrinsic/extrinsic) and the strength or intensity (important/not important) of spiritual or religious commitment.

The categories also reflect the distinction made earlier between spirituality and religion (see Chapter 1), although in concept and practice there is considerable overlap. The typology is a rationally derived schema based on religious and psychological theory and counseling experience as well as limited research available in this area. Because it is designed to approximate the dynamic complexities of counseling practice, it includes practice-oriented categories that reasonably extend the more limited set of broad categories proposed by Worthington (1991) as a current guide to scientific research.

The categories below should not be understood as a way of pigeonholing clients in a rigid or fixed way. Clients usually have characteristics from more than one category, and because of life or counseling experiences, their primary orientation may move from one category to another. Also, categories overlap. Nonetheless, they suggest the wide range of client attitudes toward spirituality and religion and are useful in characterizing the predominant orientation of a client vis-à-vis spirituality and religion.

1. Religiously committed clients. Religiously committed clients hold their religious beliefs with an efficacious personal conviction. Their religious beliefs are consciously experienced and developed as a source of significant influence (actually or potentially) on their attitudes and behavior in all important aspects of life and as a vital inner base for spiritual growth. For the religiously committed client, religion is closely akin to what Albanese (1992) calls "extraordinary—the religion that helps people to transcend, or move beyond, their everyday culture and concerns" (p. 6). It is primarily intrinsically motivating, representing a belief and attitudinal set that is pervasively important in shaping the person's general outlook and acting as a source of values used by the person in making decisions and guiding behavior. Thus, in counseling religiously committed clients, the counselor can expect that these clients will look at, or are prepared to look at, issues and problems from the perspective of their religious beliefs and values and bring these values into play in working on their problems and nurturing their development.

2. Religiously loyal clients. "Religious loyalties are the expectations passed on by family, community, and society from one generation to the next. They are often part of a package of familial and ethnic loyalties that are intergenerational in nature and often unconscious" (Albany, 1984, p. 128). As understood here, the religiously loyal client is someone for whom the cultural aspects of religion, often encompassed in the cumulative traditions and practices of organized religious institutions, serve as relatively strong norms in determining certain sets of beliefs and religious practices. The religiously committed person may also have religious loyalties, but these institutional and cultural loyalties are secondary to the deeper values of religion. These loyalties have potentially significant impact (positive or negative) on attitudes and behaviors but not in the same inwardly interactional, developmental manner as religious commitment.

Such religious loyalties are closely akin to what Albanese (1992) calls "ordinary" religion, that is, religion that is almost indistinguishably interwoven with culture and reveals "itself in the many customs and folkways that are part of a culture: expected ways of greeting people; wedding etiquette concerning clothes, manners, and obligations; habits of diet; and holiday behavior, to mention a few" (p. 7). In a somewhat more specific sense, religious loyalties are expressed in a wide variety of more or less intense and influential attachments to institutional religious traditions and practices generally or to subsets of practices, traditions, and rules of particular religions. For example, a loyal Catholic may consider church rules and practices such as Sunday Mass or Baptism or parochial schooling or simply "being a Catholic" as important parts of one's cultural-religious identity and shape some choices and behavior with these loyalties in mind.

These cultural-religious loyalties, although influential in certain choices, do not act as a person's principal value base. They are predominantly extrinsic in the sense that they contribute to certain social attitudes and behaviors but do not, as with the religiously committed person, serve as the principal source of motivation in shaping one's overall outlook on life or important life decisions. For the religiously loyal person, the use of religious concepts in counseling may be important in understanding particular types of culturally or socially oriented behavior but are unlikely to be deeply or intensely influential in understanding and making changes in many developmental, pathological, or crisis issues and problems.

3. *Spiritually committed clients.* This category, reflecting the distinction made earlier between spirituality and religion, includes clients who, while not affiliated with organized religion, have a "courage to look within and to trust. What is trusted appears to be a deep sense of belonging, of wholeness, of connectedness, and of openness to the infinite" (Shafranske & Gorsuch, 1984, p. 233). Although the religiously committed client is also spiritually committed, a separate category of "spiritually committed" is appropriate because a client may be spiritually committed but not identify with any established religion or typical religious beliefs.

Being spiritually committed typically involves an active valuing of meaning in life, with a sense of purpose guided by an altruistic attitude toward others and a vision for the betterment of the world along with a serious awareness of the tragic side of life (Elkins, Hedstrom, Hughes, Leaf, & Saunders, 1988). In counseling the spiritually committed client, the counselor can expect the client to be ready to weigh and apply these spiritual values to understanding and resolving problems.

4. *Spiritually/religiously open clients.* Spiritually/religiously open clients do not have a spiritual or religious commitment or a loyalty to religion. However, during the counseling process, these clients give evidence of an openness to the spiritual/religious dimension as a way to resolve their problems and contribute to their development and growth. Although such individuals' guiding frame of reference and resulting life-style do not include a personalized set of spiritual and religious beliefs and attitudes, their way of thinking and general attitude nonetheless suggests a compatibility with spiritual and/or religious belief and an open-mindedness that would not exclude serious consideration of spirituality and religion as potentially beneficial.

If the counselor's overall assessment of a client suggests this kind of open-mindedness to and congruence with spiritual/religious values, the client may benefit from consideration of the personal therapeutic relevance of values, beliefs, and practices rooted in a spiritual/religious perspective along with ideas and actions not associated with spirituality and religion. In this category, the client presents not as a spiritual or religious person but as one whose philosophy and life-style make it reasonable, ethical, and potentially therapeutic to include relevant spiritual and/or religious components in the client's overall search for new and altered perspectives to guide positive personal development and problem resolution.

5. *Externally religious clients.* Externally religious clients manifest an outward expression of some religious beliefs and attachments, but these outward expressions appear to carry little or no inner conviction and result in little or no significant influence on their lives in terms of religious commitment or religious loyalty. This category is not a value judgment about the client but an effort to describe complex behavior as it may affect counselors' decisions about their responsiveness to the religious dimension in counseling. Externally religious clients may initially appear to be religiously loyal, but their external religious expressions show little depth of belief and appear to have no substantive effect on their way of thinking and behaving. The externality of these clients' life perspectives and choices manifests itself, for example, in the way that religious considerations easily give way to nonreligious considerations in personal choices.

In terms of counseling, this kind of external religiousness offers little or no personal benefit in the counseling endeavor. Insofar as a client's religiousness falls into this category, the counselor has limited ethical or therapeutic justification for attempting to integrate spiritual or religious consideration into the counseling process.

6. *Spiritually/religiously tolerant or indifferent clients.* Spiritually/religiously tolerant or indifferent clients are tolerant of spirituality and religion generally and of the spirituality and religion of others, but are expressly indifferent to any spiritual or religious beliefs or influence in their own lives. When a counselor recognizes that a client falls into this category, the introduction of spiritual and religious beliefs into the counseling process is not justified therapeutically and is ethically problematic.

7. *Nonspiritual/nonreligious clients.* Nonspiritual/nonreligious clients deliberately and consciously consider spirituality and religion, conceptually and personally, as expressions of the unreal and therefore unnecessary (perhaps even harmful) to understanding reality and living effectively. They positively reject spirituality and religion but generally are not actively hostile to them or their adherents. For such a client, the counselor has no legitimate therapeutic reason for incorporating spiritual or religious beliefs, values, and practices into the counseling process.

Indeed, the counselor may find that the client's rejection of spirituality and religion is important to the client's positive development and improvement. For counselors who themselves are spiritually or religiously committed, a counseling process that involves the explicit rejection of spirituality or religion as part of a client's therapeutic progress may prove to a challenge. However, just as it has been argued that nonreligious counselors should respect and be ready to use effectively the spirituality and religiousness of their clients, so too must spiritually/religiously oriented counselors respect the nonspirituality/nonreligiousness of some clients and be ready to employ their secularity in achieving personally and socially therapeutic progress. If spiritually or religiously committed counselors cannot work this way with clients in this category, a referral is called for.

8. Clients hostile to religion. Clients hostile to religion are not only unreligious but are also in varying degrees actively hostile, in attitude and action, to religion, religious groups, and the influence of religion in society. What has been said about clients in the previous category generally applies to clients in this category.

The degree and quality of the hostility might well be a part of other counseling issues, however. Hostility toward religion may be based primarily on a rationalistic perspective that has been affectively reinforced by genuinely negative experiences with religion (e.g., religiously motivated hatred and discrimination or religiously based rejection of clear scientific evidence); in this case, it is presumed to have no relevance to counseling issues. If, however, hostility toward religion is a particular manifestation of psychologically detrimental hostility associated with a variety of cognitive distortions, the counselor's treatment of that hostility may well include clarification of religious as well as other distortions. It is important to note that clarification of psychosocially harmful religious distortions in the case of the religiously hostile client, unlike clarification of such distortions in religiously committed or religiously loyal clients, is within a larger nonreligious or rationalistic context. Thus, clarifications for the religiously hostile clients are not carried out with a view of using positive religious ideas or values as part of the change process. Rather, the purpose is to facilitate a healthy rationality that will support positive development and the resolution of emotional and behavioral problems while leaving the client to his or her own views about religion.

These eight categories provide a schema for initially organizing information gathered about clients' spirituality and religiousness. The methods for obtaining this information include formal or direct assessment procedures as well as the assessment activities nested in the overall counseling process. This taxonomy does not represent a diagnostic schema for labeling or distinctly classifying clients, but a way of reasonably organizing spiritual and religious information about clients with a view to determining whether and how the spiritual/religious dimension may be incorporated into the counseling process with specific clients.

A Typology of Potential Connections between Clients' Issues/Problems and Spirituality/Religion

The second general typology for systematically determining the pertinence of spirituality or religion for each client is made up of four broad categories of client issues and problems with varying degrees of spiritual and religious relevance. The purpose of this typology is to give counselors a cognitive framework for organizing information about clients' issues in order to assess the potential connections between major categories of client problems/issues and spirituality/religion.

The four broad categories in this typology indicate varying degrees of likelihood that religion *might* be associated with a specific issue or problem that a client presents in counseling. They provide an additional way for the counselor to think carefully about the potential relevance of spirituality and religion with particular clients. Used in conjunction with the previous typology of client spirituality and religiousness, this typology of issues and problems is another guide to the counselor in translating spiritual and religious information into counseling decisions about including the spiritual/religious dimension in counseling.

The boundaries between this typology's categories are not hard and fast. Depending on individual circumstances, specific issues and problems may fall into more than one category. Also, people may experience a specific issue in religious or nonreligious (e.g., psychological) terms under different circumstances and at different times. However, the categories do provide a way of understanding primary or predominant connections between specific issues and problems and the spiritual/religious dimension. In this respect, the categories provide the counselor with an additional perspective for considering the appropriateness of responding to the spiritual/religious dimensions of a specific issue or problem.

1. Predominantly or specifically spiritual/religious issue/problem. The highest probability that the inclusion of the spiritual/religious dimension in counseling will be therapeutically beneficial is with those issues that are primarily spiritual or religious in nature or are directly related to some spiritual or religious factor. These might include difficulties such as fear of losing one's faith, guilt consciously and directly connected to a distinct sense of sin or some violation of religious strictures, indecision about devoting oneself to a religious vocation, or interpersonal conflicts associated with differences of opinion about religious beliefs and practices. Other close connections between the spiritual/religious dimension and counseling issues might include a strong reliance on spiritual/religious beliefs and practices to help one in difficult circumstances. In cases like these, spirituality and religion may play an important role in the very nature of the client's problem, or they may have a strong bearing on how issues are explored and understood and how new directions and solutions are formulated.

When the spiritual/religious dimension is so directly and substantially implicated in the client's problems, the counselor has a therapeutic obligation to respond with understanding to this dimension of the client's concerns and help the client sort out the relevance of this dimension to the client's development and problem resolution. This is not to say that the client's spirituality or religion will necessarily be the therapeutic core aspect of the client's concern. Indeed, as we will note later, the client's overt spirituality/religiousness may be masking nonspiritual/nonreligious issues and problems that are at the heart of the client's difficulties. In any case, for clients with problems in this category, the counselor should respond directly to the spiritual/religious aspect to explore its relevance to the client's improved self-understanding and problem resolution.

Issues with a significant spiritual/religious component may be presented by religiously or spiritually committed clients or religiously loyal clients. A religiously hostile client may have a problem with a significant negative relationship to religion. However, it is primarily religiously/spiritually committed or religiously loyal clients for whom spirituality and religion are likely to be implicated in their problems. The counseling issues of clients who are unconcerned about religion, only superficially concerned, indifferent, or negative do not fall into this category.

For the religiously or spiritually committed client, a problem with a significant religious aspect portends important life choices involving religious values and beliefs, for example, choosing a religious career, ending a long-term relationship incompatible with one's beliefs, or changing one's behavior or belief to deal with guilt-laden behavior. The counselor in these cases needs to be respectful and empathic and to learn, from the client and from consultation and study if necessary, enough about the client's specific beliefs to facilitate the counseling process.

A religiously committed client's religion may be so consciously important and so much in the forefront of the client's usual decision making that it may be masking a basically nonreligious psychological problem, for example, unresolved anger toward a parent, very fragile sense of self-esteem, or confusion about one's sexual identity. Here too the counselor needs to respond with understanding to the client's religiousness but with an increasingly discriminating effort to help the client identify the core, basically nonreligious problem or issue.

With the religiously loyal client, religion may be implicated strongly as a cultural issue—for example, whether to marry inside or outside one's religious tradition. In a case like this, the issue is not so much making a choice that is deeply formative in terms of one's religious beliefs (as with a religiously committed client) but primarily preserving, defending, or asserting one's cultural-religious identity, for example, by insisting that one's fiance marry into one's religion or at least be married in one's religious institution.

In the case of a religiously loyal client presenting a problem with a significant religious component, the counselor's general approach is to understand the religious component as a form of cultural patterning that strongly shapes the client's attitudes and behavior within a more or less culturally-religiously circumscribed identity. That is to say, religion is acting not only to influence one's sense of self but also to set fairly distinct limits on the changes one permits oneself. In this regard the religiously loyal person is unlike the spiritually or religiously committed person whose spirituality or religion is not only an important part of one's psychosocial identity but also acts as an internal force for change and the challenging of external limits. Thus, with the religiously loyal person, the understanding and resolution of a religiously significant problem is more like negotiating an adjustment of problematic or challenging life events within the limits of one's religious loyalties rather than using religious convictions as a source of serious change in life perspective or life-style. For religiously loyal clients the external forms of religion are likely to prevail in some negotiated development of a solution. For the spiritually or religiously committed person the core formative values of spirituality and religion are called on to help one change oneself and one's environment as necessary for the sake of a maturing personal integrity and a more just and growth-supporting environment.

Of course, in the particularities of each religiously committed or loyal client, there will be subtle differences in the actual interplay and reciprocal influence of religion, spirituality, and secularity. Intrinsic spiritual or religious commitment does not have unlimited effects on behavior, and religious loyalties are not without life-changing effects. But the basic emphasis (commitment or loyalty) that characterizes each spiritual/religious person will have different effects on problem solving. The alert and informed counselor can shape a spiritual/religious assessment of the client according to these overlapping categories insofar as they reflect the relevance of spirituality and religion to the client's life development and problems.

2. Nonspiritual/nonreligious issues/problems with a significant spiritual/religious component. This general category is made up of those issues or problems that are not directly spiritual or religious in nature but are significantly affected by spiritual and religious beliefs and practices. These include issues such as converting from one religious tradition to another for the sake of marrying or making peace in the family, or suppressing one's religious practice for career advancement. The line between problems such as these and those in the previous category is not hard and fast, and indeed, as counseling progresses, the role of the spiritual/religious dimension may shift from a background influence to the foreground or vice versa. However, the distinction is conceptually and practically useful because it guides the counselor in recognizing and integrating a potentially significant spiritual/religious component in the case of a problem that, because of its predominantly nonspiritual/nonreligious appearance or character, might not easily reveal its spiritual/religious aspect.

145

Indeed, for counselors in secular settings, it may be expected that counseling problems and issues that fit this general description are far more likely than category one problems—those that are directly religious. These latter are more likely to be taken to counselors who have an explicit identification as a religious or pastoral counselor or who have an association with a religious institution. But it can be expected that spiritually or religiously committed and religiously loyal individuals who experience indirectly spiritual/religious problems as primarily psychosocial concerns will confer with counselors in secular settings. We noted earlier how the combined nonreligious atmosphere of a secular counseling setting and the primarily nonreligious nature of clients' problems may exercise a subtle but powerful influence toward neglecting the spiritual or religious aspect of such problems, even when this aspect is implicated as a major part of the problem. Explicitly recognizing a general category of nonspiritual/nonreligious issues with a significant spiritual or religious component provides a counterbalance to influences that tend to obscure spirituality and religion; it enhances a way of thinking about spirituality and religion in the assessment part of counseling that explicitly establishes spirituality and religion as legitimate elements in an overall understanding and treatment of clients for whom spirituality and religion show themselves to be consequential.

Several examples illustrate how spirituality or religion may be an important background aspect of a presenting problem. Anne, a 28-year-old single woman, notes on her intake form that her major issue is a relationship problem. Also, along with other information on the intake form, she writes that she is a Baptist and checks that religion is very important to her. She tells the counselor that she has become very attached to—maybe fallen in love with—a 31-year-old man, John, whom she has been seeing for the past six months. Their relationship has become increasingly serious, and she is confident that he loves and cares about her. She believes that he may soon ask her to marry him. She says that he always treats her well, and he seems like a kind and pleasant person. He has a regular job at the same professional level as hers. He doesn't seem to have any big problems, such as drinking or violent behavior. Anne says that she has come to counseling because she is concerned that John is not very communicative about his emotions or his thoughts. This tends to make her feel unsure about him and triggers some old feelings of insecurity on her own part. Although he is kind and attentive, his reserve is troublesome. Anne also says that one element of her concern is that over the past several years she has become increasingly serious about the spiritual/religious dimension of life. Once or twice she tried to discuss this with John, but he good-naturedly avoided the discussion by saying something like, "I'm not personally interested in religion; it's okay for others, but I'll just stick to the business of this life."

In this example, religion is intermixed with the client's major internal conflict over feelings of attraction to John, supported by his several positive traits, and her concern about his emotional reserve and his reluctance to share his inner life with her. In the context of this major, apparently central relationship issue, Anne also notes the contrast between her increasing valuing of religion and John's benign indifference. Religion is not the presenting or principal issue, but it certainly appears to have an important bearing on how Anne will think through and resolve her problem. The counselor's progressive assessment of Anne's situation needs to account for the relationship dynamics between Anne and John (perhaps calling for couples counseling) and help Anne to weigh how and to what extent her religious convictions will influence her decisions about John.

Another example in this category is Maureen, 34 years old, married for 10 years, with a daughter, seven, and a son, five. Her husband, Ted, is a professional consultant who has to work long hours and spend several weeks a year away from the family. Maureen writes on the intake form that her major presenting problem is her deep unhappiness related to marital, relationship, and sexual issues. As part of the other intake information she notes that they are Catholics; she subsequently tells the counselor that they attend church "fairly regularly; being Catholic is important to them." Maureen says there are no "really big problems" that she can point to between Ted and her, but she has become increasingly unhappy ("unfulfilled") in her marriage. Their relationship, including occasional sex, seems to have become routine. Maureen tells the counselor of her pervading sense of unhappiness, especially with her marriage. In the second session, she reveals that she has recently begun an affair with another woman. She is strongly drawn to this other woman and greatly enjoys their relationship, including their sexual intimacy. She feels deeply torn about this, because of her husband and family and because she

147

never thought that "as a good Catholic" she would have a relationship like this.

Religion does not appear as intrinsically motivating for Maureen as it did for Anne; it does, however, form a potentially
important part of the overall picture of Maureen's struggle. The
counselor in this case is faced with helping Maureen sort through
several important issues, including her marital relationship, parental responsibility, sexual identity and/or sexual needs, desire
for intimacy, sense of responsibility and guilt, and the relevance
of her religion—all bearing on her evolving sense of self. With so
many significant issues to consider, the counselor (particularly in
a secular setting) might give little attention to the religious aspect,
unless sensitive and prepared to assess the religious part of Maureen's case. For Maureen religion may not constitute a significant
part of her evolving exploration and understanding of herself and
her decisions in this part of her life. However, the counselor cannot
assume this or simply neglect to help Maureen include her religion
as part of her overall look at her situation.

Art, a client in his early 40s, comes to counseling for what he
describes as vague and pervasive feelings of emptiness, dissatisfaction, and joylessness in his life. On his intake form he writes that
he has primarily a career problem. He notes that he is Jewish, and
on a problem checklist part of the intake form, he checks "Spiritual Issues" as somewhat important. He tells the counselor that
he has been successful in his family business career. He mentions
that he has been sexually unfaithful to his wife on a few occasions
but that he truly loves her, is generally satisfied with his family
life, and has no desire to leave his wife or family. Despite his
career success and generally satisfactory marriage and family life,
he still feels deeply dissatisfied. At one point, while talking about
his childhood and adolescent days, he mentions, almost in passing, that he had been raised in a religiously Jewish home, had
participated regularly in synagogue services and activities with his
family, and had once thought of becoming a rabbi. But he found
that he had a talent for all phases of his family business, was able
to advance quickly, and was soon making very good money. His
work soon came to dominate most of his time and attention. Until
recently he was satisfied with his work, but increasingly he is
coming to feel dissatisfied and wonders if he should change his
career.

Like Anne and Maureen, Art presents with several significant interrelated issues focusing on a central secular issue; for Art the focus is on his career and the course of his life. Religion is in the background, fleetingly acknowledged but also appearing as a potentially significant element in the life of a person who is seeking a renewed sense of purpose. Without a category that helps the counselor to consider explicitly the potential role of religion in Art's continuing search for meaning and fulfillment, the counselor might miss or downplay how the client's religious roots can affect his self-exploration and search for direction.

These three examples are representative of an unlimited variety of ways that spiritually or religiously oriented or rooted clients may present issues that are more or less significantly affected by their spirituality or religiousness. By having a typology of problems and issues that includes spirituality and religion as an indirect but significant element, the counselor is prepared to make assessments that will give due weight to the potential significance of these elements in the client's shifting of perspectives and action planning for change.

3. Nonspiritual/nonreligious issues/problems with a potential connection to the spiritual/religious dimension. Issues or problems in this category, unlike those in the previous two, do not have a necessarily inherent connection with spirituality or religion, nor do clients present these problems with explicit reference to spirituality and religion. On the other hand, by their very nature these issues have a plausible connection to the spiritual/religious dimension; they thus have some potential for inviting a spiritual or religious perspective for understanding them better. This category generally includes issues with a potential for raising questions such as those about the meaning of life or life events, the possibility of life beyond death, hope and trust for the future, the interconnectedness of humans and the universe, or the ethical implications of significant decisions. In the concrete, these questions may be tied to the death of a loved one, a family breakup, an unwanted or unexpected pregnancy, a public disgrace, serious financial hardship, serious illness, or alcoholism.

For nonspiritual or nonreligious individuals, none of these matters has spiritual or religious significance; it is clearly possible to take a nonspiritual/nonreligious stance toward them. On the other hand, because of questions they may raise about meaning in life (and death) or peoples' vulnerability in the face of tragic events, they invite the possibility of seeking enlightenment and direction in spiritual and religious perspectives on life. For spiritually and religiously oriented individuals this may be an obvious connection. Also, for those described above as spiritually and religiously open clients, these issues may turn their open-mindedness in the direction of therapeutically pertinent spiritual and religious beliefs. When spiritually/religiously open people are confronted with problems like those noted above, spirituality or religion may provide alternative perspectives helpful to the client in understanding and acting constructively on such problems.

This category of religiously relevant issues is not without conceptual and practical difficulties. Conceptually, the line between nonspiritual/nonreligious problems with a potential connection to spiritual/religious concerns (this category) and nonspiritual/nonreligious problems with a significant religious or spiritual component (previous category) is certainly permeable and movable. Spiritually oriented people would note, for example, that several of the broad issues in this category are significantly spiritual by their very nature. On the other hand, there is no doubt that many approach these problems from a nonreligious, nonspiritual point of view. Unlike the previous category, issues and problems in this category are not only conceptually separable but also are *in fact separated* from spirituality and religion for many people. Thus this category of issues provides the counselor with a further refinement for broadening assessment to possibly include the spiritual/religious dimension when it is conceptually but implicitly connected to a religiously open client's presenting problem even though the client initially makes no religious connection to the problem.

A practical difficulty with categorizing client issues as *potentially* amenable to a spiritual/religious perspective is that the counselor is put in the position of initiating the client's consideration of this perspective. This is likely to strike many counselors as an ethically dubious counseling response. Spirituality and religion represent an array of beliefs and values, diverse to be sure, but all with serious implications for guiding persons' thinking and behavior. Given the axiom that counselors, *precisely in the practice of counseling*, are not to impose their own values or induce clients in the direction of values contrary to their clear self-awareness and free choice, what leeway does the counselor have to *initiate* the client's incorporation of spiritual/religious views into the client's self-exploration? Should the counselor avoid introducing a consideration of this universe of beliefs and values even when the client's issues appear to have significant philosophical and existential connections with a spiritual and religious perspective? Why should the counselor specifically avoid spirituality and religion when it is likely that the counselor is going to rely on a set of humanistic values that are widely accepted by the majority of mental health professionals, including counselors (Jensen & Bergin, 1988; E. W. Kelly, in press)? We have already seen that counselor as well as client values play a significant role in counseling, so that the issue is not whether these values will come into counseling but how they should be used for the therapeutic benefit of clients according to their awareness and self-determined development. Counseling is centrally concerned with respecting the client's self-determination according to freely chosen values; thus there are no easy answers to the question of values in counseling, especially those explicitly associated with spirituality and religion.

With respect to counselors in secular settings, the position proposed here is that *in principle* the counselor may ethically introduce spirituality and religion as a potential source of ideas, beliefs, and values in this category of problems and issues under the following conditions: (a) the counseling process has progressed to a point where the client is cognitively and affectively prepared to consider with free awareness alternative ideas and values that may be therapeutically beneficial to his or her development and problem solving; (b) the counselor raises the spiritual/religious perspective as one of several that the client may find pertinent to his or her self-exploration; (c) the counselor does not advance a specific expression of spirituality or religion but facilitates the client's consideration of options consistent with previous or current client beliefs; (d) the counselor does not move beyond his or her knowledge and competence with respect to specific aspects of spirituality and religion and allows clients to conduct their own search for specifics through referrals and personal study; (e) insofar as clients come to actively consider spirituality or religion in their self-exploration and developing self-understanding, the counselor keeps his or her focus on the counseling or therapeutic relevance and benefit of these ideas and beliefs and maintains neutrality with regard to development of particular spiritual or religious beliefs; (f) if a client chooses to discuss the spiritual/religion dimension as part of his or her self-exploration, the counselor facilitates the client's weighing of the advantages and disadvantages for the client; (g) if a client is disinclined to consider spirituality and religion in exploring this category of issues, the counselor drops them from the presentation of alternative perspectives; or (h) in the case of minors counselors should avoid introducing the spiritual/religion dimension without first consulting with their legal guardians, because in practice (if not in principle) such an initiative opens the counselor to heated criticism and perhaps legal action that significantly outweighs any therapeutic benefit that may be temporarily gained.

With these guidelines in mind, the category of nonspiritual/nonreligious issues and problems with a potential connection to the spiritual/religious dimension is useful for counselors as an important part of thinking systematically about the spiritual/religious aspect in assessment. In these issues, spirituality and religion do not leap out as explicit elements in the client's evolving self-understanding but rather are inherent in the issues themselves, thereby bidding the counselor to raise them for the client's explicit consideration.

4. *Nonspiritual/nonreligious issues/problems with little apparent or close connection with the spiritual/religious dimension.* This category includes the many issues and problems that are predominantly related to achieving personal objectives or overcoming problems in a primarily secular, nonreligious sphere of life. Some spiritual and religious individuals may argue that no spheres of life are completely disconnected from the spiritual/religious dimension (just as others may argue that spirituality and religion are irrelevant to life). The pan-religious view, regardless of its merits one way or the other, is not useful to much of counseling; indeed, it may distract from a therapeutic/developmental focus and open the door to unethical value persuasion. Many issues have little or no spiritual/religious connection to developmental and therapeutic counseling, and many clients are nonreligious, nonspiritual, or not interested in bringing their spirituality or religion to bear on the issues they bring to counseling. A few examples might include dissatisfaction with one's career or current working conditions, a teacher's problems managing difficult high school students, problems with being overweight or having a smoking habit, relationship and marital conflicts and sexual problems, specific phobias, a lack of assertiveness and low self-esteem, and chronic bedwetting. In the evolving assessment of these and similar issues

with clients who do not bring up spirituality or religion themselves, the counselor can consider the spiritual/religious dimension to have no direct therapeutic significance for these clients and to be an inappropriate perspective to include in the counseling process.

With these background typologies providing a framework for organizing spiritually or religiously oriented information, we can now turn our attention to general and specific assessment procedures that include the spiritual/religious dimension.

Assessing spirituality and religion: a general approach

Intake

A first step toward including the spiritual/religious dimension in the assessment component of counseling is to make it a regular part of the intake procedure and the initial exploratory phase of the counseling process. This step can be implemented fairly easily in most instances. It is a simple but important step that signals to the client that spirituality and religion are acceptable aspects of the counseling process, and it sets the stage for the client or counselor to bring them subsequently into the counseling process when appropriate. Though not a specific or formal assessment in itself, this initial step is an opening to elaborating later, as appropriate, on this aspect of clients' lives in subsequent, more expansive assessments.

The intake form may include one or two items that ask clients for very general information about their spirituality or religion. For example, the intake form used at The George Washington University Counseling Laboratory has two such items on a relatively brief form. The first is in the section on general identifying information (e.g., name, address, occupation, etc.) asking for "Religious/Spiritual Orientation." Spirituality and religion occur a second time in a 23-item checklist of past and current problem areas. The purpose of these items with respect to spirituality and religion is to (a) obtain a preliminary indication about the relevance of spirituality and religion for each client, (b) obtain information that the counselor or client might subsequently refer to at appropriate points in the counseling process, (c) initiate client self-reflection that is explicitly open to spirituality and religion, and (d) indicate to the client that these are acceptable elements to include in the counseling process. The typical procedure is for the client, who has been assigned to a counselor intern on the basis of a brief telephone interview, to fill out the intake form before beginning the first counseling session. The counselor then quickly reviews the completed form in the presence of the client and has the client clarify any response or ask any questions about items that may have been unclear. The intention here is not to probe into issues but to ensure that the form has been completed clearly.

Because spirituality and religion are an explicit part of the form, they constitute from the beginning of counseling, along with other information, an acceptable and potentially relevant dimension of the counseling process. Whether they actually come into play, of course, depends on the intake response of the client and how the remainder of the counseling process unfolds. A review of 51 representative intake forms in a recent nine-month period in The George Washington University Counseling Laboratory showed that 29 (57%) clients indicated a specific spiritual or religious heritage and that 15 (29%) checked ethical/values/spiritual issues as being a problematic area in the past (6), present (6), or the past and present (3). Thus counselor interns and their supervisors were aware from the beginning of counseling that spirituality and religion were a current area of concern with nine (17%) clients and were previously an area of concern for six (12%) other clients.

Initial Self-exploration

A second part of a general approach to spirituality and religion in assessment is connected with the counselor's responsiveness to the client's initial self-exploration. Whereas the information on the intake form is a general, static indication of the client's concern (or lack of concern) with spirituality and religion, the client's unfolding expression of himself or herself in the beginning of counseling offers an evolving picture whose details the counselor's responses help to fill in with deepening empathy and specificity. For example, Margaret was a client in marriage counseling whose initial description of her marriage included several religious images and values associated primarily with conservative Protestant-Christian belief. My responses to her reflected her religiousness so that she was able to expand on how religion specifically shaped her perspective on her marital problem and also gave her husband an opportunity to respond directly to this aspect of their marriage. Religion was not the central focus of their marital stress but was an important contextual variable in understanding and attempting to resolve their problems (e.g., religious values of faithfulness, responsibility, compassion, and forgiveness were all woven into the counseling process).

Another example was Stanley, a 25-year-old single male, who wrote Judaism as his religious heritage on the intake form but checked that spirituality and religion had never been a problem. Stanley presented himself and his problem with absolutely no sign of interest in spirituality or religion; indeed, his description of himself and his behavior was thoroughly secular and materialistic. However, he also spoke of a dissatisfaction with his many fleeting sexual liaisons and expressed a desire for a deeper, more personal relationship with women other than those with whom he had one-night stands. He said that he found it hard to meet "other kinds of women." This led to a discussion of values and a consideration of young women who attended synagogue. Stanley and I talked briefly about this idea, but he rather quickly came to the conclusion that he did not want to get involved with synagogue, even to meet someone like he was talking about. We never again considered anything religious as part of his effort to solve his problem. I might hypothesize that later in life Stanley might reconsider the values of Judaism, but at this time he was indifferent to religion (in its spiritual and cultural aspects), and it formed no significant part of the way he conceptualized his problem. For him religion was not an appropriate element of counseling in the secular or general sense.

A third example is Allen, a 25-year-old single male, who gave Catholicism as his religion and checked that ethical/values/spiritual issues were problematic for him in the past and currently. Allen's counselor was a second-semester master's intern who helped Allen over many sessions to discuss a pervasive despondency related primarily to his failure in relationships with women. The counselor was able to facilitate Allen's self-reflective exploration of himself, his troubled relationship with his mother, and the attitudes and behaviors that seem connected with his relationship failures. However, the counselor, despite a number of cognitive and behavioral strategies to have Allen change, felt stuck because of his lack of progress. During a session near the end of the counselor's internship, Allen explicitly raised his religious concern, saying that his relationship with Christ was very important to him. In a subsequent supervision session the counselor said that this remark made him feel very uneasy because he was fearful of entering an area that he knew little about; thus the counselor let Allen's statement pass and moved on to some other topic. As it turned out, the graduating intern was able to bring about Allen's smooth transition to a rising second semester intern, a mature, committed Christian woman who was well disposed to allow Allen's inclusion of religion in counseling if therapeutically pertinent.

These three sample cases illustrate how a readiness to incorporate spirituality and religion in counseling, explicitly operationalized in the intake procedure, can open the counseling process to the spiritual/religious dimension. At the same time, the diversity of these cases with respect to spirituality and religion shows that the counselor must be prepared to follow up or drop these issues as they fit each client's particular needs and interests. In Margaret's case the counselor's assessment might be viewed primarily as an evolving component of the overall counseling process, allowing the client to elaborate gradually on the specifics of her already fairly clear and definite religious beliefs as these affect her marital relationship. With Stanley the proper approach is to discontinue consideration of the spiritual/religious dimension unless Stanley himself brings it back into the picture. In the case of Allen a next step would be to facilitate discussion of his religious perspective and, depending on the development of this issue in the overall counseling process, to assess Allen's religiousness in greater depth.

A General Assessment Approach

A variation on this general approach to an initial assessment of the client's religious interest and concern is that presented by Midelfort (Yost, 1986). This approach, used by Midelfort (1962) in family therapy, consists of a semistructured interview that can be integrated rather easily into the counseling process. In this method, the counselor in the first session asks family members their ethnic origins and religious affiliation. If the members disavow any religious affiliation, the counselor then asks them to briefly present the philosophy or belief system that governs their views, particularly those related to healing. If they do not strongly claim any ethnic affiliation, the counselor asks them to select one from those they enumerated. The rationale for this method is that clients' religious, spiritual, and/or ethnic heritage is a source of potentially healing factors that clients can apply to their own development and problem solving. Later in the counseling process the counselor can invite clients to claim from their heritage those elements that will promote healing—whether the healing is in the physical, emotional, cognitive, social, or spiritual realms.

In this process the counselor takes care to enter the family's life (or individual client's life) where an opening occurs. This is a process of beginning empathically where clients are as they present themselves and of continuing to explore with them until there is a "natural opening" to the religious or ethnic elements—that is, to a point in the counseling process where they can be reintroduced as aspects of the client's own life that may have a healing affect on the family's or individual client's current concern. In this situation the counselor then responds to clients in religious and ethical terms that are consonant with their own statements about their ethnic and religious affiliation and are likely to be a source of strength for improvement and development. (It should be noted that clients may also uncover or claim elements from their cultural or religious heritage that are sources of debilitation and distortion as well as sources of strength.)

This general approach, reflecting Midelfort's own therapeutic and philosophical convictions, is proactive with respect to the potentially positive therapeutic effects that may be achieved by a client's serious consideration (and perhaps reevaluation) and use (or reworking) of values inherent in his or her own religious, spiritual, philosophical, and cultural heritage. It is not, however, a values-intrusive approach because it invites people to uncover and use their own heritage, including their spiritual/religious heritage. Given that values are a part of the counseling process, and given counselors' concern that values be used ethically and effectively (Norcross & Wogan, 1987), this method of having clients explicitly identify their core cultural, religious, and philosophical heritage provides an ethical way of therapeutically incorporating values that arise from the client's self-identified perspective. It is a way of taking an informed first step in determining the relevance of specifically spiritual/religious values in the client's life and ascertaining if further, more specific assessment of spirituality and religion may be proper and useful.

Assessing spirituality and religion: bridging from the general to the specific

Moving from a general assessment of a client's spiritual and religious heritage to more specific assessments of spirituality and religion raises questions of *when* a specific assessment is indicated, *what* precisely is to be assessed, and *how* this assessment is to be made.

A secular setting for counseling is assumed in addressing here the question of *when* a more specific spiritual or religious assessment is indicated. Unlike spiritually or religiously based counseling (e.g., Christian or Islamic counseling), which establishes a presumption for making a religious assessment with particular belief content, general (secular) counseling necessarily builds on a far more ecumenical philosophical and scientific base. This ecumenical base implies that counselors are prepared to use a wide range of diverse beliefs for the therapeutic and developmental benefit of the client. Thus the *when* of specific spiritual/religious assessment in counseling is based not on a spiritual or religious belief system that is presumed to be shared by the counselor and client (e.g., Judaism, Buddhism, Christianity, New Age) but on initial information from the client suggesting that spirituality or religion in some form is likely to be therapeutically significant. This is achieved in part by the simple measure described in the preceding section on a general approach to assessing spirituality and religion. In addition, the nature of the client's problem (e.g., a serious illness, compared with career planning) and the client's use or nonuse of spiritual or religious concepts and terms (e.g., language suggesting a religious commitment or loyalty, compared with a secular perspective) provide further clues to the advisability of facilitating exploration of the spiritual/religious dimension and/ or using an assessment instrument to enhance understanding of the content and quality of the client's beliefs.

The use of specific methods for assessing the client's spirituality and religion also depends on the counselor's theoretical orientation and the requirements of the counseling setting. A person-centered or existential-humanistic counselor who works in a set-ting with no requirements for specific assessments and diagnoses is not likely to use an assessment instrument of any kind. In this case, it is the counselor who is, so to speak, the instrument of assessment, facilitating the client's progress through counseling primarily on the basis of the therapeutic/counseling relationship and folding in "assessment" as a part of the client's ongoing self-exploration and expanding self-understanding. In this approach to counseling, the issue of assessment is not the instruments or interview methods that are used but the counselor's way of being and responding in relationship to help the client expand and deepen his or her self-presentation and come to more self-actual-izing experiences of the self. With respect to spirituality and religion, the "assessment" demands of this predominantly human-istic approach are principally to ensure the counselor's respectful openness to the spiritual/religious dimension and an informed readiness to facilitate a clarified integration of that dimension into the client's overall development and problem resolution.

Counseling approaches with a cognitive, behavioral, person-environment (trait-factor), and clinical/medical emphasis—and systematic eclectic or integrative approaches that include these orientations—are more likely to incorporate the use of specific assessment methods and tools. Therefore, in determining when a spiritual/religious assessment is appropriate, I am assuming coun-seling approaches that use specific assessment techniques and counseling settings in which such assessments are either required or typical.

Spirituality/Religion in Commonly Used Assessment Instruments

Bridging from a general assessment of spirituality and religion to a more specific assessment may involve the use of instruments that include spirituality and religion as a subset of a more comprehen-sive assessment (e.g., personality, interests, wellness). This may not be as easy as it first appears, especially if the counselor would like to use one of the more widely used standardized instruments. For example, Watkins and V. L. Campbell's (1990) extensive presentation of major assessment methods typically used in coun-seling shows that these instruments contain next to nothing pro-viding information specifically about clients' spirituality or religion, except for a very few religiously oriented occupational designations on the Strong Interest Inventory, the Kuder Occupational Interest Survey, and Holland's Self-Directed Search. A review of the extensive indexes in *The Eleventh Mental Measurements Yearbook* (Kramer & Conoley, 1992) and *Test Critiques* (Keyser & Sweetland, 1994) also yields very little information about spiritual/religious elements in tests other than those specifically related to religion, spirituality, and values. To date there are no reports of a comprehensive study to identify the spiritual/religious elements nested in the large array of general and specialty assessment instruments that are available for counselor use. Such a study, highlighting explicitly spiritual/religious elements in commonly used assessment instruments, would be particularly helpful for counselors in secular practice to identify specifically spiritual/religious attitudes, interests, cognitions, and behaviors as these are embodied within more generalized reports of personality styles, personal and interpersonal cognition and behavior, ways of coping, career interests, clinical traits, and needs and temperament.

Assessment instruments with spiritual/religious items. It is possible and useful, however, to identify several instruments in which spirituality or religion are a subset of a larger array of factors. For example, the *Family Environment Scale* (FES) (Moos & Moos, 1981), a 90-item instrument to measure the social-environmental attributes of families, contains specifically spiritual/religious items and yields a Moral-Religion Emphasis subscale score along with nine other subscale scores. Thus, in using the FES for broad assessment purposes (i.e., obtaining a client's perceptions of the social climate of the family in general), the counselor also obtains information directly about clients' perceptions of religion in their families. Another example is the *Mooney Problem Checklist-C* (MPC-C) (Mooney, 1950), which contains 20 (of 330) items specifically addressed to spiritual/religious concern; this instrument has the definite potential for opening a client to a discussion of spiritual/religious concerns. Also, the *Campbell Interest and Skill Survey* (CISS) (D. Campbell, 1992) has eight items that directly elicit responses regarding religious, spiritual, and moral interests, a basic scale (of 29 basic scales) for "Religious Activities," and an occupational scale for "Religious Leader." Moreover, the CISS has an interest/skill patterns scale showing the relationship of respondents' interests to skills (four combinations of high and low) and indicating whether a client is advised to pursue, explore, develop, or avoid particular basic interests and occupations.

Wellness instruments. Another group of assessment instruments with a spiritual element consists of measures of wellness and holistic functioning. The *Life Assessment Questionnaire* (LAQ), developed for use primarily with college students, measures 10 dimensions of overall wellness, including the spiritual dimension (DeStefano & Richardson, 1922; National Wellness Institute, 1983; Palombi, 1992). The *Wellness Inventory* (WI) was designed as a measure to stimulate growth-oriented approaches to personal issues (Palombi, 1992; Travis, 1981). Included among the 12 dimensions of the WI are two spiritually oriented categories ("Finding Meaning" and "Transcending") that correlate significantly with the "Spiritual Dimension" of the LAQ (Palombi, 1992). The *Holistic Living Inventory* (HLI) yields scores suggesting optimal functioning on four dimensions of holistic living, including "Spiritual Functioning" (Stoudenmire, Batman, Pavlov, & Temple, 1985, 1986). The *Wellness Evaluation of Lifestyle* (WEL) (Witmer, Sweeney, & J. E. Myers, 1994) is based on a holistic model for wellness and prevention over the life span, with spirituality listed as the first of five major life tasks (Witmer & Sweeney, 1992). The WEL has 111 items and yields scores on the spirituality life task as well as four other life tasks, 16 dimensions of wellness, and a total wellness score.

The FES in the realm of family functioning; the CISS in the realm of career exploration; and the LAQ, LI, HLI, and WEL in the realm of holistic wellness are representative of nonreligious assessment procedures that a counselor in secular practice may find useful for gaining an initial estimation of clients' spiritual and religious interests and attitudes in the context of a more comprehensive assessment. In this way instruments such as these can become part of the information bridge that may alert counselors to the potential developmental and therapeutic relevance of spirituality and religion in helping clients constructively work on the problems they bring to counseling.

If general assessment procedures indicate that spirituality or religion may be a significant part of a client's issues, more specific forms of spiritual and/or religious assessment may be worthwhile in the counseling process. We now turn our attention to these more expressly spiritual and religious assessment procedures.

Spiritual and religious assessment: specific procedures and instruments

When spirituality and/or religion appear to be a likely major factor in the client's self-presentation, the counselor may help the client by assessment procedures that are focused directly on the spiritual/religious dimension. The remainder of this chapter is devoted to a discussion of several models, methods, instruments, and diagnostic schemes that deal directly with the spiritual/religious dimension. Assessment procedures for this dimension may be generally categorized in line with the distinction between spirituality and religion. Some procedures deal primarily with spirituality in the holistic sense irrespective of particular religious content, while others tap spiritual attitudes and particular specific religious beliefs and behavior. The following discussion of several procedures is organized according to this general distinction.

Models for Spiritual and Religious Assessment

Various models illustrating the relationship of spirituality/religion to other dimensions of life provide a conceptual framework for understanding and using specific methods of spiritual and religious assessment. The several models presented here have many characteristics in common, and all make a distinction between spirituality and religion.

Witmer and Sweeney (1992) include spirituality as the center of their comprehensive conceptualization of a holistic model of wellness and prevention (see their "Wheel of Wellness and Prevention" in Figure 1). As the primary life task, spirituality represents a fundamental sense of oneness in the inner life and with others, purposiveness or meaning in life, hope or optimism, and moral values nurturing one's own well-being and that of others. Spirituality is integratively infused into primary self-regulating and self-enhancing traits, and in conjunction with other major life tasks (work, friendship, and love), is realized in and influenced by major societal institutions including religion. The Wheel of Wellness and Prevention model provides a comprehensive framework for understanding and integrating spiritual and religious assessment in counseling and has recently been developed into an as-

FIGURE 1

A Holistic Model for Wellness & Prevention Over the Life Span

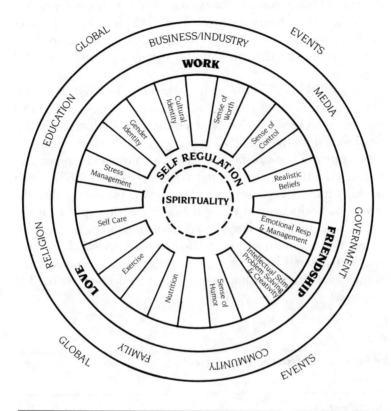

sessment instrument (WEL) that includes a score for spirituality as well as other areas of life.

Also in the sphere of spiritual assessment (as distinct from religious assessment), C. W. Ellison (1983) has developed a *Spiritual Well-Being Scale* (SWBS) built on a model of spirituality with a vertical (transcendental, religious) component and a horizontal (social-psychological) component. Like Witmer and Sweeney, C. W. Ellison regards spirituality as an integrative force interwoven in the whole of the person (Ellison & Smith, 1991). In their discussion of spirituality in nursing practice, Stallwood and Stoll (1975) (Carson, 1989) also present a conceptual model of human nature as a dynamic whole with spirit at the center, expressing itself as an inner harmony and outer connectedness through all the biological, intellectual, emotional, voluntary, and moral aspects of the total person. This model is designed to make nursing assessments sensitive to the spiritual factors (strengthening or distressing) that may affect a patient's particular medical needs.

Farran, Fitchett, Quiring-Emblen, and Burck (1989), also writing from the nursing perspective, present a model for spiritual assessment and intervention in which the spiritual dimension (distinguished from the religious) is conceptualized as encompassing "the totality of one's being and serves as an overarching perspective which unifies the various parts of the person" (p. 188). Their model, which is explicitly multidisciplinary, brings together the developmental stages of the spiritual dimension; practical approaches to understanding the spiritual dimension; life experiences, events, and questions related to the spiritual dimension; and attitudes and behaviors signifying expanded or altered functioning in the spiritual dimension. (Their model is reproduced in Figure 2.)

FIGURE 2

A Model for Spiritual Assessment and Intervention

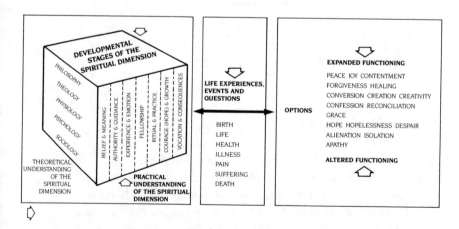

Note. From "Development of a Model for Spiritual Assessment and Intervention" by Carol J. Farran, George Fitchett, Julia D. Quiring-Emblen, and J. Russell Burck, 1989, *Journal of Religion and Health, 28,* p. 186. Reprinted by permission.

Although Farran et al. (1989) base their model on what they call a unifying approach, as contrasted with an integrated approach, to the spiritual dimension, their perspective is congruent with Witmer and Sweeney's, C. W. Ellison's, and Stallwood and Stoll's conceptualizations—all of which show spirituality to be a core, integrative, meaning-oriented dimension of human existence that infuses all major aspects of human life and has the potential to influence (and be influenced by) all human functioning in a variety of positive and negative ways with varying degrees of intensity. The chief implications of these models for spiritual assessment procedures are twofold. First, spiritual assessments, while reflecting categories that embrace religious and nonreligious belief systems (Hay, 1989), should focus on elements especially related to spirituality (e.g., meaning in life, a sense of transcendence, attitudes toward a Higher Power [God], inner harmony, connectedness with the universe, etc.) as distinguished from particular religious belief and observance (e.g., church attendance, belief in doctrines associated with specific religions, etc.). Second, such assessments provide a measure of spirituality (e.g., spiritual well-being, spiritual health, holistic living) that is distinct from other dimensions of human functioning while also showing a functional association with other related areas of life.

Expanding on these two points, Hay (1989) has proposed five basic principles to guide the development and use of spiritual assessment tools. These principles can be summarized as follows:

1. The categories of spirituality should encompass religious and nonreligious belief systems, thus making assessment inquiries applicable to religious and nonreligious persons.

2. Spiritual assessment categories need to use language that bridges and serves religion and psychology. A diagnostic language of spirituality is needed that respects the integrity of psychology and religion, as well as that of nonreligious philosophies.

3. Though spirituality may be generally relevant to all needs, the spiritual dimension may not be as assessable as the physical and psychosocial unless the patient's suffering is so acute that the patient identifies spiritual needs separate from the physical and psychosocial.

4. Varied human systems—physical, psychological, social, and spiritual—have inherent resources to effect healing and, in addition to various outside interventions, can be activated by spiritually oriented actions to exert their own natural healing power.

5. Account must be taken of the way in which spiritual development occurs in human experience, namely within a community context that enhances inner personal resources that give rise to meaning expressed in belief systems (often including religious belief systems).

The models and principles presented here are practically useful in guiding a counselor's general approach to spiritual assessment and conceptually important in the formulation of specific assessment methods and tools. We now turn our attention to the latter.

Spiritual Assessment and Diagnosis

Spiritual assessment procedures provide formal instruments or interview methods for measuring a client's spiritual well-being—a dimension of an individual's overall well-being involving an internalized set of beliefs and values by which a person experiences a sense of human and universal connectedness, transcendence open to the infinite, meaning associated with ultimate concern, and life purpose (see, e.g., Carson, 1989; C. W. Ellison, 1983; Elkins et al., 1988; Moberg, 1984; Shafranske & Gorsuch, 1984; Witmer & Sweeney, 1992). Apropos our earlier distinction between spiritual/religious maturity and immaturity and spiritual/religious well-being and distress, C. W. Ellison (1983) hypothesizes that spiritual health and spiritual maturity may not be the same as spiritual well-being. Spiritual health and maturity are seen as an underlying state of sound and well-developed spiritual soundness, whereas spiritual well-being is the experienced expression of this underlying state. However, Ellison's effort to assess differentially spiritual well-being and spiritual maturity has not proven successful (Sappington & Wilson, 1992). Indeed, in light of the SWBS's (*Spiritual Well-Being Scale's*) positive relationship with a variety of other measures of personality (C. W. Ellison & Smith, 1991), one can assume that the SWBS measure of spiritual well-being is a reasonably good indicator of a more lasting state of spiritual health.

Insofar as human spirituality embraces spiritual well-being and spiritual health/maturity, it may be understood as existing on a continuum running from a positive sense of spiritual well-being, spiritual health, and optimal spiritual functioning to a negative sense of spiritual distress (Carpenito, 1993) involving a variety of spiritual and spiritually related problems. It is important to note here that this spiritual distress (which includes religious and non-religious forms of belief) does not necessarily signify either spiritual immaturity or even deep spiritual unhealthiness; it certainly does not represent a pathological understanding of spirituality or religion. As noted earlier, spiritual distress (an absence of the experience of spiritual well-being) may occur as a crisis in an otherwise spiritually healthy or mature person, as an expression of underlying spiritual/religious immaturity, or as a mixture of varying degrees of crisis and spiritual immaturity.

Described more specifically, spiritual well-being (C. W. Ellison, 1983; Moberg, 1984) in its most positive expression consists of a securely held set of meta-empirical and natural beliefs and values giving rise to an inner hopefulness about the ultimate meaning and purpose in life, a deep peace that is a source of joy in living as well as courage to confront suffering forthrightly, and an actively benevolent connection with others and the universe. The absence of spiritual well-being may indicate spiritual distress, a condition described in the *Handbook of Nursing Diagnosis* as "the state in which an individual or group experiences or is at risk of experiencing a disturbance in the belief or value system that provides strength, hope and meaning" (Carpenito, 1993, p. 301; see Table 1). In the fourth edition of the *Diagnostic and Statistical Manual of Mental Disorders* (DSM-IV) (American Psychiatric Association, 1994), a clinical condition associated with spiritual or religious problems is described as "distressing experiences that involve loss or questioning of faith, problems associated with conversion to a new faith, or questioning of spiritual values that may not necessarily be related to an organized church or religious institution" (p. 685).

In the case of highly spiritual/religious individuals who concentrate on the development of their inner life (e.g., through meditation, prayer), spiritual distress may manifest itself as a "spiritual emergency" (S. Grof & C. Grof, 1989)—"a difficult and explosive personal crisis, varying in degrees of intensity, involving some kind of spiritual awakening, typically triggered by a stressful emotional spiritual event" (Oldenburg, 1994, p. D5). The cognitive, affective, and behavioral manifestations of spiritual emergencies, like other forms of spiritual distress, may mimic in some respects certain mental disorders (e.g., bipolar depression). An understanding of the distinctive diagnostic elements of spiritual distress and spiritual emergency provides the counselor with a way to distinguish emotional and behavioral disturbances associated

TABLE 1

Spiritual Distress

DEFINITION

Spiritual Distress: The state in which an individual or group experiences or is at risk of experiencing a disturbance in the belief or value system that provides strength, hope, and meaning to one's life.

DEFINING CHARACTERISTICS

Major (Must Be Present)

Experiences a disturbance in belief system

Minor (May Be Present)

Questions credibility of belief system

Demonstrates discouragement or despair

Is unable to practice usual religious rituals

Has ambivalent feelings (doubts) about beliefs

Expresses that he or she has no reason for living

Feels a sense of spiritual emptiness

Shows emotional detachment from self and others

Expresses concern—anger, resentment, fear—over the meaning of life, suffering, death

Requests spiritual assistance for a disturbance in belief system

RELATED FACTORS

Pathophysiological

Loss of body part or function	Pain
Terminal illness	Trauma
Debilitating disease	Miscarriage, stillbirth

Treatment-related

Abortion	Isolation
Surgery	Amputation
Blood transfusion	Medications
Dietary restrictions	Medical procedures

Situational (Personal, Environmental)

Death or illness of significant other

Embarrassment at practicing spiritual rituals

Hospital barriers to practicing spiritual rituals

Intensive care restrictions	Lack of privacy
Confinement to bed or room	Lack of availability of special foods/diet

Beliefs opposed by family, peers, health care providers

Divorce, separation from loved ones

Note. From Handbook of Nursing Diagnosis (5th ed.) (p. 301) *by Linda J. Carpenito, 1993, Philadelphia, PA: J. B. Lippincott Company. Reprinted by permission.*

with a growth-oriented struggle with spiritual issues from similar disturbances tied to mental disorders.

Assessment instruments. Several instruments designed to measure spiritual well-being have potential value for a counseling assessment of the spiritual domain. Prominent among these is the *Spiritual Well-Being Scale* (SWBS) (C. W. Ellison, 1983; C. W. Ellison & J. Smith, 1991; Paloutzian & C. W. Ellison, 1982). A variety of research studies have shown the SWBS to be reliable and possess reasonably acceptable validity (C. W. Ellison, 1994; Ledbetter, L. A. Smith, Fischer, Vosler-Hunter, & Chew, 1991). The SWBS is reproduced in Table 2. Its brevity (20 items) makes it especially attractive for relatively nonintrusive integration into the ongoing counseling process. For those whose spirituality includes an acceptance of the concept of God, its nonsectarian content makes it appropriate for people with diverse spiritual beliefs. The three subscale scores (overall spiritual well-being, existential well-being, and religious well-being) may serve as a tentative starting point for the counselor to explore the distinctive characteristics of each client's spirituality (Ledbetter, L. A. Smith, Vosler-Hunter, & Fischer, 1991). The individual test items also have the potential to stimulate client exploration of a number of spiritual attitudes pertinent to the client's presenting and emerging counseling issues.

As noted earlier, C. W. Ellison (1983) conceptualized spiritual well-being as a personal experience that is related to but distinguished from spiritual health and spiritual maturity, which are understood as enduring *underlying states* that are expressed in the *experience(s)* of spiritual well-being. This distinction has potential heuristic and clinical value in that it points to what may be an enduring spiritual state (spiritual health and spiritual maturity) in comparison to spiritual experience (spiritual well-being) that has not yet passed the test of time. Noting C. W. Ellison's distinction between spiritual well-being and spiritual health, Veach and Chappel (1992) have developed an instrument they call the *Spiritual Health Inventory* (SHI). An examination of SHI items and of preliminary research results does not psychometrically justify a distinction between spiritual health and spiritual well-being. However, the SHI does appear to be a promising measure of spirituality in four factor-derived domains (personal spiritual experi-

TABLE 2

Spiritual Well-Being Scale*

For each of the following statements circle the choice that best indicates the extent of your agreement or disagreement as it describes your personal experience:

SA = Strongly Agree	D = Disagree
MA = Moderately Agree	MD = Moderately Disagree
A = Agree	SD = Strongly Disagree

1. I don't find much satisfaction in private prayer with God.	SA	MA	A	D	MD	SD
2. I don't know who I am, where I came from, or where I'm going.	SA	MA	A	D	MD	SD
3. I believe that God loves me and cares about me.	SA	MA	A	D	MD	SD
4. I feel that life is a positive experience.	SA	MA	A	D	MD	SD
5. I believe that God is impersonal and not interested in my daily situations.	SA	MA	A	D	MD	SD
6. I feel unsettled about my future.	SA	MA	A	D	MD	SD
7. I have a personally meaningful relationship with God.	SA	MA	A	D	MD	SD
8. I feel very fulfilled and satisfied with life.	SA	MA	A	D	MD	SD
9. I don't get much personal strength and support from my God.	SA	MA	A	D	MD	SD
10. I feel a sense of well-being about the direction my life is headed in.	SA	MA	A	D	MD	SD
11. I believe that God is concerned about my problems.	SA	MA	A	D	MD	SD
12. I don't enjoy much about life.	SA	MA	A	D	MD	SD
13. I don't have a personally satisfying relationship with God.	SA	MA	A	D	MD	SD
14. I feel good about my future.	SA	MA	A	D	MD	SD
15. My relationship with God helps me not to feel lonely.	SA	MA	A	D	MD	SD
16. I feel that life is full of conflict and unhappiness.	SA	MA	A	D	MD	SD
17. I feel most fulfilled when I'm in close communion with God.	SA	MA	A	D	MD	SD
18. Life doesn't have much meaning.	SA	MA	A	D	MD	SD
19. My relation with God contributes to my sense of well-being.	SA	MA	A	D	MD	SD
20. I believe there is some real purpose for my life.	SA	MA	A	D	MD	SD

*Items are scored from 1 to 6, with a higher number representing more well-being. Reverse scoring for negatively worded items. Odd-numbered items assess religious well-being; even-numbered items assess existential well-being.

ence, spiritual well-being, sense of harmony, and personal help-lessness). Like the better researched SWBS, the SHI has the advantages of brevity as well as item content that could be integrated into the counseling process. The SHI is reproduced in Table 3.

Another promising instrument for measuring spirituality is the *Index of Core Spiritual Experience* (INSPIRIT) (Kass, R. Friedman, Leserman, Zuttermeister, & H. Benson, 1991). The INSPIRIT was developed to assess two core elements of spirituality—a distinct event and an event appraisal leading to a personal conviction of the existence of a Higher Power and to a perception of an internalized relationship between the person and the Higher Power. Although it is more limited in scope than the SWBS and still in an early stage of development, initial results with the INSPIRIT suggest that this brief (seven items) scale may provide a quick and helpful method for assessing spiritually oriented clients' core experience of spirituality and their sense of a Higher Power (God) and for stimulating relevant discussion of these issues in counseling. The INSPIRIT is reproduced in Table 4.

Other instruments the counselor may wish to consider for a spiritual assessment include the longer, comprehensive instruments mentioned above, the *Life Assessment Questionnaire*, the *Wellness Inventory*, and the *Holistic Living Inventory* (HLI), all of which include a spiritual dimension or meaning/transcendence score. Possible disadvantages of these instruments for counseling purposes, however, are their length and less specific spiritual focus. On the other hand, they may be useful for considering spirituality in a larger context and for obtaining evaluative and research data.

An assessment/research instrument of specific application with spirituality as expressed in Alcoholic Anonymous's Twelve-Step program is the *Brown-Peterson Recovery Progress Inventory* (B-PRPI) (H. P. Brown & Peterson, 1991). The B-PRPI is a 53-item instrument designed "to both obtain data on the actual behaviors, cognitions, and beliefs of those successfully utilizing a twelve step recovery program, as well as provide a method for measuring progress in the acquisition of such behaviors, cognitions, and beliefs in the treatment or research setting" (p. 23). Developed with the participation of self-identified members of AA and several other types of 12-step programs, the B-PRPI's initial findings indicate that it distinguishes successfully between individuals before and during progressive participation in a 12-step program, detects

TABLE 3

Spiritual Health Inventory

For each of the following statements circle the choice that best indicates
the extent of your agreement or disagreement.

SA = Strongly Agree	D = Disagree
MA = Moderately Agree	MD = Moderately Disagree
A = Agree	SD = Strongly Disagree

1. I have a sense of internal support or strength in dealing with illness or other problems.   SA   MA   A   D   MD   SD

2. I experience a sense of harmony with the world and the universe as they exist.   SA   MA   A   D   MD   SD

3. I believe in God, a Creator, or a Higher Power.   SA   MA   A   D   MD   SD

4. God, the Creator, or Higher Power is so powerful that nothing I do makes any difference.   SA   MA   A   D   MD   SD

5. I believe my life has meaning.   SA   MA   A   D   MD   SD

6. It is my experience that developing and maintaining spiritual health requires effort and work.   SA   MA   A   D   MD   SD

7. I *do not* believe that anything can be done to develop spiritual health.   SA   MA   A   D   MD   SD

8. I have an internal experience of being accepted for who I am.   SA   MA   A   D   MD   SD

9. I *do not* pray to God, a Creator, or a Higher Power.   SA   MA   A   D   MD   SD

10. I believe my life has purpose.   SA   MA   A   D   MD   SD

11. I experience the presence of God, the Creator, or Higher Power in my life.   SA   MA   A   D   MD   SD

12. I have *no* experience of peace with myself or with others.   SA   MA   A   D   MD   SD

13. I believe that God, the Creator, or my Higher Power will do things for me or to me.   SA   MA   A   D   MD   SD

14. I have had a spiritual experience or a sense of spiritual awakening.   SA   MA   A   D   MD   SD

15. I experience a sense of awe when I consider life and the universe.   SA   MA   A   D   MD   SD

16. I *do not* believe there is such a thing as spiritual health.   SA   MA   A   D   MD   SD

17. My experience of God, the Creator, or Higher Power leaves me with a sense of humility.   SA   MA   A   D   MD   SD

18. I am grateful for all I have received from life.   SA   MA   A   D   MD   SD

Note. From "Measuring Spiritual Health: A Preliminary Study" by Tracy L. Veach and John N. Chappel, 1992, Substance Abuse, 13, pp. 142–143. Reprinted by permission.

TABLE 4

INSPIRIT

Instructions:
The following questions concern your spiritual or religious beliefs and experiences. There are no right or wrong answers. For each question, circle the number of the answer that is most true for you.

1. How strongly religious (or spiritually oriented) do you consider yourself to be? (strong; somewhat strong; not very strong; not at all; can't answer)

2. About how often do you spend time on religious or spiritual practices? (several times per day—several times per week; once per week—several times per month; once per month—several times per year; once a year or less)

3. How often have you felt as though you were very close to a powerful spiritual force that seemed to lift you outside yourself? (never; once or twice; several times; often; can't answer)

    People have many different definitions of the "Higher Power" that we often call "God." Please use your definition of God when answering the following questions.

4. How close do you feel to God? (extremely close; somewhat close; not very close; I don't believe in God; can't answer)

5. Have you ever had an experience that has convinced you that God exists? (yes; no; can't answer)

6. Indicate whether you agree or disagree with this statement: "God dwells within you." (definitely disagree; tend to disagree; tend to agree; definitely agree)

Continued

changes consistent with measured changes in psychiatric symptomatology (e.g., depression, self-concept, MMPI clinical scores, and clinical mood measures), and provides useful clinical information, such as the particular nature of presenting problems and specific deficit areas of clients who are not making progress. For counselors working with clients in 12-step programs, the B-PRPI may be beneficial for identifying and stimulating discussion of specific problem areas (e.g., hostility or resentment toward others or toward spirituality).

Assessment interview methods. Counselors may use assessment interview methods to achieve a better understanding of clients' level and quality of spiritual attitudes and functioning. Depending on the counselor's theoretical orientation, the specific needs of the client, and the particularities of the counseling process, counselors may weave spiritual interview assessment methods into the

TABLE 4 *Continued*

INSPIRIT

7. The following list describes spiritual experiences that some people have had. Please indicate if you have had any of these experiences and the extent to which each of them has affected your belief in God.

   The response choices are:
   I had this experience and it:

   4) Convinced me of God's existence;
   3) Strengthened belief in God; or
   2) Did not strengthen belief in God.
   1) I have never had this experience.

A. An experience of God's energy or presence

B. An experience of a great spiritual figure (e.g., Jesus, Mary, Elijah, Buddha)

C. An experience of angels or guiding spirits

D. An experience of communication with someone who has died

E. Meeting or listening to a spiritual teacher or master

F. An overwhelming experience of love

G. An experience of profound inner peace

H. An experience of complete joy and ecstasy

I. A miraculous (or not normally occurring) event

J. A healing of your body or mind (or witnessed such a healing)

K. A feeling of unity with the earth and all living beings

L. An experience with near death or life after death

M. Other _____

Note. From "Health Outcomes and a New Index of Spiritual Experience" by Jared D. Kass, Richard Friedman, Jane Leserman, Patricia C. Zuttermeister, and Herbert Benson, 1991, Journal for the Scientific Study of Religion, 30, pp. 210–211. Reprinted by permission.

overall counseling process as appropriate in qualitative assessment (see Goldman, 1990), or they may use a set of relevant questions and leading/guiding responses as a relatively discrete part of the exploratory component of counseling. The creative counselor can use the models of spirituality presented above, along with the specific elements of these models, as background information to facilitate a client's self-exploration in special areas of spirituality as these are pertinent to each client's expanding exploration of his or her distinctive issues and problems. For example, the counselor may help clients to explore more deeply and expansively their own attitudes, beliefs, and activities toward meaning and hope in life, ultimate concern, connection with a Higher Power (God), and the transcendent.

Stoll (1979) has developed a spiritual assessment guide for nurses that counselors might readily adapt for use. Her guide is divided into four areas of concern: "The person's concept of God or deity [Higher Power], the person's source of strength and hope, the significance of religious practices and rituals to the person, and the person's perceived relationship between his spiritual beliefs and his state of health" (p. 1574). Within each of these areas, Stoll recommends several questions that the counselor may use to help the client explore more deeply. The following list of questions is taken from Stoll, with several variant phrases in parentheses as suggestions of how counselors might adapt them in making a spiritual assessment in counseling practice.

With respect to the concept of deity, the counselor could use or adapt the following questions from Stoll (1979):
- Is religion [spirituality] or God [Higher Power] significant to you? If yes, can you describe how?
- Is prayer helpful to you? What happens when you pray?
- Does God [or a Higher Power] function in your personal life? If yes, can you describe how?
- How would you describe your God [Higher Power] or what you worship? (p. 1574)

With respect to source of hope, Stoll proposes the following questions:
- Who is the most important person to you?
- To whom do you turn when you need help? Are they available?
- In what ways do they help?
- What is your source of strength and hope?
- What helps you the most when you feel afraid or need special help? (p. 1575)

In the area of spiritual or religious practices, the following questions may be useful:
- Do you feel your faith (or religion) [or spiritual beliefs] is helpful to you? If yes, would you tell me how?
- Are there any religious [or spiritual] practices that are important to you?
- Has being sick [discouraged, worried, upset, distressed, unsure, confused, uncertain, etc.] made any difference in your practice of praying? Your religious [spiritual] practices?

• What religious [spiritual, inspirational] books or symbols are helpful to you? (pp. 1576–1577)

With respect to the relationship between spiritual/religious beliefs and health, emotional and mental well-being, and development, the counselor may adapt the following responses:

• What has bothered you most about being sick (or what is bothering you)?

• What do you think is going to happen to you?

• Has being sick (or what has happened to you) [or the problem or issue that you want to resolve] made any difference in your feelings about God [Higher Power] or the practice of your faith [or spiritual beliefs]?

• Is there anything that is especially frightening [concerning, troubling] or meaningful to you now? (p. 1577)

Apropos the skillful integration of these or similar questions or guiding/facilitative responses into the overall counseling processes, Stoll notes that the timing of these assessment inquiries will affect how clients respond. The counselor will use these and similar questions and responses not as a fixed method of inquiry but as a process guide for facilitating the client's and counselor's enhanced understanding of the client's spiritual beliefs and practices as these are relevant to the client's issues and problems.

In the context of hospice care work, Hay (1989) has developed a comprehensive assessment interview guide that describes four types ("diagnostic categories") of spiritual and spiritually related problems that reflect the overlap in psychosocial-spiritual functioning. These four types of problems or diagnostic categories, along with defining characteristics and assessment components, are presented in Table 5. Of particular note is Hay's inclusion of historically oriented assessment items (e.g., "past and present spiritual disciplines and adaptive techniques . . ." and "past and present participation in communities which reflect belief system") (pp. 26, 28) that may be helpful to the client and counselor in understanding the contribution of current crises and/or spiritual/religious immaturity to the client's current spiritual problems.

Spirituality in relation to other areas of functioning. A major purpose of spiritual assessment is to help the counselor understand how spiritual well-being or spiritual distress is associated with other major client issues and problems. On the positive side, C. W. Ellison and J. Smith's (1991) review of research conducted

TABLE 5

Spiritual Diagnoses: Four Categories

Spiritual suffering

I. **Problem:** Spiritual suffering
II. **Definition:** Inter-personal and/or intra-psychic anguish of unspecified origin

III. **Defining characteristics**
1. Pain
2. Insomnia
3. Non-compliance with care plan
4. Diminished or extinct involvement in available support systems
5. Low level of conscious awareness of factors in self development
6. Withdrawal/isolation
7. Conflict
8. Anxiety, fear, mistrust
9. Anger
10. Depression
11. Guilt
12. Unforgiving
13. Low self worth
14. Low quality of life
15. Hopelessness
16. Grief
17. Lack of sense of humor

IV. **Assessment**
1. Conscious awareness of factors in personal development
2. Nature and causes of spiritual support system breakdown
3. Relationship between interpersonal behavior and belief system
4. Whether suffering due to immediate circumstances or long-standing concerns of guilt and/or conflict
5. Religious history as causes, e.g., community conflict, spiritual leader relationship
6. Explore issues of guilt, blame, remorse and forgiveness in personal context

Inner resource deficiency

I. **Problem:** Inner resource deficiency
II. **Definition:** Diminished spiritual capacity

III. **Defining characteristics**
1. Low level of elements which animate and empower
2. Low aspirations in personal and community goals
3. Diminished will to persevere
4. Inadequate possession or use of spiritual disciplines and adaptive techniques leading to diminished coping skill

IV. **Assessment**
1. Level of awareness of elements which animate and empower
2. Level of aspiration to achieve goals
3. Willingness to carry out personal, community and care plan goals
4. Past and present spiritual disciplines and adaptive techniques, e.g., meditation, prayer, visualization, relaxation, guided imagery, reading, sharing, nature contact, laughter/humor, art, music, poetry, etc.

Continued

TABLE 5 *Continued*

Spiritual Diagnoses: Four Categories

Belief system problem

I. **Problem:** Belief system problem

II. **Definition:** Lack of conscious awareness of personal meaning system

III. **Defining characteristics**
1. Expressions of life's meaninglessness
2. Questioning adequacy of present belief system, religious or non-religious
3. "Why me?" "Why am I suffering?" and related questions
4. Isolation from communities sharing belief system

IV. **Assessment**
1. Nature of belief system, philosophy, or world view which gives meaning to life
2. Perspective on meaning of diagnosis and prognosis
3. Consistency of relationship between belief system and interpersonal relationships
4. Past and present participation in communities which reflect belief system

Religious request

I. **Problem:** Religious need

II. **Definition:** Specifically expressed religious request

III. **Defining characteristics**
1. Absence of ordained and/or lay religious leadership
2. Desire for sacramental or devotional expressions of religion
3. Separation from traditional affiliation
4. Spiritual suffering due to unresolved issues of religious nature
5. Diminished inner resource due to atrophied spiritual disciplines

IV. **Assessment**
1. Nature and source of religious belief system
2. Adequacy of local congregational resources in meeting needs and requests
3. Adequacy of clergy in meeting needs and requests
4. Presence of support system from local congregation

Note. From "Principles in Building Spiritual Assessment Tools" by Milton W. Hay, 1989, The American Journal of Hospice Care, 6, pp. 26–29. Reprinted by permission.

with the SWBS suggests that spiritual well-being is positively correlated with self-ratings of health, perceived health in the elderly, acceptance of kidney disability, health assertiveness, less anxiety and greater hopefulness in dealing with a cancer diagnosis (see also Mickley, Soeken, & Belcher, 1992), internal locus of control, hardiness and hope in AIDS patients, self-actualization as measured by the Personal Orientation Inventory, and self-esteem. Spiritual well-being has also been shown to be correlated negatively with high blood pressure, frequency and amount of pain, degree of impairment in cancer patients, social isolation and loneliness, despair and hopelessness, depression, stress, aggressiveness and conflict avoidance. Although, as C. W. Ellison and J. Smith note, more research is needed to refine these results, current data suggest that the SWBS measure of spiritual well-being is a valid and useful indicator of spirituality in relation to major areas of physical and psychosocial functioning. The counselor in professional practice may find that this measure provides information that helps a client work on a number of important life issues.

Progress in the spirituality of the 12-step program, as measured by the B-PRPI, has been shown to have a significant relationship with decreases in depression and hopelessness scores; mood scores of tension, anger, fatigue, and confusion; and clinical measures of the MMPI (H. P. Brown & Peterson, 1991). For clients who are actively working on or drawing inspiration from 12-step beliefs and practices, the counselor may find that assessments of 12-step spirituality can guide client and counselor toward exploring, gaining perspective, and changing direction in several interrelated problem areas.

Religious Assessment and Diagnosis

For many people spirituality is inextricably intertwined with their particular system of religious beliefs and practices. For such people a counselor may find it helpful to use formal or systematic assessment methods that tap the more specifically religious aspects of a client's functioning. Because the primary purpose of this book is to discuss the spiritual and religious dimension in the context of secular or general counseling, a caveat is in order at this point. It bears repeating that a counselor in a nonreligious setting doing general counseling needs to consider carefully the therapeutic value and ethical propriety of a specifically religious assessment (as distinguished from a broader spiritual assessment). Three conditions need to be met for the counselor to proceed with a religious assessment. First, the counselor must be reasonably confident of his or her understanding of the pertinent elements of the client's religion or at least confident that he or she can empathically and respectfully learn about the client's religion from the client and from study and consultation as necessary. Second, the client must be aware and accepting of a religious assessment. Third, the counselor must be able to make it clear to himself or herself and to the client how a religious assessment is therapeutically relevant to the client's developmental and problem-solving progress.

Religious diversity and assessment. In addition to the issue of counselor expertise in doing a religious assessment, there is the problem of conducting a religious assessment that is sensitive to the many differences among various major religions and, indeed, the differences within these religions. Moreover, the counselor who is prepared to make a religious assessment is faced not only with the difficult point of religious diversity, both theological-institutional and personal-interpretive, but also with the currently quite modest developmental stage of *formal or systematic* religious assessment procedures (e.g., assessment instruments, structured interview methods). Current formal or systematic religious assessment methods—for example, paper-and-pencil instruments and structured interview methods—appear to be developed almost entirely from the Christian perspective (or, given the diversity within Christianity, one might say from *certain* Christian perspectives).

This is not to say that religious assessment is confined, either in the literature or practice, to Christianity. The point is that whereas several formal instruments and structured interview methods exist for assisting with religious assessments in the Christian tradition, religious assessment with clients of other major religions relies on criteria contained in less structured interview guidelines that must be adapted according to the belief and practice content of a specific religion (Lovinger, 1984; Rizvi, 1989; Spero, 1985). Spero (1985), for example, in his description of several cases of religious assessments with religious Jewish clients proposes a set of eight diagnostic characteristics for discriminating healthy or mature religion from unhealthy or dysfunctional religion; these are: (a) relationship of religion to overall life-style; (b) recency and disrupting effects of religious intensity/involvement; (c) history of religious crises or disruptions; (d) regressive or fixated level of religious functioning in association with mature object-relations development and ego functioning; (e) fear of religious backsliding and reactive rigidity or scrupulosity in religious belief and practice; (f) continued unhappiness following religious conversion; (g) resolving personal issues such as identity formation through the idealization of a religious movement or leader; and (h) the counselor's sensing of religious countertransference with a religiously immature client. Spero also provides a lengthy list of questions to probe more deeply and expansively into the client's religiousness. To conduct this kind of religious assessment according to the salient beliefs of a religious client would require a counselor who is either thoroughly conversant with the client's religion or who has sufficient knowledge and sensitivity to learn from the client. Even in the latter case, the counselor would likely have to limit himself or herself to selected religious content directly pertinent to client problems or, if a more expansive religious assessment seems appropriate, refer the client to a counselor who is competent in the client's religion and/or consult with such a counselor or a member of the client's clergy.

A *comprehensive* religious assessment includes a formal assessment instrument as only one part of several methods for exploring a client's religious beliefs and practices. For example, Eimer (1989) describes a five-part religious assessment method that includes pertinent demographic information, questions for initially determining the role of religion in the client's problem, a 40-question structured interview, and a chronological account of the client's religious history. While such a comprehensive religious assessment may be therapeutically useful for clients whose concerns and problems are heavily interwoven with their religion, it is very likely that a counselor in general secular practice (e.g., community mental health center; public and private schools; employee assistance counseling units; human service agencies such as rehabilitation, drug abuse, sexual abuse counseling centers; college counseling centers; in-patient psychiatric units; private practice) will find it appropriate to refer a client to and/or consult with a pastoral counselor, chaplain counselor, or counselor specializing in religious issues.

Rather than making a comprehensive religious assessment, a counselor in secular practice is more likely to use a religious assessment instrument or interview procedure as part of a general assessment related to the client's presenting concerns and any specialty purpose of the setting in which the counselor is working (e.g., substance abuse, women's issues). It is with this context in mind that the following religious assessment methods are presented.

The procedures described below include a mixture of general spiritual and religious elements and various specifically Christian beliefs and perspectives. Although these methods and instruments are directly applicable to Christian clients, a resourceful counselor might be able to adapt more ecumenical parts of them for use with clients of other religious traditions. Such adaptations would void the particular psychometric qualities of the method but nonetheless would provide a practical framework for a potentially useful qualitative assessment.

Religious Status Inventory and Religious Status Interview.
Malony (1985a, 1988, 1992, 1993a, 1993b, in press) has developed what is probably the most thoroughly articulated and researched interview procedure for conducting a formal religious assessment from a Christian perspective, *The Religious Status Interview* (RSinT). This structured interview procedure has been developed into inventory form as *The Religious Status Inventory* (RSinV) (Massey, 1988). Originally, the principal conceptual foundation of the RSinT and RSinV was the notion of "religious maturity" (Malony, 1985a) or "optimal religious functioning" (Malony, 1988); more recently Malony (in press) has adopted what he proposes as the more specifically religious concept of "theological functioning."

The concept of religious maturity has been formulated in several different but closely related ways (Worthington, 1989). Allport's (1950) conceptualization of religious maturity was presented in Chapter 2. Other formulations include that of Feinsilver (1960), who proposed a simple and useful 3-R test for religious maturity. This test involves asking if a person's religion is (a) reasonable (i.e., does it come to terms with modern thought), (b) responsible (i.e., does it generates social concern), and (c) related (i.e., does it connect people to others and to the physical world). Strunk (1965) elaborated on the characteristics of religious maturity to include (a) social concern and involvement rather than withdrawal and isolation, (b) social involvement arising from cognitive and spiritual awareness rather than unthoughtful behavior, (c) integration of religion with social concern, and (d) a spiritual awareness that includes a personal conviction of a transcendental power greater than oneself (summarized in Worthington, 1989).

Building on Pruyser's (1971/1991; 1976) earlier work in religious diagnosis, Malony's (in press) most recent reconceptualization of religious maturity as "theological functioning" is composed of eight dimensions that form the basis of items for the RSinT and the RSinV. These eight dimensions are:

1. Awareness of God: The extent to which persons affirm and are conscious of the transcendent reality of God in their lives.

2. Acceptance of God's Grace and Steadfast Love: The extent to which persons understand and experience the truth that God loves and accepts them totally.

3. Knowing God's Leadership and Direction: The extent to which persons depend on God for guidance in doing good, handling stress, and solving problems.

4. Being Ethical: The extent to which persons feel mandated by God to live lives of justice and love.

5. Being Repentant and Responsible: The extent to which persons, in interaction with this God, take responsibility for their own feelings and behavior.

6. Involvement in Organized Religion: The extent to which persons join with, seek support from, and are actively engrossed in the life of the church.

7. Experiencing Fellowship: The extent to which persons are related to others, inside and outside the church, as children of God.

8. Affirming Openness in Faith: The extent to which persons are growing, elaborating, and being willing to change at the same time that they hold onto the essentials of their faith.

Malony stresses that these eight dimensions, the RSinT, and the RSinV are based on Christian theological affirmations. This is reflected in several concepts (e.g., grace) and terms (e.g., fellowship). At the same time, the eight dimensions continue to reflect strongly the broader concepts of religious maturity as formulated by Allport, Feinsilver, and Strunk. Furthermore, they portray a set of beliefs, attitudes, and practices that—with appropriate variations in terminology and some shift in the meaning of specific concepts—could be adapted for assessments of religious maturity with people of religions traditions other than Christianity.

The RSinT is an interview guide of 33 open-ended questions with instructions for rating answers to each on a five-point scale. The questions are related to the eight dimensions described above and may be used to obtain subscale scores as well as a total score. The RSinV is a 160-item instrument calling for responses on a five-point scale of "Not true of me" to "True of me." It yields seven factor-derived subscale scores that approximate but do not exactly coincide with Malony's eight dimensions of "theological functioning." For counselors whose religious competency and approach to counseling accommodates an in-depth religious assessment of Christian clients, the RSinT and the RSinV will provide a wealth of religious information potentially relevant to clients' life development and resolution of emotional, mental, and behavioral problems.

The use of the RSinT or the RSinV in counseling in secular settings would take the counselor and client very deeply into the religious value world of the client (in this case, Christian clients). It bears repeating that counselors working in general, secular practice (i.e., not in religious or pastoral counseling) need to assure themselves that the three conditions noted previously for pursuing a religious assessment are clearly established. A major thesis of this book is the potential therapeutic value of counselors' knowledgeable and respectful approach to spirituality and religion in counseling. Notwithstanding this support for a competent inclusion of spirituality and religion in counseling, it must be emphasized that the more deeply and extensively the counselor explores this dimension with the client, the more expert the counselor must be in this area and the more confident the counselor must be that this exploration is conducive to the client's self-determined welfare. Indeed, the extent of religious competence implied by the use of the RSinT and similar instruments suggests that the counselor has a kind of specialty competence akin to pastoral or religious counseling. In the absence of this religious competence the counselor working with a highly religious client whose religion appears very relevant to the counseling should probably make a referral and/or seek appropriate consultation.

Other religious assessment instruments. Several other instruments purport to measure some aspect of religious maturity within a Christian perspective (Bassett et al., 1990). Examples of these include the Shepherd Scale (Bassett et al., 1981), a 38-item instrument for distinguishing Christians from non-Christians; the Christian Life Assessment Scales (CLAS) (Do. E. Smith, 1986), a 64-card Q-Sort procedure providing individualized information on eight religious (Christian) traits (e.g., love, kindness/goodness, faithfulness, self-control), four roles, and one general orientation factor; and the Character Assessment Scale (CAS) (Elzerman & Bolvin, 1987; Schmidt, 1983), a 225-item instrument purporting to measure eight character traits based on biblical principles concerning moral conduct (e.g., truth, respect, concern). Although many of the elements measured by these instruments have general applicability across different religions (e.g., concern for others, kindness/goodness, respect for self and others, self-control, physical health), the instruments themselves, in terms of background concepts and terminology, are designed and intended for clients who are Christian, thus limiting their suitability in counseling settings established for clients from diverse religious and philosophical perspectives.

Given the increasing diversity of religions in the United States and other countries and the growing acceptability of including religious issues in counseling and psychotherapy, it is hoped that counselors and behavioral scientists of major religious traditions other than Christianity will design religious assessment instruments based on beliefs and terminology in their particular tradition. The development of such tradition-specific instruments would have value for informing the practice of counseling and for expanding our comparative knowledge of religious similarities and differences, especially as these are pertinent to human development, counseling, and psychotherapy. A possible prelude to this kind of interreligious study is Bassett et al.'s (1990) comparison of five primarily Christian-oriented assessment instruments, with results indicating four basic religious maturity factors: (a) personal commitment as manifested in living, (b) personal commitment as expressed in belief, (c) relationship with others, and (d) perceptions of God as sustainer and protector. Expanding this kind of research to include religiously diverse instruments would give further insight into common elements of religious maturity while respecting religiously distinctive beliefs and practices. It is not unthinkable that development of assessment procedures along these lines would yield assessment instruments applicable to several major religious traditions, for example, by containing alternative sections specific to different religious traditions as well sections applicable to all respondents.

Religious history. A religious history is another potentially important religious assessment element in counseling approaches that include a formal or systematic inquiry into the client's developmental history. Benner (1991), noting that counselors routinely inquire about a client's medical, vocational, and family history but typically omit anything about religion, argues that a religious history may not only provide valuable information about the client but also may open the door to exploring spiritual/religious concerns. Barnhouse (1986) and Faiver and O'Brien (1993), writing from the general mental health perspective, and Eimer (1989), writing from the pastoral care perspective, recommend that a religious history be a typical part of an overall client assessment. A religious history includes material such as religion of family of origin; how religion was practiced in the home and how this practice affected the client's upbringing; relationships with significant others in the religious arena; changes in religious affiliation and practice; current and changing patterns of attendance at religious services; experiences of religion as supportive or frightening; consultation with one's clergy about problems; the influence of the religious media; and development of ideas of God.

Reflecting many of these same categories of information, Little and Price (1985) and Ludwick and Peake (1982) describe their development and use of structured religious history forms for use with children and adolescents in clinical settings. Although these are based on a Christian perspective, many of the items could be generalized to other religions and other items changed to reflect different religious perspectives. Indeed, I have used a shortened and adapted version of the Ludwig and Peake form with counseling students from Jewish, Islamic, and Buddhist backgrounds and consistently received favorable feedback that the selected items were appropriate and provoked serious self-reflection.

A client's religious history has a close relationship with his or her religious development as conceptualized formally in Fowler's (1981) and Oser's (1991) theories (see Chapter 2). Although these theories were developed with interview formats designed primarily for research, Oser (1991) has noted that his research, using religiously oriented dilemmas, was conducted in semiclinical interviews—an indication that it may be appropriate for certain clinical uses. Butman (1990) has proposed that Fowler's interview form might be adapted for counseling/clinical purposes. For example, Part I (Life Review) and Part II (Life-shaping Experiences and Relationships) of Fowler's (1981) interview guide would be helpful in obtaining an in-depth religious history, while Part III (Present Values and Commitments) and Part IV (Religion) would be helpful in understanding the structure and expression of a client's faith. Noting the length of Fowler's interview guide, Barnes, Doyle, and B. Johnson (1989) developed a brief, objective instrument that shows promise for identifying three "styles of faith" similar to Fowler's stages three through five, which are regarded as most typical of adults. Because Fowler's stages represent faith development largely irrespective of particular religious content, his interview guide lends itself to counseling adaptations across different religious traditions (see, e.g., Grossman's [1992] application of Fowler's theory to Judaism).

Conclusion

This chapter has shown that there is a multipurpose rationale, a set of sound framing concepts, and a variety of methods available to counselors for including spiritual and religious issues in counseling and clinical assessments. The assessment of spiritual and religious elements opens the counseling process to incorporating this potentially important dimension. A proficient assessment of spiritual and religious aspects of the client's life enables the counselor and client to appraise the degree of their importance in the client's life, the extent of their substantive depth in the client's thoughts and attitudes (e.g., mature or immature), their qualitative influence on the client's functioning (e.g., experienced as spiritual well-being or spiritual distress), their relevance to the client's concerns in counseling, and how and to what extent they may be integrated effectively into various counseling approaches and therapeutic methods and interventions. These spiritually and religiously informed counseling approaches, methods, and treatment interventions are the topic of the next chapter.

CHAPTER FIVE

Counseling Approaches and Techniques: Treatment Intervention and the Spiritual/Religious Dimension

T he purpose of this chapter is to describe approaches, procedures, and techniques for integrating spirituality/religion into the treatment and change components of counseling. These include approaches and techniques for working with client cognitions, affects, imagery, attitudes, language, and behavior, especially as these affect the action-oriented purpose of bringing about positive change in clients' lives.

There is a growing body of counseling and clinical literature presenting principles and reporting cases that exemplify the integration of the spiritual/religious dimension in a variety of counseling approaches and describe techniques with different kinds of clients and problems (I. R. Payne, Bergin, & Loftus, 1992). Although research on spirituality and religion in counseling and psychotherapy is gradually expanding, most approaches and techniques described in the relevant literature are in the form of case reports and counseling/clinical applications of theories and concepts associated with the relationship of religion, spirituality, and pastoral care on the one hand and counseling, psychotherapy, psychology, and human development on the other. The spiritually and religiously informed approaches presented in this chapter provide counselors with an array of carefully reasoned and experientially based methods and techniques that address specific kinds of spiritual and/or religious issues and concerns that clients bring to counseling.

The rich diversity of approaches and techniques for working with the spiritual/religious dimension in counseling reflects a combination of several interrelated factors, including distinctive applications of different theoretical approaches to counseling, a variety of developmental concerns and clinical problems, client diversity at different stages of life development, and a wide array of religious, spiritual, theological, and psychosocial concepts and practices. Given this multidimensional influence of diverse factors, it is difficult to organize approaches and techniques neatly into discrete categories or avoid overlap of similar concepts and practices among categories. The approach taken in this chapter is to use an organization of material that moves from introductory principles and concepts and general counseling approaches to more specific techniques applicable to special populations and specific issues.

Introductory principles and concepts

Three Major Perspectives

Techniques that address the spiritual/religious dimension in counseling may be described from three broad interrelated perspectives: (a) the nature and content of the client's spiritual/religious beliefs and practices, (b) the way the client is interpreting and using these beliefs and practices, and (c) the counselor's personal/therapeutic response to the nature and client use of his or her beliefs and practices. Given the subjective interpretations that each person gives to the objective content of spiritual/religious ideas, it may be difficult at times to distinguish between the first two perspectives (i.e., the objective content of belief and the personal interpretations of the belief content). However, the distinction is therapeutically important for at least two reasons. First, the distinction should encourage the counselor to look beyond general and sometimes stereotypical ideas to explore more deeply the distinctive interpretations that characterize each client's beliefs and practices. Second, the distinction between the objective and subjective aspects of spirituality/religion raises the question of alternative formulations of belief and practice, which can be used to help clients examine their current beliefs and practices and rethink or transform beliefs and practices in ways that are personally and socially beneficial. We will see uses of these two perspectives and the distinction between them in several of the techniques to be described later. With respect to the third perspective (i.e., how the counselor responds to the client's spirituality/religiousness), we will see how this plays out so that the counselor's use of various approaches and techniques is thoughtfully shaped to each client's distinctive spiritual/religious needs.

Positive and Negative Effects of Spirituality and Religion

Spiritual and religious beliefs and practices, considered objectively in terms of content and subjectively in terms of personal interpretations, may be viewed on a continuum from positive to negative effects on personal-social development and behavior, with a variety of mixed effects. It bears repeating that assessments of the negative and/or positive effects of spiritual/religious beliefs require careful and respectful sensitivity to how diverse beliefs and practices are interwoven and expressed in various ways across different cultures, spiritual/religious traditions, family lives, and individual personalities. Within the relational context of this thoughtful sensitivity, techniques addressing the spiritual/religious dimension are shaped in part by how spiritual/religious beliefs contribute beneficially to psychosocial development and problem resolution or how they contribute to causing, maintaining, and/or masking intrapersonal and interpersonal problems. Treatment approaches and techniques need to incorporate criteria and assessment procedures that distinguish between healthy/mature and unhealthy/immature expressions of spirituality and religion and between experiences of spiritual well-being and spiritual distress.

General counseling approaches to spiritual/religious issues

Malony (1993a) has proposed four general counseling approaches based on information obtained in a religious assessment; these are disregarding, annihilating, correcting, and encouraging spiritual or religious beliefs, attitudes, or practices of clients, depending on how these affect the client's life development and overall psychosocial functioning. These four approaches correspond to negative, mixed, and positive influences of spirituality and religion.

Based on a modest expansion of Malony's categories and a renaming of three of them to broaden their meaning, I propose four general approaches designed as a substantive framework to clarify the purpose of specific spiritually/religiously oriented techniques in light of how the spiritual/religious dimension affects the client's welfare. The four general approaches—deferring, invalidating, reworking, and encouraging—are by no means discrete but weave in and out of the counseling process as the client's self-presentation and needs evolve and change.

Deferring Approaches

Deferring approaches include counselor decisions to temporarily sidestep, disengage from, or disregard spiritual or religious information that the client brings to counseling. The counselor may choose to sidestep a client's effort to bring religion into counseling because it may have little to do with other issues that the counselor thinks are more germane to the counseling process. In this case, the intention is not to persistently disregard religion as the counseling process evolves but rather to sidestep it to redirect the client's attention to another aspect of self-presentation.

Lovinger (1990) offers an example of this kind of response when he recommends, as a general rule, that the counselor, in response to a client's question early in counseling about the counselor's own religious beliefs (e.g., "Are you saved?" or "Do you believe in God?"), respond not with a direct answer but in a way that will lead the client to explore the meaning of the question. Some counselors consider a direct response to such a question a sign of openness; however, a direct response may convey what the client interprets as a troubling value difference, which can stress the gradual forming of a working alliance. Or if a direct response indicates a similarity of client and counselor beliefs, the client may settle into a feeling of easy assurance that makes the confrontations and life-changing demands that are an inherent part of counseling more difficult. The question may mask a client's deeper pain or vulnerability, and a direct answer may result in the client's adding yet another layer of protection from exploring more influential psychosocial sources of the client's problems. Thus, while respectful of the question, the counselor may choose to deflect it with a response that opens the client to explore the meaning(s) underlying the question. It may help if the counselor responds with invitational empathy: "I value your question, especially because it suggests something of importance to you. Rather than respond to it directly, I think it might be helpful if you were to talk a bit more about salvation (or belief in God) and how it's important to you." If the client accepts the counselor's respectful invitation to elaborate on the meaning of the question, the client has an opportunity to deepen self-exploration rather than adding to his or her protective layer. However, as Lovinger notes, if a deferring-redirecting response does not deter the client from pressing the question, then a direct answer is preferable to an evasion.

Clients' use of spirituality or religion to mask more influential determinants of behavior or to project or displace nonreligious psychosocial issues is noted regularly in the literature. Pattison (1982), for example, notes that "it is not unusual to find religious issues used as a 'stalking' horse to present and represent an underlying family conflict" (p. 147). He describes the case of a young Jewish family in which strong religious disagreements arose unexpectedly in attempts to resolve disputes connected with a Bar Mitzvah for the children. Although there were some genuine religious differences between the spouses, Pattison notes that the question of religious differences moved to the background when underlying conflicts related to issues of trust, sharing, and reciprocity were resolved. The therapist came to recognize the religious disputes as a projection of more therapeutically pertinent issues, gradually disengaged from discussion of religious issues, and redirected the family's attention to the underlying issues of family dynamics. In this case, the therapist did not altogether sidestep the religious issues but worked through them as a way of uncovering more influential dynamics, leaving the religious issues to the side. It is worth noting, however, that spiritual/religious issues may not only serve as "stalking horses" for other issues but also may have significance in their own right. For example, in the case presented by Pattison, although marital-interpersonal issues lay beneath religious disputes as the key source of the presenting problem, the deepening of religious conviction did turn out in this case to be an important therapeutic change.

A counselor may purposefully choose to disregard spiritual/ religious information obtained from a client assessment because "the counselee's religion is very weak and unformed" and it seems therapeutically preferable to "work instead with stronger determinants of behavior," especially if time limitations are a factor (Malony, 1993a, p. 111). This is a purposeful counselor choice in view of the client's self-presentation and needs and the circumstantial requirements of counseling. But it need not be an unalterable choice. For example, while noting that a client had checked the area of religious concerns on the intake form, a counselor-trainee whom I was supervising chose to work with the client within her completely nonreligious discussion of painful interpersonal issues. This appeared to be an acceptable and workable course until the client herself brought up her emotionally strong religious beliefs as part of her problem. At this point, the deferring approach to the religious dimension yielded to a deliberate counseling effort to help the client explore and clarify the religious aspects of her problems.

Invalidating Approaches

The term invalidating represents a strongly directive and ethically precarious approach to any value-laden issues the client brings to counseling. It is used here as similar to what Malony (1993a) calls "annihilating" approaches, which are intended to eradicate a clearly psychosocially noxious spiritual or religious belief or practice. Malony understandably notes that "many counselors might shy away from annihilating another person's faith because they either don't know enough about a given religion or fear that they might be imposing their interpretations or values into the situation" (p. 111). Despite this caution, he cites instances of religious beliefs that are clearly pathological, extremely self-debilitating, or imminently dangerous to others. These might include, for example, a command by God to commit suicide or seriously harm others, claims to be Jesus or the devil, and religiously justified practices of child sexual abuse.

An invalidating approach presents counselors, especially in secular practice, with important ethical, legal, and therapeutic decisions. Ethical codes of professional helping associations (e.g., American Counseling Association, American Psychological Association, American Association of Marriage and Family Therapy) all require counselors and therapists to take effective action to protect the client and/or others when the client presents as a clear and imminent danger. Most certainly, this requirement holds in cases where the client's rationale or motivation is spiritual or religious. Furthermore, counselors must follow legal and institutional requirements to ensure adequate protection for clients in such cases. Although this book does not include a detailed discussion of these particular ethical and legal requirements, counselors have an obligation to be well-informed from the many sources in which ethical and legal requirements and issues of counseling are presented (see, e.g., American Counseling Association, 1992; Herlihy & Golden, 1990; Pope, 1991).

When a noxious belief does not present ethical demands for protective action or when such action has been appropriately taken and the client continues in counseling, the counselor is faced with the therapeutic decision of whether and how to use invalidating approaches. From a purely technical perspective, the decision to use an invalidating approach may not be particularly difficult for counselors who follow a rational emotive brand of cognitive therapy. Ellis (1989b) unabashedly presents a rationale and procedures for eliminating self-defeating (irrational) ideas—what he calls a "hardsell approach to talking people out of their disturbances" (p. 14). However, even when spiritual or religious beliefs are clearly deleterious, a therapeutically invalidating approach is very likely to involve more than a direct, frontal strike at the offending belief, if indeed such an approach is used at all. Because noxious spiritual/religious beliefs usually represent some kind of unhealthy, pathological distortion of a larger, benign system of belief (e.g., child sexual abuse rooted in or justified by a distortion of Christian beliefs of love or obedience, or messianic delusions rooted in a distortion of beliefs of a person's oneness with God), an invalidating approach often takes the tack of "untwisting the illusion" (Imbrie, 1985) from its distorted association with healthy spirituality and religion. In this approach, the counselor can acknowledge and respect the client's general religious sense, while working to help the client uncover the psychosocial sources of his or her religious distortions, recognize and turn loose unhealthy spiritual/religious beliefs, and achieve a healthy mental and emotional status that can integrate a mature or at least undistorted spirituality and religiousness.

The precise focus of an invalidating approach is a specific psychosocially destructive belief or set of beliefs. Because such beliefs do not occur in a psychosocial or spiritual/religious vacuum, however, an invalidating approach is often complemented by more complex approaches. This takes us to the next set of approaches, those of reworking.

Reworking Approaches

Generally comparable to Malony's category of correcting approaches, reworking approaches include a set of related methods for helping clients to make personally and socially beneficial shifts in beliefs and practices that are in themselves or in the appropriate context compatible with positive human development and functioning but as a result of negativizing influences have become disruptive and problematic for the client. The negative and problem-producing influence of spirituality and religion in these cases takes several different forms, including the following: (a) adhering with emotional rigidity to immature expressions of belief inadequate to the client's life circumstances (e.g., clinging to anthropomorphic childhood belief symbols that are incompatible with one's general intellectual development and growing knowledge of modern science); (b) unqualifiedly emphasizing one belief out of context with related beliefs (e.g., a single-minded, punitive insistence on right behavior in children with neglect for understanding and loving patience); (c) overgeneralizing or misapplying a belief to incompatible areas of life (e.g., applying a belief in accepting God's will to a passive, self-justifying acceptance of avoidable emotional abuse); (d) having powerfully negative emotions and self-defeating thoughts entangled with religious belief and imagery (e.g., experiencing a pervasive fear and anxiety intertwined with images of a fierce God, hell, and damnation from the preaching of a tyrannical father); (e) being trapped (emotionally, cognitively, and/or physically) in a relationship, institution, or community whose religiously asserted authority is psychologically debilitating (e.g., a wife and children constantly browbeaten by a husband harshly asserting a belief in his God-instituted rights of authority or the member of a cult that abusively restricts freedom of thought and action); (f) misapplying spiritual or religious beliefs and practices as solutions to problems whose causes and features call for a reasonable use of nonreligious solutions (e.g., overextending a belief in spiritually positive thinking or imagery or healing prayer to preclude reasonable medical treatment for cancer or arthritis); and (g) experiencing distress and/or acute doubt about a long-held and mature belief (e.g., a painful bewilderment and anger at the death of a child that eclipses one's usually firm belief in a benevolent God).

All problem types outlined here involve a misconstruing of spiritual and religious beliefs and practices that in more mature forms, more positive developmental and psychosocial circumstances, or more supportive and congenial environments might be generally free of personal and social problems, indeed could be contributory to a person's overall well-being. Therefore, unlike inherently harmful beliefs, these beliefs may be susceptible to *reworking* techniques in counseling, that is, techniques that disentangle a belief from the cognitive, emotional, and/or social web that is causing it to be part of the client's problem rather than a supportive or at least neutral factor in the client's life.

Reworking approaches involve a *rethinking/reexperiencing* process in which the counselor facilitates the client's reflective talking about spiritual and religious beliefs and practices in a therapeutically safe environment. This rethinking/reexperiencing process includes methods of (a) *refocusing and redirecting*, that is, facilitating the client's comparative consideration of related beliefs; (b) *reframing*, that is, helping the client to consider expanded, deepened, or alternative meanings for spiritual/religious beliefs; (c) *relabeling*, that is, helping a client consider alternative language in which to express the substance of a belief more helpfully; and (d) *revitalizing*, that is, helping the client to recapture the positive cognitive and emotional force of a formerly supportive belief or practice that has waned or become eclipsed under stressful developmental, psychosocial, or environmental circumstances.

Clients' problems, even relatively mild and simple ones, always have several interwoven facets (e.g., cognitive/affective; interpersonal/intrapersonal; intrapsychic/environmental; family, work, religion, and other areas of life). When spirituality and religion occur as problematic factors in a client's issues, it is almost certain that there will be disturbances in other aspects of the client's functioning. The counselor's responsibility with respect to the spiritual/religious dimension, therefore, is not only to explore and understand the particular quality of and consequent treatment for problematic and disturbing spiritual/religious beliefs but also to assess how problems in other areas of the client's development and functioning are connected with spiritual and religious issues.

Encouraging Approaches

When a client's spiritual and religious beliefs show themselves as a mature and positive force in the client's development and functioning, the counselor might explore how the client can use these beliefs as aids in the developmental and healing processes. In this case spirituality and religion are not part of the problem but a potential part of the solution. Encouraging approaches occur in two basic, interrelated forms, *applying* and *enhancing*. Both approaches involve the positive application of healthy spiritual/religious beliefs and practices. The distinction is that *applying* refers to methods for having clients use their already fundamentally mature beliefs in the developmental and healing processes, whereas *enhancing* refers to methods in which the counselor helps a client to identify and further develop a relevant but not yet well-formed spiritual/religious belief or practice.

For example, a counselor working with a religiously mature and committed client who is experiencing debilitating sadness because of a spouse's adultery and desertion may find that brief periods of prayer for strength, peace, and hope are a supportive complement to cognitive-behavioral strategies. Later in this chapter we will examine more carefully the question of prayer in secular counseling, its potential benefits and drawbacks, and criteria for including it in counseling. The point here is that if the counseling process has brought out that a client values prayer as part of a mature spirituality/religiousness and if process criteria indicate that prayer in this case is appropriate and potentially beneficial, the counselor might well explore (based on the criteria to be discussed later) in an encouraging way how the client can use prayer in the current distress. If the same conditions prevail except that the client's prayer is not well developed in relation to the distress he or she is experiencing, the counselor may choose to enhance the client's prayer, for example, by suggesting appropriate readings about prayer (see, e.g., Carmody & Carmody's, [1990] *Prayer in World Religions*). Alternatively, the counselor can make an informed referral to a member of the clergy, spiritual director, or congenial prayer support group that can help with prayer.

It is not uncommon that mature, highly religious persons will call upon their religious faith in times of crisis and distress. However, it also happens that such persons may become so immersed in their problems and efforts to solve them that they neglect to energize their spiritual/religious beliefs on their own behalf. Because in this book the assumption is made—amply justified in theory and research (see Chapter 3)—that healthy, mature spirituality and religion are supportive of positive development and good mental health, it makes eminent therapeutic sense for a counselor to engage the client positively in actively applying this life dimension to resolving problems.

The four general approaches described here represent several substantive ways in which the counselor can address the spiritual/religious dimension according to the diverse negative and positive effects that spirituality and religion, understood objectively and subjectively, are having on the client's development and functioning. Implementation of these approaches depends on the general response of the counselor as well as the counselor's specific methods for working with the spiritual/religious dimension. Before moving to a discussion of specific methods and techniques, we need to consider two points that have a more general effect on the counselor's responses: client-counselor value convergence and counselor countertransference.

Value convergence and countertransference

Value Convergence

Research indicates that the religious belief or nonbelief of the counselor generally does not have appreciable differential effects on counselor attitudes toward clients or on client outcomes, although there may be circumstances (e.g., in the case of highly religious clients) where some differential effects may occur (see Chapter 1). On the other hand, research does show that value convergence—that is, the phenomenon of clients' values moving toward those of the counselor/therapist—occurs in counseling, albeit in complex ways that are not entirely clear, predictable, or usable in treatment (see Chapter 3). Based on extensive reviews of studies on the influence of values in counseling (Beutler & Bergan, 1991; T. A. Kelly, 1990), pertinent research allows us to summarize two key findings of value convergence with reasonable confidence: (a) over the course of counseling rated as beneficial by the counselor, client values converge toward those of the counselor, and (b) whether value convergence occurs depends in large part on particular, complex patterns of initial client-counselor value similarity and dissimilarity.

Value convergence in counseling clearly has implications for the counselor's response to the spiritual/religious dimension. Spirituality and religion are inherently value-laden. What is more, the general approaches described earlier involve various methods for significant value interaction between the counselor and client, and indeed for various kinds of value influence. Therefore, when counselors use any of these general approaches for responding to spiritual and religious issues, they need to ensure that their work is ethically appropriate and therapeutically effective. Tjeltveit (1986) has described four forms of unethical value influence. Counselors can use these as a kind of "do-not-do" checklist to ensure that their work with spiritual and religious issues remains ethical. These unethical value influence actions are:

1. Eliminating or reducing the freedom of clients to choose their own values. This may occur in four ways: (a) imposition of counselor values, for example, in the form of insisting that the continuance of counseling is contingent on accepting the counselor's values; (b) judgmentalism or moralism, which involves the counselor conveying a condemnatory or censorious attitude toward the client; (c) propagandizing, which refers to the counselor promoting limited value options; or (d) selective reinforcement of certain values, signaling to the client value options that are more acceptable to the counselor.

2. Failure to provide clients with adequate information about counseling, including the likely use of methods for clarifying, rethinking, and altering values, and the potential benefits and risks involved in working with values in counseling.

3. Failure to abide by assurances (e.g., promises, contracts) that value changes will not occur without the client's aware, voluntary, responsive participation in these changes.

4. Counselor's lack of competence in using methods that involve value changes.

The client's *informed consent* is the major counterbalance to unethical counselor influence of client's values. Informed consent in this case involves a clear informing of the client at each stage of counseling so that the client has sufficient information to begin and proceed through counseling with an awareness commensurate with his or her ability to use the information beneficially. Understood in this sense, informed consent is infused throughout the counseling process, often in the background of the counselor's work as a kind of open and unconditional respect for the client's dignity and rights, and occasionally in the forefront in terms of the counselor's discussing explicitly with the client the kind of value interaction and influence that may occur. The self-awareness that this kind of values work entails on the counselor's part brings us to the second major issue in counselor responsiveness to clients' spirituality or religion, the possibility of counselor countertransference.

Countertransference

The counselor's response to spiritual/religious issues is susceptible to unconscious influences rooted in the counselor's own developmentally shaped attitudes toward spirituality and religion. Countertransferential responses reflect a spiritually/religiously biased reaction rather than a straightforward reflection of the client's self-presentation. The spiritually/religiously countertransferential response is distorted by how the client's self-presentation triggers some unconsciously held attitudes toward spirituality and religion in the counselor. At the level of deliberate self-awareness counselors may sincerely intend to respond to value issues with self-congruent (undistorted) honesty and nonjudgmental respect (e.g., by using an informed consent procedure); however, this is no guarantee that the counselor's responses will not be influenced by attitudes outside the counselor's immediate awareness. This is especially probable in the spiritual/religious dimension, which tends to be laden with emotions intertwined with significant relationships and events in one's development and associated with strong negative or positive opinions about the value and validity of religion in general or specific religious beliefs and practices. These nonaware attitudes may be predominantly positive or negative, or they may represent a complex mix of negative and positive attitudes toward different forms of spirituality and religion.

The counselor can take steps to guard against spiritual/religious countertransference and, if countertransference does occur, recognize, remedy, and even turn to positive use these client-inappropriate but self-revealing responses. The general caution is for the counselor to be clear about his or her own attitudes and values about spirituality/religion, cognizant of the countertransference phenomenon in general, and especially alert to the possibility of countertransference when the client brings spiritual and religious issues into counseling. Following Spero's (1981) specific suggestions, counselors can increase their general awareness of spiritual/ religious countertransference by being alert to: (a) apparent counselor-client similarities in spiritual/religious values that do not have the same origin and function in the client as in the counselor; (b) shared spiritual/religious values and traditions that may lead to collusive avoidance rather than clarifying, perhaps challenging, exploration of beliefs and practice; (c) counselor-client dissimilarities in spiritual/religious beliefs, practices, and development that may lead to the counselor's negative or dismissive reaction to the spiritual/religious dimension of clients' behavior; (d) counselor's religious enthusiasm that may lead to misfocusing on spiritual/ religious issues at the expense of more pertinent dynamic factors; and (e) intrusions of interested third parties (e.g., clergy, relatives, teachers) whose spiritual/religious convictions may spark strong affective reactions by the counselors.

Knowledge of typical countertransferential expressions can help counselors to recognize countertransference when it happens and alter their response. Six particular manifestations of countertransference as described by Lovinger (1984) and slightly reworded here involve: (a) extended "philosophical" discussions that have no developmental or therapeutic aim; (b) arguing with clients about their doctrine because the counselor regards it as destructive or theologically incorrect, even though it is normative for the patient's denomination; (c) avoiding religious topics if the client raises them or labeling them to the client as "resistance"; (d) interpreting too quickly, and without sufficient exploration, spiritual/religious matters in nonspiritual/nonreligious psychosocial terms; (e) failing to explore significant shifts in the client's religious orientation, especially shifts toward the counselor's denomination; and (f) interpreting the client's acquisition or rejection of a religious orientation as a sign of progress or regression without adequate exploration.

Counselors' understanding and awareness of spiritual/religious countertransference not only aids them in avoiding or correcting this type of distortion in responding to clients but also may spur counselors to clarify their own attitudes toward spirituality and religion as well as the life-history roots of these attitudes. Counselors who become self-aware of the kinds of countertransference described here might benefit by consultation with colleagues who are experienced and broadly informed regarding spirituality and religion in counseling and human development.

This concludes our discussion of introductory concepts, general counseling approaches, and general response issues of value convergence and countertransference. We now turn our attention to more specific approaches, methods, and techniques, as applied to several different kinds of issues and client populations, as described in a growing body of literature on approaches, techniques, and treatment applications for working with the spiritual/religious dimension in counseling. As we shall see, some techniques are closely connected with particular theory-based approaches to counseling and psychotherapy (e.g., cognitive self-inquiry of spiritual/religious beliefs in the cognitive-behavioral approach). Other methods occur more eclectically across a variety of approaches (e.g., the use of spiritual/religious language or symbols in developing therapeutic strategies). Some techniques involve the use of spiritual or religious practices (e.g., meditation or the 12 steps in helping anxious and addicted persons) as an integral part of or adjunct to counseling. Certain techniques apply spiritual and religious concepts and practices to particular problems (e.g., considering God to be an influential member of a family in distress) and particular client populations (e.g., incorporating elderly peoples' typically high regard for spirituality and religion). From the large body of literature available, I have attempted to select a representative cross section of approaches and techniques and describe them in a manner useful for integrating them into practice, and to provide references for more extended study.

Theory-based approaches to counseling and psychotherapy with the spiritual/religious dimension

Some techniques and methods of treatment have a primary association with particular approaches to counseling and psychotherapy, although they frequently have eclectic applications across various approaches. I will first discuss several major approaches to counseling and psychotherapy as they broadly apply to the spiritual/religious dimension, then move to a discussion of more specific techniques with special issues and populations.

Cognitive-Behavioral Approaches

Given the significant cognitive component of spiritual and religious beliefs and the current prominence of cognitive-behavioral therapy and counseling (CBT/C), it is not surprising that CBT/C techniques have been applied to the spiritual/ religious dimension. Propst (1988) describes a 10-step process for integrating spiritual and religious concepts and CBT/C in the treatment of depression and anxiety disorders. Although her presentation is from the Christian perspective, the process is applicable to different spiritual/religious beliefs, depending on the client's particular belief system, and could be applied to issues and problems other than depression and anxiety. Adapting primarily Beck's (Beck, Rush, Shaw, & Emery, 1979) comprehensive process-oriented CBT approach, Propst presents a method involving the typical CBT steps, namely, relationship building, diagnosis, presentation of CBT rationales to client, developing client's affective and cognitive self-awareness, cognitive restructuring, dealing with anger and passivity [assertion training], relaxation skills training, communication skills training, and assigning beneficial homework.

Noting that the distinctive core of CBT/C is cognitive restructuring—the transformation of persistently self-defeating thoughts and thinking processes into positive or at least neutral thoughts and healthy ways of thinking—Propst presents Christian beliefs that can be used to help clients achieve healthy thinking in six basic areas of cognition susceptible to self-disturbing polarities: perception of undercontrol versus overcontrol; attention focused on past versus future; avoidance or denial of positives versus negatives; defeatism versus perfectionism; external versus internal focus; and meaninglessness versus rigidity of belief. Examples of Christian-based healthy beliefs to replace these polarities include the following: (a) for overcontrolling or undercontrolling clients, beliefs about control based on the biblical model of Jesus who lived in charge of his life while recognizing that this control was not an exclusive, unlimited control but exercised in the context of influential people and events; (b) for clients overgeneralizing from past mistakes, beliefs based on the example of Jesus calling Peter's attention to his present love of Jesus, rather than his betrayal of Jesus, as the guiding force in his life; and (c) for perfectionistic clients, beliefs formed by Paul's declaration of God's outgoing love for sinful, broken humanity, saying "in effect that even though we are *not* okay, we *are* okay [italics in original]" (Propst, 1988, p. 112).

The CBT/C approach described by Propst is clearly applicable in different spiritual/religious belief systems. For example, Prest and Keller (1993), employing a cognitive-constructivist framework within family therapy, present several cases in which clients were helped to replace or reframe self-defeating beliefs with widely held spiritual beliefs. These included: the belief that "human beings are manifestations of God" as a way to help a client in "relanguaging" a highly depreciating and negatively emotional relationship with his father; and a belief in God as strong, caring, and involved in the dark places of peoples' lives rather than a "wimpy" God in charge of only the light moments of life as a way of helping a despondent religious person. Miller (1988) describes the use of biblical-based beliefs—namely, the right to rest and relaxation for God's servants, grace as an unmerited gift of God's acceptance of persons' imperfection, and attentive interest in others rather than anxious self-consciousness—in the effective cognitive-behavioral treatment of a depressed, insomniac, self-critical young seminarian.

Counselors who are sufficiently conversant with Jewish, Islamic, Buddhist, or noninstitutional spiritual belief systems could make CBT/C applications of relevant beliefs from these systems as appropriate to particular clients. Furthermore, recent research suggests that nonreligious therapists trained in CBT/C with religious content can be just as effective as religious therapists in using religiously based CBT/C (Propst et al., 1992). Thus it appears that counselors of different religious beliefs or no religious belief can be trained to provide CBT/C with spiritual/religious content from various traditions pertinent to clients' belief systems. While counselors certainly need to exercise professional care not to work outside their area of competence and knowledge, those who receive appropriate training and supervision may find that CBT/C with appropriate spiritual/religious content is a particularly congenial approach to building relationships with highly spiritual/religious clients and just as effective as similar approaches using nonreligious content (W. B. Johnson & Ridley, 1992; W. B. Johnson, Devries, Ridley, Pettorini, & Deland, 1994).

Methods that emphasize a straightforward behavioral approach are also applicable to the spiritual/religious dimension. Miller and J. E. Martin (1988) note several applications, including the use of behavioral change techniques for people having difficulty following desired spiritual/religious activities, the inclusion of "spiritual" behavior in overall behavioral assessments, and embedding behavioral change programs into faith systems for more lasting change. H. P. Brown, Peterson, and Cunningham (1988b) describe a behavioral/cognitive approach to the use of 12-step spirituality in counseling with clients who are alcoholics or otherwise addicted. Stressing especially the behavioral component, they encourage the client's use of a "Daily Spiritual Behavior Checklist," which includes 10 actions based on 12-step spirituality, including morning prayer/meditation, contact with sponsor, performance of "caring" behavior toward spouse, listening to cassette or reading assigned material, conducting nightly self-evaluation, nightly prayer/meditation, attendance at 12-step meetings (three nights a week), weekly attendance at aftercare, and daily self-reinforcement behavior (H. P. Brown, Peterson, & Cunningham, 1988a). Building on the client's distinctive belief system and assuming the readiness and openness of the client, the counselor can adapt this technique of a behavioral checklist to include potentially therapeutic spiritual/religious behaviors that encourage and support specific client action on problems.

Another example of behavioral treatment with religious issues is Greenberg's (1987) report of the successful use of *in vivo* exposure and response prevention in the case of an Orthodox Jewish father's compulsive ritual handwashing. To alleviate the father's anxiety about inadvertently bringing milk and meat into contact during mealtime, the therapist, after describing and modeling what he wanted the client to do, had the client put butter on his hands and actively participate in handling bottles, food, and cutlery at mealtime without wiping his or his children's hands. His anxiety was initially very high, but it gradually decreased over a three-week treatment period. It is noteworthy that this treatment was effective in reducing religiously based compulsive behavior while carried out in a manner that respected the client's adherence to ritual law rather than having the client violate his religious conviction. This is a striking example of how counselors can integrate effective treatment of a disorder based in a religious belief with a respect for the client's right to the belief.

Object Relations Approach

Object relations theory, a major development in psychoanalytic/psychodynamic theory, is broadly characterized by a shift in emphasis from instinctually motivated behavior as proposed by Freud to motivation rooted in internalized relationship patterns with significant others, especially the mother-infant relationship but including other significant relationships in the course of one's early development. The now expansive literature of object relations theory and the role of religious imagery in object relations development require the reader to go to other sources for a full treatment of these topics (e.g., Lovinger, 1984; Rizzuto, 1979; Spero, 1992). However, in line with the more general purpose of this book to describe various treatment approaches to spirituality and religion in counseling, at least a brief note about the object relations approach is in order.

Although there is not complete unanimity among major object relations theorists, substantial convergence exists on the critical importance of internalized relational patterns based on early significant relationships and the impact of these internalized relational patterns on early development of habituated patterns of thought, feeling, and behavior. These internalized relational patterns are the "objects" (i.e., people, such as good mother, bad mother, supportive father, punishing father, etc.) of "object-relations" and are *internal* to the individual, as distinguished from real objects (i.e., persons) as they exist outside the individual. The developing individual goes through a gradual process of identification, separation, and individuation with respect to these significant internalized others (i.e., object-relations) with more or less mixed success at each stage of development, depending largely on the quality of the relationships. In this developing individuation-separation process, the individual uses available family and cultural symbols (e.g., from religion and art) to help bridge (i.e., to separate while maintaining a link between) the individual's internal and external worlds. In this bridging function, religious images that are culturally, familially, or otherwise important become filled with the affectively charged object relations they are associated with. Thus the quality, valence, and psychosocial impact of an individual's personalized spirituality/religiousness are significantly influenced by the quality and dynamics of object-relations. While the spiritual/religious dimension of the individual's life becomes internalized as separate, distinctive objects (e.g., images, fantasies, concepts of God, the supernatural, religious law, divine favor and retribution, etc.), these religious objects (internal to the individual) are cognitively and affectively influenced and shaped at an unconscious level by their association with significant object-relations (i.e., internalized relational patterns with all their positive and negative intrapsychic energy and interpersonal ramifications).

It is critical, ontologically and psychologically, to emphasize the distinction between the psychological reality of object representations and the ontological reality of the people and phenomena they represent. The internal formation of spiritual/religious objects does not constitute their total and certainly not their objective reality. Nevertheless, there is a complex and dynamic association between psychologically subjective objects and the ontologically objective objects they represent, and it is a difficult philosophical/scientific task to establish the independent ontological validity of the spiritual/religious realm. A full discussion of these topics is beyond the scope of this book. However, given the highly reasonable assumption that the transcendent, meta-empirical dimension of existence as represented (albeit quite imperfectly) in spirituality/religion is *objectively* real (see Chapter 2), it is worth noting that an individual's internal distortions of spirituality and religion (and the disorders that are connected with these distortions) are subject to beneficial *psychological* change that many also involve an *ontologically objective* reality, a benevolent transcendent Reality inherently oriented toward positive human development.

Counseling and psychotherapy based on object relations theory involve a counselor's relationship with the client (unconditional positive regard, empathy, patience, and acceptance rooted in the counselor's own object-relations-forming experiences of these interpersonal qualities) that does not repeat or reinforce unsatisfactory relationship patterns based on the client's distorted object relations from past relationships (Spero, 1992). In this therapeutic environment—empathically accepting, carefully noncollusive, and selectively interpretive—the client can gradually work through the distortions of internalized object relations and the associated distortion of spiritual/religious objects. The approach integrates humanistic and psychodynamic theory (see, e.g., Cashdan, 1988; Kahn, 1991; E. W. Kelly, 1994a), with individual counselors and therapists stressing one or the other, depending on theoretical orientation and clients' needs.

Spero (1992) offers two highly illustrative examples of an object-relations approach involving the spiritual/religious dimension. Working predominantly in the psychoanalytical tradition of object-relations theory, he describes his work in helping an anxiously conflicted young Jewish man and a narcissistically conflicted Catholic nun gradually uncover the psychodynamic (object-relations) sources of their distress. In this process the therapist helped the clients disentangle multiple religious distortions from their object-relations connections, thereby enabling them to move toward healthier psychosocial and religious functioning. These cases, which involved intensive therapy over long periods of time, cannot be reduced to a few, easily replicable techniques. On the other hand, the object-relations theory and the humanistic-dynamic approaches they involve are available to counselors as a base of understanding how a client's spirituality/religion can be distortedly entangled with past negative relationships and how a genuinely humanistic (Rogerian) but dynamically noncollusive relationship provides a therapeutic place for the client to work through intertwined relational and spiritual/religious distortions. Without necessarily undertaking a lengthy therapeutic process of personality restructuring, counselors can make valuable use of object-relations theory and approaches to enhance their understanding of clients' spiritual and religious issues and problems, the connection of these problems with the clients' overall psychosocial functioning, and humanistic/noncollusive ways to help clients work toward mature, healthy levels of psychosocial and spiritual/religious functioning.

Humanistic-Existential Approaches

Humanistic and existential approaches to counseling, including transpersonal approaches, are in many respects congenial to the integration of spiritual and religious issues. For example, the primacy assigned to the inherent healing/developmental power of the therapeutic relationship (characterized by the counselor's unconditional positive regard, genuineness, and empathy) in the person-centered approach (Kirschenbaum & Henderson, 1989) is conducive to a counseling process in which clients feel safe and supported in bringing spiritual and religious issues to counseling. I have written elsewhere (E. W. Kelly, 1994a) how relationship-centered counseling and therapy not only provide a humanizing relational core but also integrate a broad range of techniques that extend and shape the relationship to the particular needs of each client. This humanistically integrative approach to counseling explicitly embraces spirituality and transcendent meaning as integral to a comprehensive understanding of a full relationship-centered model. This means that the counselor is prepared to facilitate the client's developmental and healing process at all levels, including the spiritual/religious.

Existentialism addresses the key human issues that are at the heart of religion and in many respects define spirituality: meaning, freedom, responsibility, personal authenticity, and bewilderment and anxiety in the face of suffering and death. In some formulations existential thought is nontheistic (although not necessarily nonspiritual in the broad sense) (e.g., Sartre, 1960, and probably Heidegger [see Kovacs, 1990; Lescoe, 1974]). The psychotherapeutic expression of nontheistic existentialism is oriented toward making responsible, personally authentic, and self-actualizing sense of life without resorting to theism or life meaning beyond death (see, e.g., Ofman, 1976; Yalom, 1980). Existentialism in this sense may take the form of nontheistic spirituality in that it affirms the human's capacity for creation of meaning, active freedom, and responsible human connectedness that transcends the downward pull of apathy, nonmeaning, and isolation, although it sees no escape from the ultimacy of death (see, e.g., R. May, 1969).

Theistic existentialism, on the other hand, understands the questions of meaning, freedom, responsibility, and death not only in a horizontal dimension (humanly interpersonal), but also as open to a vertical dimension toward Being—an objective reality of infinite transcendence open to humanity (see, e.g., Kierkegaard, 1909/1959; Marcel, 1960/1951; Pax, 1972). The counseling and psychotherapeutic applications of theistic existentialism are thus oriented toward an honest and responsible engagement in life and death as a way of creatively living and making meaning of our interconnected existence (being) as we have it at each moment *and* as being open to the eternity of transcendent Being—"the state of being grasped by the Spirit, namely the divine presence" (Tillich, 1961/1984, p. 171).

At the core of all existential counseling and therapy is the authentic *encounter* between therapist and client, in which the therapist is fully present with the client with an honest and responsible self-authenticity that acts as a kind of invitation expressed in a variety of interpersonal ways but always technique-free. Nontheistic existential therapy envisions the therapeutic encounter as the vehicle for the client's achieving greater autonomy, authenticity, and intrinsic meaning that is strictly "finite, individual, and mortal" (Wilber, 1986, p. 137). Theistic existential therapy understands this developmental achievement within the larger context of a genuine opening to eternal transcendence.

Humanistic-existential approaches do not fit well with the more technique-oriented purpose of this chapter. With the possible exceptions of paradoxical intention in Frankl's (1946/1984) logotherapy and the directions of gestalt therapists for clients to focus on their affect and body movements, humanistic and existential approaches are nontechnical. I have included them here, nonetheless, because they represent therapeutically powerful ways for the counselor—via an authentic relationship opening the client to progressively deeper self-exploration and honest personalized meaning-making—to facilitate the inclusion of the client's spiritual and religious perspectives (positive and negative) in movements toward greater personal congruence and effective action. In particular, the transpersonal extension of the humanistic-existential orientation focuses special attention on the transcendental-spiritual core and context of human existence and emphasizes methods (e.g., meditation) that develop and use peoples' spiritual resources (Weinhold & Hendricks, 1993).

This concludes our review of theory-based approaches to spiritual/religious issues in counseling. We turn our attention now to intervention methods and techniques that occur eclectically across different theoretical approaches.

Methods employing spiritual/religious imagery, language, and belief

Spiritual/religious beliefs and practices are often clothed in distinctive imagery and language that signify and convey the cognitive content and affective intensity of a person's faith. There are many examples, including images and language of a predominantly benevolent or punishing, involved or disinterested, all-supreme or collaborative God; of law, obedience, sin, grace, forgiveness, miracles, life after death, and revealed truth and spiritual/religious authority. For the spiritual/religious person, these images and associated language are interwoven in individuals' psyches across the course of their personal development. Depending on the nature of that development (e.g., benevolent or threatening, intense or tepid, reasonable or dogmatic), spiritual/religious imagery and language become more or less important, affectively laden elements in framing life issues and problems.

While noting that spiritual/religious imagery and language may be significant aspects of how spiritual/religious clients conceive issues and express problems, it is especially important not to lose sight of their *inherent content* value for the believer, that is, their significance as a *real* realm of actuality (e.g., God, angels, supernatural influence and intervention, divine benevolence and justice, transcendental consciousness). Spiritual/religious images and language are the distinctive, personally important way that individuals convey what they believe. The use of religious images and language in counseling is not simply a matter of adeptly using images and language acceptable to the client but also understanding and respecting that these images and language represent realities that form a significant part of the client's view and experience. Attention to spiritual/religious imagery and language involves the counselor in respectful attention to the beliefs that underlie the images and language.

The counselor's respectful use of client's spiritual/religious imagery, regardless of particular techniques, conveys to the client that the counselor is "able to hear things worth paying attention to" (Lovinger, 1984, p. 185). The counselor who hears a distraught client's brief reference of "praying to God that my family can get through this crisis" and responds to that faith—even if spirituality is not a prominent aspect of finding a solution in this case—demonstrates a respectful attentiveness conducive to strengthening the counselor-client relationship and opening all doors to further client exploration. Beyond this general effect, the counselor can formulate a number of specific interventions that use spiritual/religious imagery and language as a way of effectively tapping a client's beliefs.

Because of the great diversity of spiritual/religious beliefs and language, the purpose here is to present a few representative techniques or approaches involving the therapeutic use of spiritual/religious images and language and the beliefs that they represent. The examples described here, while necessarily limited, nonetheless indicate how images, language, and beliefs from different spiritual/religious traditions can be used in counseling.

Exploring and Resolving Client Problems

Counselors can use spiritual/religious images, language, and the beliefs they represent to help clients through their reluctance or confusion in discussing painful, embarrassing, or suppressed problems and issues. For example, Bullis and Harrigan (1992) describe their use of the New Testament image of Jesus as a door through which the seeker finds healing and support (John 10:9) to help a reluctant client discuss his experience of sexual abuse. In this case, the therapist helped the client to divulge his painful memories by visualizing "Jesus leading him through a door . . . a comforting, sustaining sacred image" (p. 310) that enabled the client to remember, confront, and eventually resolve the effects of this trauma.

Lawrence (1983) describes a similar example of using the comforting and strengthening image of and belief in Jesus to help a resistant Christian client deal with childhood sexual abuse. The client was a young woman full of self-hatred, shame, anger, and conflicted feelings toward her father. To help the client confront and work through these deeply ingrained, self-defeating patterns of thinking and feeling, the counselor combined the approach of inner healing prayer with gestalt and transactional techniques in which the client was supported in talking about her terrible trauma:

> Ruth was asked to be her Child and reexperience her feelings about her father and herself. In prayer, Jesus was asked to be present and to minister to this Child. Ruth was then asked to take another chair and to "Be Jesus" and, since he speaks through his people, to let him speak through her to her Child. As Jesus-in-Ruth sat and looked at her Child, Ruth began to cry. When Jesus-in-Ruth spoke, he told her he understood her feelings and that he loved her and forgave her. At this point Ruth returned to Adult stage again and stated, rejoicing and crying at the same time, "Now I can forgive myself!" (p. 161)

Presented from the perspective of transactional analysis, this case also has implications for how a religious image/belief of great significance to a client might be woven into standard counseling techniques from other perspectives. For example, a number of adaptations of cognitive-behavioral approaches can incorporate the use of corrective religious beliefs that employ religious images and language (see, e.g., Propst, 1988; Propst et al., 1992; Craigie

213

& Tan, 1989; W. B. Johnson et al., 1994; Tan, 1987), several of which are described above in the section on cognitive-behavioral approaches.

Severe life crises—serious illness, loss of a loved one, extreme financial crises, divorce—frequently provoke a keen sense of dependence on God in religious and religiously open persons (Craigie & Tan, 1989). This in turn initiates a spiritual and psychological readiness to adopt or revitalize healthy, humanizing beliefs that had formerly been resisted or ignored. For spiritual/religious clients going through life-shattering crises, beliefs from their spiritual/religious traditions may provide support and guidance in making life-enhancing changes. Diverse spiritual/religious traditions contain beliefs that encourage an earnest search for and personal application of deeper religious knowledge. For example, Christians believe in the "truth that will make you free" in being faithful to the teachings of Jesus; in Islam the believer holds that advancing in the knowledge and accomplishment of Allah's will as revealed in the teachings of the Prophet in the Qur'an is the path of a good and fulfilled life (see, e.g. Khouj, 1986); a prayer in modern Judaism calls on the Lord to "open our eyes that we may see and welcome all truth," whether from ancient revelations or present-day seers, "for Thou hidest not Thy light from any generation of Thy children that yearn for Thee and Thy guidance" (*Union Prayerbook* as cited in L. Brown, 1945, p. 731); and a healthy spirituality (as distinguished from organized religion) involves a progressively nondistorting awareness of one's inner and perceptual worlds, "whenever the heart opens fully to love without fear" (Vaughn, 1991, p. 117).

The counselor can use spiritual/religious beliefs and the images and language of these beliefs as a way of helping and supporting the client-in-crisis to refocus from pain and loss to the possibility of renewing or accepting beliefs that offer the opportunity for healthy growth. This, of course, is not a simple process, in counseling or in the client's life. Each client reacts differently to life crises, some by opening up to positive change, others by closing down. But for spiritually and religiously oriented or open clients who have been deeply affected by life crises and in the counseling process have reached a state of readiness to make important positive cognitive shifts, the counselor may effectively use the powerfully motivating language and beliefs of authentic spirituality and religion.

The counselor who understands that for some clients spiritual/ religious language, imagery, and beliefs represent *influential realities* is in a position to consider their potential impact on understanding and resolving the client's concerns. In discussing this impact of religious belief in the family, Pattison (1982) has described the phenomenon of "sacralization," referring to a "patterning of family structure and functions [including attitudes, values, and interactions in family life] provided by a religious framework" (p. 144), making religion an intrinsic part of family life. Sacralization has the advantage of providing consensual support in the family in times of crisis when suited to the current needs of the family and its members. On the other hand, it is a disadvantage when it is not adaptive to current needs and social demands and blocks needed change. A particular expression of sacralization is "family coalitions with the supernatural," wherein figures of the spiritual world (God, Christ, a saint, an ancestor, a spirit teacher, angels) are "invoked and drawn into the personal interactions between family members" (Pattison, 1982, p. 145). Clearly such coalitions also exist for individuals as well.

The therapeutic relevance of these coalitions is drawn out explicitly by Griffith (1986) in his description of several cases "employing the God-family relationship" (p. 609). In the cases described by Griffith, family members' relationships with God act as a substantive and influential reality in their lives. In effect, God is part of the family system (Burton, 1992). The focus is on the individual's personal relationship with God rather than on the family's consensual idea about God (family myth), with the recognition that individuals' personalized notions of God may be influential in different ways. When employing the God-family (or God-individual) relationship, the counselor does not question the validity or nature of the client's belief. In this respect, the counselor assumes a "one down position," that is, the counselor allows clients to inform him or her about their particular God-belief. In one case, Griffith described a college-age male whose excessive anxiety about his mother's safety interfered with his own development and the relationship between his parents. The therapist was able to use the son's strong belief in God as the divine orderer of nature and the son's consequent need to be obedient to God to help him recognize that his behavior implied a lack of trust in God and an interference in God's role. Where other interventions had failed, this use of the son's religious conviction of being faithful to God's powerful care stimulated him to disengage from up-setting intrusions into his mother's life. The use of religious belief in this case was also congruent with the son's development, em-ploying the son's devotion to God to facilitate a normal emotional separation from his family.

In a second case, the therapist was able to use a controlling mother's fervent Christian belief as a way of gradually applying to herself the theme of a "loving letting go" as portrayed in the biblical parable of the prodigal son. On the basis of this belief, the therapist helped the mother to use her trust in God's loving care as a way of recognizing her domineering behavior. It was also a stimulus for the mother to allow her daughter to find her own way through therapy and through a brief period of atheism to her own personalized relationship with God, herself, and her mother.

In a third case, the God-client relationship was explored by having a young woman client, whose God-images were filled with fears of condemnation and punishment, engage in a sequence of role plays and role reversals involving herself, God, and her father. By speaking to herself in the role of God, she came to experience God as at least as compassionate as she was. With this shift in her experience of God, she was able to alleviate her anxious self-blame and irrational overconcern for her sick father. In discussing these cases, Griffith notes that the methods "steered clear of theological beliefs and focused on relationships to God. . . . In each case a shift in the relationship to God coincided with shifts in the other family relationships and with remission of presenting symptoms" (p. 615).

The therapeutic use of personalized beliefs in God is available not only for bringing about shifts in family systems but also for helping clients rethink their God beliefs in ways that facilitate positive personal change. Of particular relevance to counseling is research suggesting that loving-accepting God-images are posi-tively related to self-esteem and negatively related to loneliness, whereas wrathful-rejecting-impersonal God-images are negatively related to self-esteem and positively related to loneliness (Benson & Spilka, 1973; Schwab & Petersen, 1990). An example of this relationship is found in Genia's (1992) description of a young schizotypal male whose pervasive self-devaluation was associated with the "primitive quality of [his] psycho-spiritual functioning" (p. 323). This included a distorted image of a wrathful God that reflected the transferential internalization of an often angry and disapproving minister-father who had pressed his son toward perfection. The precise cause-effect relationship between a negatively distorted God and self-devaluation is not clear and is almost certainly part of a more complex set of psychosocial factors; however, it is not unreasonable to assume that there is a circular rather than linear relationship between the two. If this is the case, the counselor working with self-deprecating and/or lonely religiously oriented clients would do well to determine the quality of the clients' God-image and help clients to rethink their God-image and achieve a loving-accepting image (Riina, 1995).

The notion of rethinking, shifting, and reframing spiritual/ religious beliefs and language raises the issue of working therapeutically with distorted, unhealthy, or immature beliefs. Striking examples of such distortions occur in seriously disturbed persons whose mental disorders involve a variety of "religious disperceptions" (Imbrie, 1985, p. 143). Imbrie (1985) describes how mental disorder may involve a distorted twisting of religious beliefs (e.g., messianic illusions in schizophrenia or narrowly selfish notions of God in antisocial behavior). Imbrie recommends an approach that does not deny the perceptions of the clients but rather enlists the strength underlying and hidden in the disperceptions—an approach to "untwist the illusion." This requires the counselor to know enough about the client's spirituality or religion so that, through a skillful combination of respect and confrontation, the counselor can help the client use his or her basic religious commitment to replace unhealthy religious beliefs with those that support healthy behaviors. Thus, the counselor helps clients reframe beliefs distorted in mental disorder; for example, Imbrie (1985), describing a client who believed that she was pregnant with the Christ child, worked to rechannel delusions by encouraging her to think of Christ as being in her heart rather than her womb.

Distortions of beliefs occur across all forms of spirituality and religion. Cunin, Cunin, and Cunin (1992) describe cases of distortions and exaggerations of Orthodox Jewish clients, for example, how the traditional emphasis on learning may be distorted into a father's stern pressure on a child to be number one (a "Godol Hador"). This may lead to anxious perfectionism, feelings of inadequacy, and unresolved anger at parents as well as a repetition of the cycle in subsequent generations. The therapeutic strategy that they recommend is to help the client find personal ways of self-calming and explore and gain new perspectives for mitigating the sense of failure and anger at parents, while not downplaying the family's emphasis on learning—a source of healthy and harmonious living.

Propst (1992) describes the case of a middle-aged single female whose avoidant personality disorder involved fears of rejection and anticipation of hurt that were tied to an overly cheerful notion of Christian faith. Noting that risk taking and an openness to struggle and sacrifice are integrally connected with authentic living in healthy Christian belief, Propst recommends that these beliefs become an important part of cognitive therapy by helping an avoidant client to replace avoidant wishful thinking with beliefs that give support in actively facing painful situations.

Whipple (1987) describes how certain Christian fundamentalists' religious beliefs about gender roles, as well as their suspicion of secular counseling, may hinder battered women from ending the cycle of violence in their marriages. Because of Christian fundamentalists' strong belief in the supremacy of the Bible, the counselor's task is to use the Bible itself as a source of teachings for helping the battered wife understand that abuse against a wife is contrary to God's will and that working with a counselor to stop such abuse is in line with God's will. As the problems of clients show themselves to be deeply intertwined with strong and highly content-based religious beliefs, the more likely is consultation and/or referral to sympathetic clergy and religious authorities called for, procedures that will be discussed later in this chapter.

Forgiveness

Forgiveness based in spiritual/religious belief is receiving increased theoretical attention as a potentially beneficial process in client improvement, although research is still sparse (McCullough & Worthington, 1994). Based on their review of relevant literature (see, e.g., Enright, Eastin, Golden, Sarinopoulos, & Freedman, 1992; North, 1987), McCullough and Worthington (1994) define the therapeutic technique of forgiveness "as a problem-solving strategy [consisting of] a complex of affective, cognitive, and behavioral phenomena in which negative affect and judgment toward an offender are reduced, not by denying one's right to such affect and judgment, but by viewing the offender with compassion, benevolence, and love, while realizing that the offender has no right to them" (p. 4). Writers on forgiveness argue that forgiveness has the potential for positive changes in the forgiver's affect and well-being (e.g., reducing sadness, self-deprecation, anxiety, anger and the desire for retaliation, and restoring a sense of well-being), improved physical and mental health, restoration of a sense of personal power, and reconciliation of the offendee and offender (McCullough & Worthington, 1994). While forgiveness has a close association with religion, there is also evidence that counselors in general positively value forgiveness (E. W. Kelly, in press) and are open to using forgiveness techniques (DiBlasio & Benda, 1992; DiBlasio & Proctor, 1993). Thus, forgiveness can be regarded as a potentially healing process that is suitable for and congenial to counselors in secular and religious settings.

While forgiveness is generally thought to have beneficial psychosocial effects, the specific forgiving process for each client requires careful consideration of the client's life history and current intrapsychic attitude as well as the interpersonal dynamics between the client and offender. Forgiveness is properly seen as a gradual transformational process, not a singular event, in an offended client (Human Development Study Group, 1991; Smedes, 1984), with a preforgiveness stage and forgiveness stage. The preforgiveness stage consists of honestly recognizing the offensive event, consciously experiencing the consequent hurt and anger, and gathering relevant information to understand—*not* acquiesce to—the motivations of the offender. The forgiveness stage consists of reframing one's perceptions of the offender in a genuinely broader context while recognizing the possibly permanent changes in oneself; releasing one's desire to retaliate; and wishing the offender well, while not necessarily becoming actually reconciled with the offender if this is undesirable or impossible (Rosenak & Harnden, 1992; Human Development Study Group, 1991). Furthermore, the psychological effects on the client may be such that he or she, even while going through the process of forgiveness, may retain a need to maintain a degree of inner guardedness against subsequent hurt (Davenport, 1991).

While one may expect individual differences among clients, the counselor who attempts to facilitate the process of forgiveness in a deeply hurt client is likely to employ a wide range of relational, psychodynamic, and cognitive-behavioral skills. These are a complex group of skills that enable the counselor to respect the client's

219

capacity to change despite frailties and confusions and to help the client gradually move inward so that the client can: (a) honestly acknowledge the offending event, (b) understand and experience the consequent hurt and anger while dropping defenses, (c) transform self-blame into self-compassion and self-forgiveness, (d) empathically reframe the offender as a complex, three-dimensional human being, (e) decide to take a humanizing (rather than dehumanizing stance as did the offender) toward the offender, and (f) allow and encourage oneself to experience a sense of release from the psychic and interpersonal negativity that the offense and its consequence entailed (Davenport, 1991; Enright et al., 1992; McCullough & Worthington, 1994).

The powerful and pervasive role of forgiveness in Christian faith and beliefs about human connectedness and altruism inherent in spirituality are particularly congruent with a therapeutic approach to forgiveness. However, given the complexity of the forgiveness process and the potential pitfalls of superficial and emotionally unhealthy forgiveness, counselors need to take care that religious imperatives or spiritual convictions about forgiveness do not lead them to harmful shortcuts in the forgiveness process. Also, counselors need to recognize that clients differ in the relative importance they attach to forgiveness, either in terms of their personalized view of spirituality or as a consequence of the relative importance of forgiveness in different spiritual and religious systems. Thus, counselors' therapeutic use of forgiveness is tempered by the complexity of the forgiveness process and by the value that the client places on it in comparison with other curative factors (e.g., achieving justice).

Willingness/Release/Letting Go

"Willingness implies a surrendering of one's self-separateness, an entering-into, an immersion in the deepest processes of life itself," the spiritual processes "of an experienced and interpreted relationship among human beings and the mystery of creation" (G. G. May, 1982b, pp. 6, 23). It stands in contrast to "willfulness . . . [which] is the setting of oneself apart from the fundamental essence of life in an attempt to master, direct, control, or otherwise manipulate existence" (p. 6). Fleischman (1986) describes this willingness as "release," a spiritually and religiously based letting go of inordinate struggles to control all the events, feelings, and persons in one's life (see also Trout, 1990). For the spiritually oriented client who is tied up in stress and anxiety related to a drive to control (e.g., one's family, one's career, one's image), the willing process of release can be seen as reflected in the great religious teachings on trust in the benevolent will and purposes of God, as seen, for example, in the Psalms, the Gospel, and the Qur'an.

Release from the control struggle, or letting go of the fear and the pressures of the past and the future, is a gradual attitudinal/cognitive/behavioral process that can be reinforced in the spiritual/religious client by turning to an attitude of trust in the meaningful purposes of God and the deep processes of life. This is not a process of passivity, resignation, dependency on authoritarian direction, or obedience to some guru. It is rather a turning loose of the uncontrollable and the unnecessary, a positive spiritual realignment of one's life and a joining of one's resources with healing and life-enhancing processes of reality. An example of this spiritual release was a divorced female client whose persistent anger and depression were tied in part to her frantic efforts to reverse what was clearly a losing custody contest. Several weeks into counseling the client gradually came to recognize how circumstances worked against her gaining custody. With a revitalized religiousness, she told the counselor of her evening prayer: "I placed them in God's hands." With this she was able to achieve a peaceful although still painful, acceptance of her new situation and to devote her attention to improved ways of relating to her children.

Spiritually and religiously based practices

Several practices closely associated with spiritual and religious beliefs may be beneficially integrated into counseling and psychotherapeutic treatment, depending on the particular mix of client, counselor, setting, and problem variables. These practices include meditation, prayer, ritual, the 12-step program, and related activities rooted in spiritual or religious belief.

221

Meditation

Meditation has a long and venerable history in the major world religions (Goleman, 1988) and in recent times has been adopted in counseling and psychotherapy as a method for alleviating a variety of mental, emotional, and physical problems, especially those related to stress (H. Benson, 1993; Carrington, 1993). There are a variety of meditation methods, reflecting different spiritual/religious and philosophical/scientific beliefs, assumptions, and practices. However, across all varieties of meditation, the core *methodological* emphasis is on the training of attention (Goleman, 1988)—an attentiveness that is calm, alert, and focused (Odajnyk, 1993; Shafii, 1985). Although a highly cognitive activity, meditation involves the whole person in a psychophysiological experience (Carrington, 1993; Shafii, 1985) that Shafii (1985) characterizes as "active passivity" (e.g., sitting quietly while being inwardly alert and focused) and "creative quiescence" (e.g., inwardly calm while being open to expanded awareness) (pp. 90–91).

This calm but alert attentiveness is practiced in two basic forms (Carrington, 1993; Goleman, 1988; Odajnyk, 1993). One is *concentration* or fixed meditation in which the meditator fixes his or her mind on an internal or external object (e.g., a word, sound, bodily sensation, statue) while minimizing distractions and bringing the wandering mind back to attention on the chosen object. The second is *mindfulness*, in which the meditator, rather than concentrating on a fixed object, focuses alertly but nonjudgmentally on everything passing through the mind, entailing "full watchfulness of each successive moment, a global vigilance to the meditator's chain of awareness" (Goleman, 1988, p. 106; see also Kabat-Zinn, 1993). A variation of mindfulness is "discursive meditation" (Odajnyk, 1993, p. 47), in which the meditator focuses on a sequence of events, including not only unregulated passing thoughts and sensations but also a connected succession of ideas, images, or events (e.g., scenes from the life of Jesus, the changing movements in dance or music). While these basic methods highlight the major distinctions among types of meditation, most schools "are eclectic, using a variety of techniques from both approaches [i.e. concentration and mindfulness]" (Goleman, 1988, p. 107).

Meditation may be practiced as a spiritual, religious, or simply psychological-therapeutic activity (i.e., without spiritual or religious elements or intentions) or as an integral combination of a religious/spiritual and psychological activity. Although popularly associated with Eastern religions and even more narrowly with the Transcendental Meditation (TM) movement, meditation with a spiritual/religious orientation is deeply rooted and extensively practiced in Western religions (H. Benson, 1993; Goleman, 1988; Schopen & Freeman, 1992). When divested of its spiritual and religious elements and purposes, meditation also serves as a therapeutic methodology with similarities in method and effect to biofeedback techniques, progressive muscle relaxation, and visualization techniques (Carrington, 1993). Research indicates that therapeutic meditation has substantial potential benefits in the treatment of stress, chronic pain, anger and hostility, anxiety and depression, insomnia, and symptoms related to medical problems such as cancer and AIDS (H. Benson, 1993; Carrington, 1993). The overlap between spiritual/religious forms of meditation and nonspiritual/nonreligious forms makes it appealing as well as beneficial to clients with varying degrees of spiritual/religious commitment.

A meditation approach particularly well suited to the stress-related problems typically encountered in counseling uses a fairly simple method emphasizing training in attentive concentration with a physical calm or relaxation. Various meditation practices and more advanced stages of meditation are certainly important for those seeking spiritual growth and enhanced mind-body health (D. P. Brown, 1986; Gawler, 1989), but the simple steps of the early stages of meditation can be readily incorporated in counseling (Carrington, 1993). A simple and proven meditation method developed at the Mind/Body Medical Institute at Harvard Medical School (H. Benson, 1993) incorporates the basic principles of concentrative meditation for achieving a therapeutic relaxation response. This method, under the title of "How to Elicit the Relaxation Response," is reproduced in Table 6. Apropos the incorporation of the spiritual/religious dimension in counseling, Benson (1993) notes that research indicates that religiously prayerful meditation (or meditative prayer; see, for example, Foster, 1992; Poloma & Gallup, 1991; Shafii, 1985) produces the same kind of physiological changes as nonreligious meditation (e.g., transcendental meditation), leading the Harvard Mind/Body

T A B L E 6

How to Elicit the Relaxation Response

Some general advice on regular practice of the relaxation response:

- *Try to find 10 to 20 minutes in your daily routine; before breakfast is a good time.*
- *Sit comfortably.*
- *For the period you will practice, try to arrange your life so you won't have distractions. Put the phone on the answering machine, and ask someone else to watch the kids.*
- *Time yourself by glancing periodically at a clock or watch (but don't set an alarm). Commit yourself to a specific length of practice, and try to stick to it.*

There are several approaches to eliciting the relaxation response. Here is one standard set of instructions used at the Mind/Body Medical Institute:

Step 1. Pick a focus word or short phrase that's firmly rooted in your personal belief system. For example, a nonreligious individual might choose a neutral word like *one* or *peace* or *love*. A Christian person desiring to use a prayer could pick the opening words of Psalm 23, *The Lord is my shepherd*; a Jewish person could choose *Shalom*.

Step 2. Sit quietly in a comfortable position.

Step 3. Close your eyes.

Step 4. Relax your muscles.

Step 5. Breathe slowly and naturally, repeating your focus word or phrase silently as you exhale.

Step 6. Throughout, assume a passive attitude. Don't worry about how well you're doing. When other thoughts come to mind, simply say to yourself, "Oh, well," and gently return to the repetition.

Step 7. Continue for 10 to 20 minutes. You may open your eyes to check the time, but do not use an alarm. When you finish, sit quietly for a minute or so, at first with your eyes closed and later with your eyes open. Then do not stand for one or two minutes.

Step 8. Practice the technique once or twice a day.

Note. "How to Elicit the Relaxation Response" Copyright 1993 by Consumers Union of U.S., Inc., Yonkers, NY 10703-1057. Reprinted by permission from CONSUMER REPORTS BOOKS, January 1993.

group to "recommend that our religious patients consider using such prayer when they elicit the relaxation response and that nonreligious patients use any sound, word, or phrase with which they are comfortable" (p. 241). For religious clients who are unfamiliar with or even suspicious of meditation, learning that it is a widely respected form of prayer and an acceptable therapeutic method provides a bridge to its effective use in counseling.

In addition to individually focused methods of meditation, Sweet and C. G. Johnson (1990) describe an interpersonally oriented method—Meditation Enhanced Empathy Training (MEET)—designed to foster an empathically friendly and accepting manner toward others as well as enhanced self-esteem. In this method, the counselor builds into the client's growing meditative skill empathic and prosocial statements and images that go gradually from beneficence toward oneself to beneficent wishes for others. Initial case studies with this method suggest that meditation that explicitly introduces benevolent images and statements may have therapeutic benefit for clients who feel angry, hostile, or suspicious toward others.

Prayer

Prayer is primarily an expression of the pray-er's relationship to a Higher Power. Some discussions of prayer in counseling focus primarily on meditative forms of prayer (see, e.g., Canda, 1990). However, this is too restricted and tends to cloud the intentional differences between nonreligious, therapeutic methods of meditation and meditative prayer. The prayers of many believers take a variety of forms for diverse purposes (Brohi, 1987; Carmody & Carmody, 1990; Foster, 1992; Poloma & Gallup, 1991; Poloma & Pendleton, 1991; Schachter-Shalomi, 1991), including, for example, spontaneous/free-form or formal/written oral prayers for thanksgiving, praise, petition, and repentance. While the spiritual value of prayer in virtually all spiritual/religious traditions is understood to depend on the inner sincerity of the pray-er (i.e., prayer is not magic but the expression of personal involvement with a Higher Power), the manifestations of prayer occur in many different ways. Forms of prayer that are likely to be associated with counseling are petitions (e.g., for relief, change, or divine support and guidance for oneself or others) and thanksgiving.

The association of prayer with counseling may occur in several ways, including (a) the private prayer of a counselor for clients, (b) a counselor referral to or collaboration with religious specialists for client prayer activities outside counseling as a result of the client's interest in prayer, and (c) the in-session use of prayer by the client and/or the counselor (Canda, 1990). A religious counselor's benevolent *private* (i.e., out-of-session) prayers for clients' welfare present little or no direct conflict with secular counseling; indeed, counselors who integrate altruistic prayer into their own healthy attitudes toward themselves and others may enhance mind-body benefits in the counseling relationship (Canda, 1990; Dossey, 1993). This aspect of prayer and counseling is important, but it is related primarily to the personal spiritual/religious life of the counselor and is not developed here. The issue of collaboration with religious specialists for clients' prayer interests will be discussed below in the section on referrals and consultations. The focus of this section is primarily on clients' discussion of prayer and request for prayer during counseling.

The role of prayer in secular counseling is controversial and problematic. Lovinger (1990), for example, writing from a positive perspective of working with religion in counseling, cautions that although "there is nothing wrong with prayer, [nonetheless] it is a deliberate act . . . [that] does not deal well with [the] automatic patterns of feelings, attitudes, and behaviors" characteristic of many client problems. "If the client persists in insisting that prayer *should* [italics in original] help with the problem, then the meaning of prayer needs to be explored" (p. 169). The concern here is that the client's discussion of prayer, not to mention a request for prayer during counseling, may divert attention from the need for deeper exploration of and psychological change in troublesome aspects of the client's intrapersonal and interpersonal life.

Other problematic issues about prayer in counseling involve the following: (a) potentially inappropriate intrusion of the counselor's religious values, which may be contrary to the client's self-determination; (b) the inappropriate mixing of religious practice with the secular and scientifically based practice of counseling and psychotherapy in secular settings; (c) the potential incompetent use of a spiritual/religious activity by a counselor uninformed about prayer in general or a client's distinctive prayer beliefs; and (d) the conviction of some nonspiritual/nonreligious counselors that prayer is a futile and unscientific activity based on illusory beliefs. Any seriously positive approach to prayer in secular counseling must take these concerns into account.

The first condition for determining the acceptability of prayer in secular counseling is a reasonable confidence that prayer *in general* has beneficial potential for personal development and therapeutic change, or at least is not inconsistent with these purposes. It is beyond the scope of this book to address differences of opinion on this issue. My approach is to adopt the position that prayer represents a reasonable, humanly valuable expression of spiritual/religious belief on the grounds that personal spirituality/religiousness, which includes prayer, is generally congruent with good mental health (see Chapter 2). Moreover, considerable, albeit mixed, research evidence and extensive personal experience support the positive psychosocial and physical benefits of prayer (Dossey, 1993; Frank, 1973; Poloma & Pendleton, 1991). The practical consequence is that prayer *in general* may have an appropriate role during counseling and psychotherapy. However, it is necessary to consider other conditions to determine whether prayer is appropriate in specific counseling cases, and if it is, how it might be properly incorporated.

Whether and when to include prayer *in* counseling depends on the following conditions (modified from Canda, 1990):

1. *Needs and interests of the client.* (a) The counselor determines whether prayer represents a generally healthy spirituality in the client and if prayer at this moment in counseling will enhance the counseling process and/or the client's developmental/therapeutic progress, or if it is likely to misrepresent the process or distract from legitimate therapeutic work. (b) The client makes an explicit request for prayer, or the counselor can readily infer an active interest on the client's part.

2. *Beliefs and competence of the counselor.* (a) In line with the importance of counselor integrity and genuineness in counseling, the counselor has a positive regard for prayer as part of his or her belief system. (b) The counselor is knowledgeable and adept in prayer consistent with the client's beliefs.

3. *Counselor-client relationship and counseling setting compatible with spiritual expressiveness.* (a) The explicitly spiritual/religious act of prayer calls for a counselor-client relationship that includes a mutually congruent spirituality between the counselor and client. (b) The counselor works within the policy and spirit of the counseling setting (e.g., public or private) with respect to spiritual/religious expression in counseling.

If the counselor can make an affirmative determination of *all* these conditions, then he or she can consider a therapeutically well-focused inclusion of prayer in counseling at the client's initiative. In terms of how this is to be done, a low-key approach is for the counselor to quietly and respectfully let the client pray. Indeed, this quietly accepting approach may be the most comfortable way for many counselors to include prayer in counseling effectively. For a counselor and client whose spiritual/religious beliefs are robust and congruent, the counselor may accept the client's invitation for an active role in a therapeutically germane prayer. In either method (respectful passive acceptance or active participation), it is critical for the counselor to have assessed the existence of the determining conditions and to ensure the appropriate integration of the prayer into the ongoing developmental and therapeutic activities of the overall counseling process.

Ritual

Increasing recognition is being given to the potentially beneficial effects of rituals, religious and secular (Imber-Black, Roberts, & Whiting, 1988), as a part of and as an adjunct to counseling and psychotherapy. Imber-Black and Roberts (1992) describe five purposes of rituals: (a) shaping, expressing, and maintaining relationships; (b) facilitating change by making and marking transitions; (c) facilitating healing from betrayals, trauma, and loss; (d) expressing belief and making meaning; (e) celebrating life with joy and festivity.

For spiritually/religiously oriented clients, religious rituals may provide a congenial form of ceremonial, formally structured activities that create or enhance a sense of relatedness, meaning, and transcendence (Zuesse, 1983; Olson, 1993) with healing effects pertinent to clients' concerns. Noting the benefit of ritual in times of important or difficult transitions, Bosley and Cook's (1993) study of funeral rituals identified five therapeutic themes: memory as a tool of acceptance, affirmation of faith, emotional expression, social support, and a reconnection to family heritage. The counselor can empathically support a grieving client's participation in a religious funeral ceremony as a way to promote emotional healing, gain social support, express and experience a belief in a Higher Power or transcendent meaning, and encourage healing self-exploration and understanding. Another example of a religiously based ritual is the Jewish ritual of Bar Mitzvah—a representative form of transition rituals—which Ju. Davis (1988) describes as potentially replete with therapeutic value in helping counselors understand and help Jewish families who are experiencing high stress during their children's emergence into adolescence. Other examples of spiritual or religious rituals with potential adjunct value to counseling include ceremonies connected with premarital educational programs; first communion ceremonies for Catholic children and families; religious rituals for people celebrating marriage anniversaries; home and family religious rituals that draw families together and make the home a "sacred" place (Mazumdar & Mazumdar, 1993); blessing rituals for homes, prayer, fasting, and almsgiving rituals (e.g., as associated with Islamic observance of Ramadan); and even traditional weekly religious services that can reconnect a client to helpful values, beliefs, and persons.

Religious rituals can certainly become emptied of meaning and force over time, or people may engage in rituals in thoughtless and detached ways. However, in the case of rituals that have retained appeal and meaning or have been renewed or established in light of contemporary needs, the counselor may find that spiritually/religiously oriented clients will benefit by thoughtful and counseling-processed participation in pertinent religious rituals to cope with important life transitions and to find meaning in serious life crises.

Twelve-step Spirituality

The 12-step recovery program (see Chapter 1) originating in Alcoholics Anonymous has come to be applied widely and effectively for many addictions, including substance abuse, overeating, and sexual addictions (Buxton et al., 1987) and is recognized as a potentially powerful adjunct to counseling and psychotherapy (Khantzian & Mack, 1994). Twelve-step spirituality constitutes an integral part of the painfully honest and healing storytelling of an accepting and supportive 12-step self-help group (e.g., AA, NA, OA) that helps addicts to courageously confront the arrogance, self-centeredness, psychological denial, and self-destructiveness that undergirds their addiction (Khantzian & Mack, 1994).

The very nature of the 12-step program as a group self-help process means that it is a complement to counseling (or vice versa) rather than a part of the counseling process. An important role for the counselor is to (a) help clients understand the potential benefits of a 12-step program, (b) refer them to therapeutically pertinent 12-step programs, and (c) discuss with them any misgivings they may have about aspects of particular programs (e.g., distinctive or narrow expressions of religiosity), while helping them to appreciate the program's overall positive psychological power and essentially ecumenical spirituality. Guidelines for appropriate referrals include realistic information to the client about the probable benefits of the program as a complement to counseling, timing the referral to meet the client's needs (often early in

229

treatment), helping the client overcome defensive resistance, personally tailoring the referral to individual client needs, and preparing the client for the general nature of 12-step meetings (including their spiritual but not specifically religious nature) (Riordan & Walsh, 1994). For the client who can benefit from structured support in working with the 12-step program, H. P. Brown et al. (1988a) have developed a "Daily Spiritual Behavior Checklist," a simple weekly chart for clients to monitor themselves in 10 spiritually oriented 12-step behaviors.

Spiritual/Religious Bibliotherapy

The general technique of suggesting to clients readings that are pertinent to their work in counseling is applicable to spiritual and religious issues. For example, Malony (1985b) has described ways that the Jewish/Christian scriptures (Bible) might be used with religious clients, and Brown and Peterson (1989) have recommended specific reading assignments for spiritual evaluations in conjunction with 12-step programs. Devotional spiritual/religious literature is vast and diverse and requires that a counselor be especially familiar with readings relevant to the needs of specific clients. Without this knowledge, the counselor should consult with or refer clients to religious specialists for spiritual/religious readings that are therapeutically beneficial.

Special populations, issues, and problems

Spirituality and religion cut across all cultures and groups and may occur in many life issues and problems. However, circumstances and pressures of certain groups entail distinctive perspectives and lead to special counseling applications in the spiritual/religious dimension.

Women

Perhaps this section should be on men, because a cultural masculinism and patriarchal authority pervasive in the major world religions have contributed to many systemic inequities—not to mention oppression and abuse—to which women as a class and as individuals have been subjected throughout much of the world. On the other hand, there is the equally widespread devotedness and contribution of women to spirituality and religion as well as the paradoxical adherence (with varying mixtures of personal conviction and social coercion) of many women to spiritual/religious beliefs and systems that assign them subordinate positions to men.

A consideration of women and the spiritual/religious dimension opens the door to multiple complex issues and perspectives bearing on gender formation as a culturally embedded *social process* diversely affecting women and men rather than simply a biologically based differentiation of the sexes (Gilbert, 1992). It brings to the fore the application of feminist thinking on spirituality and religion in counseling and, at the other end of the continuum, the practical issue of counseling effectively with women whose problems are connected to their adherence to certain spiritual/religious beliefs circumscribing women's behavior and equality.

Any brief summary of feminist spirituality in counseling represents only a small piece of the rich, evolving complexity of feminist philosophy and therapy (Enns, 1993). While recognizing diverse perspectives on feminist thinking and practice, it is conceptually and practically useful to view feminism as highlighting in theory, research, and corrective action the pervasive sex-gender biases and cultural-societal-institutional inequities that have seriously adverse "political" (i.e., externally imposed limitations) and "personal" (i.e., self-concepts internalized from social constructions of women's roles) effects on women in relation to men (Gilbert, 1993). The social and personal tasks of feminist work involve recognizing and eradicating systemic biases—the "political" aspect—and helping women redefine, reexperience, and empower themselves freely in personally affirming ways—the "personal" aspect. A spiritual perspective in feminism connects the empowering revaluing of the self-in-community with questions about the larger and ultimate purposes of life (Bepko & Krestan, 1990). This connection is made explicit in a set of principles and practices that combine spiritually oriented introspective and expressive techniques (e.g., meditation, drama) focused on major issues affecting women's lives with feminist principles of consciousness raising, personal empowering, and networking (Berliner, 1992; Harris, 1989).

A spiritually oriented feminist approach (as distinguished from a standard feminist therapy practiced only by women therapists

[Dambort & Reep, 1993]) may be particularly appropriate for clients (a) whose problems involve significant external and internalized sex biases, gender devaluation, and/or subordinating abuse, and (b) whose spiritual beliefs and religious environment are potentially supportive of an empowering feminist approach. Such an approach combines principles of a "converted spirituality" (e.g., belief in a caring God who loves us as we are, respects our justifiable anger, affirms each person in her integrity and equality, calls each person to full development and responsible exercise of her gifts and power, and supports the building of relationships and communities of mutual respect and liberating care [Berliner, 1992]) with typical feminist interventions (e.g., helping clients uncover sexism in their lives, social and gender role analysis, anger work, self-disclosure, and individual decision-making skills [Chaplin, 1988; Enns, 1993]).

The application of an explicitly labeled feminist counseling approach would be resisted by clients whose religious beliefs and affiliations cast feminism as contrary to their faith. For example, Whipple (1987) discusses how a Christian fundamentalism, which emphasizes literal interpretation of Bible passages interpreted as subordinating women to men and closing off certain social roles to women, may work to hinder fundamentalist women from stopping or getting out of a violent marital relationship. In this case, "the only way that [fundamentalist] Christian battered women may be willing to do something different is if they can see *in the Bible* [italics in original] that God does not want them to be abused" (Whipple, 1987, p. 252). This approach entails the counselor's open-minded respect for the client's fundamentalist religious faith (Moyers, 1990) and a knowledgeable use (either by the counselor or a sympathetic religious specialist acceptable to the client) of biblical passages that support a counseling process and client actions to end the violence in her life.

Culture and Ethnicity

In Chapter 1 we discussed the intermingling of culture and spirituality/religion. The reciprocal, interweaving influence of culture and spirituality/religion as well as diversity within cultures should act as a caution to the counselor against making facile generalizations about clients' spirituality or religion on the basis of the their culture or ethnicity. At the same time, a recognition of the generally prominent role of religion among some cultural or ethnic groups (E. W. Kelly, 1992) can alert the counselor to consider spirituality/religion as a potentially relevant issue with clients from these groups.

For example, religion and the church have been cited as prominent sources of support for many African Americans (Allen, 1991; Carnegie Corporation, 1987–1988; Knox, 1985; Turner, 1987) and as playing a prominent role in the Hispanic family (Acosta, Groh, Hernandez, & Rathbone, 1990). A counselor's understanding of the potential connection between a client's culture and spiritual/religious perspective enables the counselor to listen with special care for how religious beliefs may be interwoven with problems presented in counseling. Knox (1985) suggests that the counselor be ready to explore with African-American clients (a) religious beliefs (including the church) as a source of hope and strength, (b) the concept of God and deity in influencing attitudes and behavior, and (c) the relationship between beliefs (including mixtures of Christian and indigenous [e.g., hexing] beliefs) and health. Acosta et al. (1990) describe the important role of religion, especially Roman Catholicism, in many Hispanic families. They note, for example, that counselors should understand the combining of a cultural "machismo" with a "pedestal" position of women and of key family events (e.g., births, baptisms, weddings) with religious significance, as well the mixing of Christian beliefs with indigenous "superstitions" accepted as a normal way of life. They also recommend that for counselors working across cultures (e.g., Anglos with Hispanics) their intellectual understanding of cultural/religious dynamics needs deepening and refining through consultation with counselors of the client's culture.

Elderly

There is substantial evidence showing that religion may have a beneficial influence in the lives of elderly people, including strong positive effects of public and private religious involvement on health status (Idler & Kasl, 1992), successful use of religious beliefs in coping, higher life satisfaction associated with the use of religious beliefs in coping, and a positive effect of prayer on life satisfaction ratings (Owens, Aoto, & Prouty, 1993; Owens & McClain, 1992; Owens, Ward, & McLeod-Winder, 1992).

233

Brink (1985) provides an illustrative example of how spiritual/ religious beliefs may be used beneficially with elderly clients in his description of short-term counseling (10 sessions) with a 79-year-old widow whose health problems necessitated her moving to live first with her son and daughter-in-law and then in a nursing home. Both situations were unsuccessful because of the client's negative style with others. Learning that this negativism was a recent development, the counselor was able to use the client's religious beliefs to (a) help her realistically accept (cognitively and with the help of prayer) her health limitations and losses, (b) have her substitute religiously based calming behavior (touching her bedside Bible) for verbally abusive behavior toward other residents, (c) facilitate her acknowledgement of suppressed guilt feelings stemming from sending her husband to a nursing home before he died, and (d) encourage her acceptance of forgiveness. Research and clinical experience indicate that counselors working with the elderly are likely to have a number of opportunities similar to those described here to integrate spiritual/religious belief into counseling care.

Gay Men and Lesbians

In addition to many of the same issues that nongays face, gay men and lesbians confront serious social prejudice, discrimination, and hostility (homophobia) that exacerbate the typical emotional stresses of developing a self-accepting self-identity (Fassinger, 1991). Before discussing highlights of affirmative counseling and psychotherapy that have been proposed for gay people in light of their special needs (Browning, Reynolds, & Dworkin, 1991; Dworkin & Gutiérrez, 1992; Shannon & Woods, 1991), the focus of this book calls for us to note the often negative role of religion toward gays and lesbians. Organized religions, particularly Western Christian religions, are a major source of stigmatizing the gay and lesbian sexual orientation as deviant and disordered (Harvey, 1993). Unfortunately, this religiously inspired depreciation continues—indeed it recently has actively intensified, especially among fundamentalist Christian groups—and is abetted by antigay doctrinal proclamations of clerical authorities. Given the concerted effort of certain religious groups and authorities to devalue the sexual orientation of gay people, it is especially important for counselors to know that there are biblical scholars, theologians, and religious leaders who provide ample evidence discrediting the noncontextual use of a few isolated Bible passages and the traditional appeal to "natural law" to support an antigay position (Comstock, 1993; Edwards, 1984; Long & J. M. Clark, 1992; McNeill, 1988, 1993; Nelson, 1982; Pronk, 1993; Scroggs, 1983; Spong, 1988).

A growing body of knowledge undergirds recent achievements in eliminating erroneous and stigmatizing characterizations of gay men and lesbians. The total elimination of homosexuality as a mental disorder category in the DSM-III-R (American Psychiatric Association, 1986) and DSM-IV (American Psychiatric Association, 1994) is supported by research showing that sexual orientation is not in itself a form or cause of pathology (Fassinger, 1991). There is a growing recognition that the devaluating myths so long and widely held about gay people are in conflict with the well-supported reality that gay and nongay people are similar to one another—except for sexual orientation—across all important life categories such as family background, career aspirations and tracks, and personal and civic virtue (Rosser, 1992). The growing realization that the devaluation of gays and lesbians is based on tragic *mis*information—the widespread persistence of which has serious deleterious effects—has led the American Counseling Association (ACA) (1994) and the American Psychological Association (APA) (1992) to formally declare in their ethical codes that any form of prejudicial action based on sexual orientation is professionally unethical.

Recent data indicate that the overwhelming majority of the nongay public (81%) opposes discrimination based on sexual orientation (Hay's study as cited in Fassinger, 1991). Despite this general attitude, despite research and experience that dispel misinformation about gay and lesbian people, and despite the concerted efforts of developmental and mental health professionals to ensure fair and informed treatment of all people regardless of sexual orientation, misinformation and bias (including overt and covert antigay attitudes among counselors and psychotherapists [Garnets, Hancock, Cochran, Goodchilds, & Peplau, 1991; Rudolph, 1989]) continue to complicate and aggravate the personal and social problems of gay men and lesbians (Fassinger, 1991; Haldeman, 1994). With respect to spirituality and religion, an affirmative approach to counseling gay and lesbian clients is designed to address these problems in several ways. In the face of

235

concerted efforts by certain religionists to devalue a gay sexual orientation on biblical or theological grounds, counselors need to be aware that spiritual, religious, and biblical scholarship provides solid philosophical and theological support for the ethical and moral neutrality of sexual orientation in and of itself (see references above). This knowledge contributes significantly to a non-homophobic stance that allows counselors to listen openly and nonjudgmentally for the spiritual/religious searchings and struggles in gay clients' lives.

Religious or formerly religious clients' struggle through internalized homophobia toward self-acceptance and self-esteem may well be connected with religious proscriptions of homosexuality. In many cases this leads to rejection of organized religion or a confused and painful effort to reconcile religious belief and self-integrity and acceptance of one's sexual orientation. Ritter and O'Neill (1989) describe how the counselor can help gay and lesbian clients whose struggles include a spiritual/religious dimension. Such help involves helping the client to (a) positively recast the spiritual image of gays and lesbians in line with scholarship and experience affirming a moral and spiritual integrity consistent with a gay sexual orientation; (b) reframe losses (e.g., rejection by the church, loss of loved ones to AIDS, feelings of not fully belonging in workplace or social groups) into opportunities for transcendence of personal pain toward spiritual growth and a heightened commitment to help others who are alienated; and (c) find a life-affirming spiritual path, either in traditional organized religion (e.g., in tolerant groups like the Quakers, Unitarians, Reform Judaism, or special denominational groups like the Catholic group Dignity [see Wagner, Serafini, Rabkin, Remien, & Williams, 1994]), alternative churches (e.g., the Universal Fellowship of Metropolitan Community Churches), or spiritual movements outside traditional religion. Connecting with a church or alternative spiritual/religious group is also helpful in providing spiritually and religiously oriented friendships and networks for mutual support and social action. Kus (1992) describes the benefits that alcoholic gay individuals can gain by actively participating in AA spirituality (e.g., in overcoming internalized homophobia as well as alcoholism and achieving peaceful self-acceptance along with sobriety).

In some cases, a gay client's internalized homophobia carries a guilty confusion making the client susceptible to suggestions of

236

"sexual orientation conversion therapy." This approach to trying to change the sexual orientation of a gay or lesbian client is rooted in the now discredited notion of homosexuality as an illness. It misapplies religiously grounded motivations to developmental and mental health counseling, is inconsistent with the ethical guidelines of ACA and APA (Haldeman, 1994), and is contrary to the spiritually healthy growth models available for counselors in their work with gay and lesbian clients. Such an approach, therefore, is without justification in a secular counseling setting.

The devastating effects of AIDS among the gay population—although certainly not synonymous with a gay orientation—make it a matter of special concern in considering spirituality and religion in counseling with clients from this population. AIDS brings many gay people face to face with the most profound losses of health, personal control, death, and loved ones and friends. These losses have "compelled many to tap deeply into themselves and to emerge with personal and spiritual resources to share with the entire community" (Ritter & O'Neill, 1989, p. 68). A spiritual perspective on AIDS complements a knowledgeable competence in the medical, psychological, and social aspects of AIDS with deepening reflections on meaning, transcendence, and hope. This is not a trivializing of the pain, anger, and sadness of disease and death or a diminishing of efforts toward health and life, but an opening to the possibility of a deeper base of understanding and peace (Fortunato, 1987; Long & J. M. Clark, 1992).

For some AIDS clients this may come in revitalized connections with their religious beliefs, and for their families in more compassionate and supportive applications of religious beliefs. This spiritual journey can take a variety forms. Fortunato (1987), for example, describes, against the backdrop of an intensified sense of mortality, the importance of living deeply in the present. Bradley's (1988) description of a young Catholic man illustrates how a counselor needs to be prepared for twists and turns of a life journey from vitality, through sickness, anger, despair, and religious disbelief, to a deep reconnection with religious faith for the sick person and his family. The counselor can gain special support for AIDS clients in the gay and lesbian community, where AIDS has helped build a "spirituality of compassion," with support groups and individuals providing service (McNeill, 1993, p. 212). A spiritual perspective on AIDS is not a Pollyanna acceptance—indeed it may involve a vitalizing struggle—but a readiness to hear and help the client's deeper questions about the meaning of life and death (Long & J. M. Clark, 1992).

Dying and Grieving

The imminence of one's own death or the death of a loved one frequently turns persons' attention to religion and spirituality. Caregivers who work with the dying and bereaved agree on the importance of exploring spiritual and religious issues with the dying and their loved ones and providing them spiritual support. Caregivers also rely on their own spiritual/religious beliefs for coping with the stress of their work (Hoare & Nashman, 1994; Millison & Dudley, 1992; D. C. Smith, 1993).

Some dying and bereaved people will bring up the spiritual/religious dimension themselves. When the counselor initiates a consideration of spiritual/religious issues, it needs to be done with a nonjudgmental readiness to hear the client's own spiritual/religious perspective. The counselor provides a gentle invitation that allows the client to explore spiritual/religious issues on the client's own terms (Speck, 1989), raising, for example, questions of meaning (Why me? Why now?), loss of one's own existence and of others, and life after death, and to express deep emotions of fear, sadness, and/or guilt. D. C. Smith (1993) suggests several methods for helping clients to explore and bring forth their own spiritual/religious resources, including open-ended questions, counselor-client dialogue based on a journey analogy, client reflections of different views of dying, picturing one's impression of the divine, and the client's forming a mental sacred shrine with important memories and objects. All of these methods are designed to invite the client to explore various spiritual aspects of dying (e.g., sources of strength, spiritual/religious beliefs, purpose of life, life after death) and to tap spiritual/religious resources for a "good" death and progressive adjustment to grief.

School counselors may be able to help children and adolescents cope with grief through group discussions, individual counseling, and nonthreatening units on grief in appropriate places in the curriculum (Balk, 1983; Costa & Holliday, 1994; Moore & Herlihy, 1993). Although religion is a very sensitive topic for public school counselors, the importance to many young people of religious beliefs about death (Balk, 1983) calls for the counselor to listen with understanding to the religious aspect of youngsters' grief and help them integrate their beliefs into their coping efforts.

Given the diversity and emotional intensity of spiritual/religious beliefs regarding death, the counselor needs to move with circumspection in helping the client to explore this domain (Dersheimer, 1990). Empathic listening is a basic requirement, enabling clients to talk about their spiritual/religious concerns and gradually develop for themselves meanings that will help them cope with painful loss and uncover possibilities for hope. For religious clients the counselor needs to understand the important role that clergy often play in helping clients to use religious resources (e.g., prayer, rituals, spiritual support). This may involve encouraging the client's spiritual/religious discussion with clergy, consultations with the client's clergy, and helping the client to integrate spiritual/religious themes from discussion with clergy into the counseling process. To work well with the dying, counselors could benefit greatly from the expertise of experienced hospice caregivers through a hospice orientation and hospice inservice education, where serious attention is given to the spiritual/religious dimension (Hoare & Nashman, 1994; Millison & Dudley, 1992).

Bowlby-West (1983) stresses the need for counselors to recognize the grieving time, sometimes very long in the case of a major loss (e.g., the death of a child [see also S. E. Johnson, 1987]). Her description of grieving in six phases, although not applicable to all cases of bereavement (Stroebe, Stroebe, & Hansson, 1993), is useful for understanding the spiritual/religious dimension in counseling grieving clients. These phases are: (a) numbness lasting from a few hours to a few weeks, sometimes interrupted by outbursts of extreme anger or distress; (b) yearning and searching (lasting months or years) for the lost person, with an intense inner struggle between an awareness of death and a desire to recover the lost loved one; (c) disorganization, despair, and hopelessness, with awareness of a discrepancy between inner ideals and reality; (d) more or less reorganization with new assumptions and a new identity; (e) transformation, involving "a release from the attachment to the dead person and an emotional experience of universal love" (p. 283); and (f) actualization, an acting on the transformation to grow into a fuller maturity. A counselor who understands the spiritual dimension of grieving helps the grieving client work with patient self-acceptance and a gradual evolution through pain toward the possibility of a greater sense of universal connectedness and inner wholeness.

Cults

As described in Chapter 1, the cult phenomenon is complex and not easy to pin down, with scholars and researchers providing alternative perspectives on the spirituality and psychology of cults (Galanter, 1989a). However, when understood in specifically non-benign forms, cults are recognized as fringe or deviant spiritual/religious groups usually led by a charismatically persuasive leader and characterized by highly consensual or coercive group norms. The cult's norms call for complete loyalty to the group and to group beliefs and practices, primarily as interpreted and conveyed by the cult leader, and discourage relationships outside the group. The cult's appeal is typically to persons—often young, but including vulnerable persons of all ages—who are dissatisfied and distressed, going through stressful life transition, and often wanting a more spiritual life within a group promising a sense of belonging and security (Deikman, 1990). Cult involvement may become a counseling and therapy concern because it draws a person away from significant life tasks (e.g., school and work responsibilities); provides a misleading and developmentally ineffectual "solution" to personal and social problems (e.g., loneliness, boredom); promotes self-defeating and/or antisocial behavior (e.g., uncritical dependency, sexual promiscuity, criminal acts); cuts off contacts with families and friends; and, if a person attempts to leave, exercises mental and/or physical coercion to thwart the departure. Those who do separate may experience periods of harassment from the cult and intense feelings of guilt and anger.

Initial levels of involvement consist of curiosity and interest, sometimes motivated by a sincere, but often dependency-laden, search for spiritual meaning and belonging or stimulated by "fun-and-games" (e.g., occult games) and superficial dabbling (e.g., in fortune telling) (Carmichael, 1993). If a counselor has contact with the person at the early "hooking" stage, the counselor should take preventive action by making empathic contact with the client, attempting to stir interest in alternative spiritual or engaging activities, and working with family or friends to provide understanding support (Sirkin, 1990). However, when a person moves through the "joining" stage (Sirkin, 1990) and becomes seriously involved in a cult ("intensification" and "social disengagement" stages), the therapeutic task becomes significantly more difficult. The ideal treatment is a combination of individual and family counseling (Sirkin, 1990).

A cult member may be brought to counseling in crisis by family members and may resist the counselor's empathic efforts with hostility, indifference, or proselytizing zeal; other family members will likely present a mixture of bewilderment, anger, pleading, and confrontation. A main task of the counselor is to maintain an open, supportive, nonjudgmental communication among the counselor, the family, and the cult member (Deikman, 1990). The purpose is to provide a therapeutic and family "place" into which the cult member can eventually move, either during the course of counseling or at a later time. The counselor also provides information for the client and family to understand why cults may appear appealing but are fundamentally unsatisfying and harmful. If the cult member does not leave the cult immediately, the counselor can work to help the family keep open and understanding communication with the cult member, providing the prospect of a welcoming and understanding home to which a gradually disillusioned cult member can return. The counselor can also provide information about sources of information and self-help groups such as the Cult Awareness Network. The counselor needs to recognize that a frustrated family might choose coercive measures like "deprogramming" to "rescue" a family member in a cult; coercive measures, however, regardless how well-intentioned and understandable from the family's perspective, are not a counseling activity. While counselors may work with the clinical consequences (e.g., family disruption, harmful disagreement among family members) of coercion, they need to understand the ethical and legal ramifications associated with involuntary and coercive actions and as a rule should seek appropriate legal and other professional consultation and/or referral.

With a former cult member, the counselor needs to understand the client's likely disorientation to ordinary life, sense of loss, and feelings of guilt, anger, and fear as well as tendencies in the family to blame, vigilantly overprotect, or stir anxiety. The work of the counselor is empathically to help the client to integrate an understanding of the negative and positive aspects of the cult experience into the gradual development or redevelopment of a reality-oriented identity and style of life; to explore alternative spiritual/ religious activities supportive of change; and to help family members to mitigate criticism, anxiety, or overprotection and be supportive in the client's difficult change. This is the stage of "realignment" for client and family (Sirkin, 1990). The counselor does not become fixed on negative and problematic issues but helps the client and family to recognize client strengths and authentic yearnings that underlay the client's cult involvement and that may now be used for a renewed engagement with life.

Satanism is a form of cult activity currently receiving attention because of its potentially detrimental effects on young people particularly (Carmichael, 1993; Ondrovik & Hamilton, 1992). Given continuing controversy on the extent of Satanism and ritualistic abuse, its precise psychological and spiritual nature, and its relationship to mental disorders (e.g., multiple personality disorders) (M. L. Rogers, 1992), counselors should evaluate client and family reports with care and an open mind. The counselor needs to seriously assess and act on client or others' reports about involvement in occult or criminal activities believed to be associated with Satanism or other cult manifestations. Counselor action includes, as described above, preventive steps to redirect initial attention or dabbling away from cult activities with understanding, good information, and alternative interests. If abuse or criminality is clear, the counselor has therapeutic, ethical, and legal responsibilities to treat and protect the client. Insofar as spirituality and religion are involved, the counselor may help the client identify the unhealthy spiritual/religious aspects of cult activity and, if possible and desirable, to develop a healthy spirituality.

Consultation and referral

The range and significance of spiritual/religious issues that may occur in counseling, as well as the intermingling of these issues with developmental and psychosocial concerns, make consultation and referral important options to the counselor. Referral and consultation between counselors and therapists and clergy and spiritual/religious specialists can be a two-way process (G. G. May, 1982a). Although the rate of cross-referrals is generally low (Chalfant et al., 1990; Ingram & Lowe, 1989), careful, well-informed referrals between counselors and spiritual/religious specialists can have benefits in helping clients sort out and integrate the psychological/developmental and spiritual/religious aspects of their lives.

Several considerations should guide the counselor in making referrals and entering consultation relationships related to spiritual/religious issues that arise in the course of counseling.

1. The counselor assesses the therapeutic significance of the client's spiritual/religious concerns. If religious language or spiritual matters are a nonproblematic, ordinary part the client's self-presentation, referral or consultation is unwarranted. However, if spiritual/religious issues are persistently intertwined with the substance of the client's concerns, are blocking counseling progress or problem solving, and/or appear as a potential resource for client improvement, a referral or consultation may be in order.

2. The counselor assesses his or her competence in working with the spiritual/religious dimension of the client's presentation. Therapeutically significant spiritual/religious material that exceeds the counselor's knowledge or competence indicates that the counselor should consider a referral or consultation. Consultation with clergy may inform the counselor about beliefs and practices pertinent to making counseling decisions and reassure the client that counseling is being carried out in accord with beliefs as interpreted by a respected religious specialist or leaders.

3. A decision about a referral or consultation with a clergyperson or spiritual specialist is based on an open discussion with the client about the reasons and potential benefits of the referral/consultation. The counselor makes sure that the client understands the reason for the referral and feels that the counselor is working in the client's best interest.

4. The choice of a spiritual/religious consultant or referral source is important. Factors to consider in this choice are the nature of the client's problem, the client's spiritual/ religious belief system, competence of the clergyperson or spiritual specialist to work helpfully with the client and collaboratively with the counselor, and the acceptability of the consultant to the client. Examples of different kinds of referrals are experienced spiritual directors for serious spiritual seekers, religious specialists for involved questions of doctrine or practice, and pastoral clergy for many questions involved in the day-to-day application of beliefs.

5. To make an informed referral the counselor will need to develop connections with clergy and religious specialists. Coun-

selors who regularly work with highly spiritual/religious clients need to establish regular resource connections, perhaps in clergy-counselor dialogue groups or in meetings between counselors and spiritual directors. If a counselor does not have regular connections suitable for a particular referral, the counselor can get some initial suggestions from the client, for example, the client's rabbi or a theology instructor. With the client's permission and assurances of confidentiality, the counselor should have an initial discussion to assess the suitability of the referral source for helping the client in a manner consistent with the client's counseling progress. This can be a sensitive issue that the counselor must handle with care; but the counselor has a responsibility not to refer the client to a religious specialist whose views or approaches to spirituality/religion may hurt rather than help a client. If the referral source turns out to be appropriate, the counselor can use this discussion to lay the groundwork for professional collaboration for the client's benefit.

6. The counselor obtains the client's permission (usually written) to consult with a clergyperson or religious specialist. The counselor protects the client's right to confidentiality by making the consultation anonymous or insisting on confidentiality with the consultant.

7. If the referral results in a continuing helping relationship, the counselor should check with the client and the referral source from time to time to ensure that the counselor and religious specialist are working in tandem for the client's benefit.

The counselor may also receive a referral from a clergyperson, religious specialist, or spiritual director (Christian, 1990). As with referrals from counselor to clergy, the counselor should receive the referral in a collegial, collaborative spirit, note the requirements for confidentiality, discuss the reason for the referral and any connections between spiritual/religious issues and the client's problem behavior and concerns, and establish an expectation for mutual consultation as necessary for the client.

Spiritual Direction

Spiritual direction is a traditional term in the Christian religion, especially Catholicism, Orthodoxy, and Anglicanism, referring to a formal, one-to-one relationship in which a person receives help and facilitation in the process of spiritual formation, that is, the deepening of one's relationship with God and related spiritual practices (e.g., prayer, meditation, fasting, charitable attitudes and behavior) (G. G. May, 1982a). There is certainly overlap between the spiritual and psychological/developmental concerns of spiritual direction and counseling/psychotherapy (Julian, 1992; G. G. May, 1982a). However, the two also diverge in content, with spiritual direction focusing on explicitly spiritual experiences (e.g., prayer and one's sense of God) and counseling/psychotherapy focusing on attitudinal, cognitive, and behavioral dynamics. They also differ in intent, with the former concentrating on the deepening relationship with God and experience of divine reality and the latter focusing on healthy, satisfying psychological development and behavior.

The overlap between spiritual and developmental/psychological concerns and dynamics means that counselors can benefit clients by understanding and working competently with spiritual/religious issues insofar as these issues are significantly intertwined with the developmental/psychological issues of counseling. However, the *differences* between these domains also mean that the counselor can help the client by appreciating the integrity of serious spiritual seekers' spiritual journeys and recognizing the complementary role that formal spiritual direction plays for some persons in their full, spiritual-psychosocial development.

Conclusion

Counselors' caring and competent attention to spirituality and religion opens them to a dimension of being, thinking, feeling, and living that for many clients is not only important in itself but may also be interwoven with the issues and concerns that clients bring to counseling. This book has attempted to describe in theory and practice the many ways that spirituality and religion influence clients' lives, highlighting procedures that counselors and psychotherapists can use to work helpfully with the spiritual/religious dimension in counseling.

However, a single book is necessarily limited in presenting the many counseling approaches available for working with the large and diverse universe of spiritual/religious belief and practice. The counselor-reader, including experienced professionals and counselors/therapists-in-training, is encouraged to continue study of the large number of listed references that have informed the writing of this book. With this study, and in consultation and supervision with other colleagues interested and experienced in the spiritual/religious dimension of counseling, counselors can build knowledgeable expertise in direct practice, collaboration, consultation, and referral for clients whose spirituality and religion may be an important element in their therapeutic improvement and life development.

References

Acosta, S., Groh, L. S., Hernandez, G., & Rathbone, B. (1990). Counseling Hispanics in the United States. *The Journal of Pastoral Care, 44*, 33–41.

Albanese, C. L. (1992). *America: Religions and religion* (2nd ed.). Belmont, CA: Wadsworth.

Albany, A. P. (1984). Clinical implications of religious loyalties: A contextual view. *Counseling and Values, 28*, 128–133.

Alcoholics Anonymous World Services. (1992). *Twelve steps and twelve traditions.* New York: Author. (Original work published 1952)

Allen, H. E. (1991). Marriage and family counseling with working class Blacks. *Urban Mission, 9*, 51–58.

Allport, G. W. (1950). *The individual and his religion.* New York: Macmillan.

Allport, G. W. (1966). The religious context of prejudice. *Journal for the Scientific Study of Religion, 5*, 447–457.

Allport, G. W., & Ross, J. M. (1967). Personal religious orientation and prejudice. *Journal of Personality and Social Psychology, 5*, 432–443.

American Counseling Association. (1992). *Ethical and legal issues in counseling.* Alexandria, VA: Author.

American Counseling Association. (1994, September). Proposed revision to the American Counseling Association Code of Ethics and Standards of Practice. *Counseling Today, 37*(3), 20–28.

American Psychiatric Association. (1986). *Diagnostic and statistical manual of mental disorders: DSM-III-R* (3rd ed. rev.). Washington, DC: Author.

American Psychiatric Association. (1994). *Diagnostic and statistical manual of mental disorders: DSM-IV* (4th ed.). Washington, DC: Author.

American Psychological Association. (1992). *Ethical principles of psychologists and code of conduct.* Washington, DC: Author.

Argyle, M., & Beit-Hallahmi, B. (1975). *The social psychology of religion.* London: Routledge & Kegan Paul. (Original work published 1958)

Assagioli, R. (1971). *Psychosynthesis: A manual of principles and techniques.* New York: Viking. (Original work published 1965)

Assagioli, R. (1993). *Transpersonal development: The dimension beyond psychosynthesis.* San Francisco: Aquarian.

Aziz, (1990). C. G. *Jung's psychology of religion and synchronicity.* Albany, NY: State University of New York.

Badri, M. B. (1979). *The dilemma of Muslim psychologists.* London: MWH.

Bagby, I. (Ed.). (1994). *Muslim resource guide.* Fountain Valley, CA: Islamic Resource Institute.

Bainbridge, W. S., & Stark, R. (1992). Client and audience cults in America. In M. E. Marty (Ed.), *Modern American Protestantism: New and intense movements* (pp. 292–307). New York: K. G. Saur.

Balk, D. (1983). How teenagers cope with sibling death: Some implications for school counselors. *School Counselor, 31,* 150–158.

Barnes, M., Doyle, D., & Johnson, B. (1989). The formulation of a Fowler scale: An empirical assessment among Catholics. *Review of Religious Research, 30,* 412–420.

Barnhouse, R. T. (1986). How to evaluate patients' religious ideation. In L. Robinson (Ed.), *Psychiatry and religion: Overlapping concerns* (pp. 90–105). Washington, DC: American Psychiatric Press.

Bassett, R. L., Camplin, W., Humphrey, D., Dorr, C., Biggs, S., Distaffen, R., Doxtator, I., Flaherty, M., Hunsberger, P. J., Poage, R., & Thompson, H. (1990). Measuring Christian maturity: A comparison of several scales. *Journal of Psychology and Christianity, 9,* 84–93.

Bassett, R. L., Sadler, R. D., Kobischen, E. E., Skiff, D. M., Merrill, I. J., Atwater, B. J., & Livermore, P. W. (1981). The Shepherd Scale: Separating the sheep from the goats. *Journal of Psychology and Theology, 9,* 335–351.

Batson, C. D., & Ventis, W. L. (1982). *The religious experience.* New York: Oxford University Press.

Beck, A. T., Rush, J., Shaw, B., & Emery, G. (1979). *Cognitive therapy of depression.* New York: Guilford.

Beit-Hallahmi, B. (1989). *Prolegomena to the psychology of religion.* Lewisburg, PA: Bucknell University Press.

Benner, D. G. (1988). *Psychotherapy and the spiritual quest.* Grand Rapids, MI: Baker Book House.

Benner, D. G. (1991). *Counselling as a spiritual process.* Oxford, UK: Clinical Theology Association.

Benson, H. (1993). The relaxation response. In D. Goleman & J. Gurin (Eds.), *Mind-body medicine: How to use your mind for better health* (pp. 233–257). Yonkers, NY: Consumer Reports Books.

Benson, P., & Spilka, B. (1973). God image as a function of self-esteem and locus of control. *Journal for the Scientific Study of Religion, 12,* 297–310.

Bepko, C., & Krestan, J-A. (1990). *Too good for her own good: Breaking free from the burden of female responsibility.* New York: Harper & Row.

Bergin, A. E. (1980a). Psychotherapy and religious values. *Journal of Consulting and Clinical Psychology, 48,* 95–105.

Bergin, A. E. (1980b). Religious and humanistic values: A reply to Ellis and Walls. *Journal of Consulting and Clinical Psychology, 48,* 642–645.

Bergin, A. E. (1983). Religiosity and mental health: A critical reevaluation and meta-analysis. *Professional Psychology: Research and Practice, 14,* 170–184.

Bergin, A. E. (1991). Values and religious issues in psychotherapy and mental health. *The American Psychologist, 46,* 394–413.

Bergin, A. E., & Jensen, J. P. (1990). Religiosity of psychotherapists: A national survey. *Psychotherapy*, 27, 3–7.

Bergin, A. E., Masters, K. S., & Richards, P. S. (1987). Religiousness and mental health reconsidered: A study of an intrinsically religious sample. *Journal of Counseling Psychology*, 34, 197–204.

Bergin, A. E., & Payne, I. R. (1991). Proposed agenda for a spiritual strategy in personality and psychotherapy. *Journal of Psychology and Christianity*, 10, 197–210.

Bergin, A. E., Stinchfield, R. D., Gaskin, T. A., Masters, K. S., & Sullivan, C. E. (1988). Religious life-styles and mental health: An exploratory study. *Journal of Counseling Psychology*, 35, 91–98.

Berliner, P. M. (1992). Soul healing: A model of feminist therapy. *Counseling and Values*, 37, 2–15.

Beutler, L. E., & Bergan, J. (1991). Value change in counseling and psychotherapy: A search for scientific credibility. *Journal of Counseling Psychology*, 38, 16–24.

Beutler, L. E., Crago, M., & Arizmendi, T. G. (1986). Therapist variables in psychotherapy process and outcome. In S. L. Garfield & A. E. Bergin (Eds.), *Handbook of psychotherapy and behavior change* (3rd ed.). New York: John Wiley & Sons.

Bordin, E. S. (1975). The generalizability of the psychoanalytic concept of the working alliance. *Psychotherapy: Theory, Research and, Practice*, 16, 252–260.

Bosley, G. M., & Cook, A. S. (1993). Therapeutic aspects of funeral ritual: A thematic analysis. *Journal of Family Therapy*, 4(4), 69–84.

Bowlby-West, L. (1983). The impact of death on the family system. *Journal of Family Therapy*, 5, 279–294.

Bradley, J. E. (1988). The bittersweet life of Jimmy Halloran. *Family Therapy Networker*, 12, 45–48, 50–51, 82–89.

Briggs, D. (1993, May 1). Mainstream religions loath to accept Islam, leaders say. *The Washington Post*, p. G10.

Brink, T. L. (1985). The role of religion in later life: A case of consolation and forgiveness. *Journal of Pastoral Counseling*, 4, 22–25.

Brohi, A. K. (1987). The spiritual dimension of prayer. In S. H. Nasr (Ed.), *Islamic spirituality* (pp. 131–143). New York: Crossroad.

Brown, D. P. (1986). The stages of meditation in cross-cultural perspective. In K. Wilber, J. Engler, & D. P. Brown, *Transformations of consciousness* (pp. 219–283). Boston: New Science Library/Shambhala.

Brown, D. P., & Engler, J. (1986). The stages of mindfulness meditation: A validation study. Part II: Discussion. In K. Wilber, J. Engler, & D. P. Brown, *Transformations of consciousness* (pp. 193–217). Boston: New Science Library/Shambhala.

Brown, H. P., Jr., & Peterson, J. H., Jr. (1989). Refining the BASIC-ISs: A psychospiritual approach to the comprehensive patient treatment of drug dependency. *Alcoholism Treatment Quarterly*, 6(3/4), 27–61.

Brown, H. P., Jr., & Peterson, J. H., Jr. (1991). Assessing spirituality in addiction treatment and follow-up: Development of the Brown-Peterson Recovery Progress Inventory (B-PRPI). *Alcoholism Treatment Quarterly*, 8(2), 21–50.

Brown, H. P., Peterson, J. H., & Cunningham. (1988a). An individualized behavioral approach to spiritual development for the recovering alcoholic/addict. *Alcoholism Treatment Quarterly, 5*(1/2), 177–196.

Brown, H. P., Peterson, J. H., & Cunningham. (1988b). Rationale and theoretical basis for a behavioral/cognitive approach to spirituality. *Alcoholism Treatment Quarterly, 5*(1/2), 47–59.

Brown, L. (1945). *The wisdom of Israel.* New York: The Modern Library.

Browning, C., Reynolds, A. L., & Dworkin, S. H. (1991). Affirmative psychotherapy for lesbian women. *The Counseling Psychologist, 19*, 177–196.

Bruner, J. (1990). *Acts of meaning.* Cambridge, MA: Harvard University.

Buber, M. (1937). *I and thou* (R. G. Smith, Trans.). Edinburgh: T. & T. Clark.

Buber, M. (1952). Religion and modern thinking. In *The eclipse of God: Studies in the relation between religion and philosophy.* New York: Harper.

Bullis, R. K., & Harrigan, M. P. (1992). Religious denominational policies on sexuality. *Families in Society: The Journal of Contemporary Human Services, 73,* 304–312.

Burton, L. A. (Ed.). (1992). *Religion and the family: When God helps.* New York: Haworth.

Butman, R. E. (1990). The assessment of religious development: Some possible options. *Journal of Psychology and Christianity, 9*(2), 14–26.

Buxton, M. E., Smith, D. E., & Seymour, R. B. (1987). Spirituality and other points of resistance to the 12-step recovery process. *Journal of Psychoactive Drugs, 19*, 275–286.

Campbell, D. (1992). *Campbell Interest and Skill Survey.* Minneapolis, MN: NCS Assessments.

Campbell, V. L. (1990). A model for using tests in counseling. In C. E. Watkins, Jr. & V. L. Campbell, *Testing in counseling practice* (pp. 1–7). Hillsdale, NJ: Lawrence Erlbaum.

Canda, E. R. (1990). An holistic approach to prayer for social work practice. *Social Thought, 16*(3), 3–13.

Caprio, B., & Hedberg, T. M. (1986). *Coming home: A handbook for exploring the sanctuary within.* Mahwah, NJ: Paulist Press.

Carkhuff, R. R. (1969). *Helping and human relations (Vols. 1 & 2).* New York: Holt, Rinehart, and Winston.

Carkhuff, R. R. (1987). *The art of helping VI.* Amherst, MA: Human Resource Development Press.

Carlsen, M. B. (1988). *Meaning-making: Therapeutic processes in adult development.* New York: Norton.

Carmichael, K. D. (1993). Counseling the cult-involved student: Guidelines and suggestions. *The School Counselor, 41*, 5–8.

Carmody, D. L., & Carmody, J. T. (1990). *Prayer in world religions.* Maryknoll, NY: Orbis.

Carnegie Corporation. (1987–1988). Black churches: Can they strengthen the Black family? *Carnegie Quarterly, 33*, 1–7.

Carpenito, L. J. (1993). *Handbook of nursing diagnosis.* Philadelphia: J. B. Lippincott.

Carrington, P. (1993). Modern forms of mediation. In P. M. Lehrer & R. Woolfolk (Eds.), *Principles and practice of stress management* (pp. 139–168). New York: Guilford.

Carson, V. B. (1989). *Spiritual dimensions of nursing practice*. Philadelphia: W. B. Saunders.

Cashdan, S. (1988). *Object-relations therapy: Using the relationship*. New York: Norton.

Chalfant, H. P., Heller, P. L., Roberts, A., Briones, D., Aguirre-Hochbaum, S., & Farr, W. (1990). The clergy as a resource for those encountering psychological distress. *Review of Religious Research, 31*, 305–313.

Chandler, C. K., Holden, J. M., & Kolander, C. A. (1992). Counseling for spiritual wellness: Theory and practice. *Journal of Counseling and Development, 71*, 168–175.

Chandler, R. (1988). *Understanding the new age*. Dallas, TX: Word Publishing.

Chaplin, J. (1988). *Feminist counselling in action*. Newbury Park, CA: Sage.

Christian, R. (1990). Making effective referrals. *Leadership, 11*, 102–104.

Chusmir, L. H., & Koberg, C. S. (1988). Religion and attitudes toward work: A new look at an old question. *Journal of Organizational Behavior, 9*, 251–262.

Clarke, J. J. (1992). *In search of Jung: Historical and philosophical enquiries*. London: Routledge.

Coles, R. (1990). *The spiritual life of children*. Boston: Houghton Mifflin.

Collins, C., & Frantz, D. (1994). Let us prey. *Modern Maturity, 37*(3), 22–26, 28–32.

Combs, A. W. (1989). *A theory of therapy: Guidelines for counseling practice*. Newbury Park, CA: Sage.

Comstock, G. D. (1993). *Gay theology without apology*. Cleveland, OH: Pilgrim.

Corbett, J. M. (1990). *Religion in America*. Englewood Cliffs, NJ: Prentice-Hall.

Corey, M. S., & Corey, G. (1992). *Groups: Process & practice* (4th ed.). Pacific Grove, CA: Brooks/Cole.

Cormier, W. H., & Cormier, L. S. (1991). *Interviewing strategies for helpers: Fundamental skills and cognitive behavioral interventions* (3rd ed.). Pacific Grove, CA: Brooks/Cole.

Costa, L., & Holliday, D. (1994). Helping children cope with the death of a parent. *Elementary School Guidance & Counseling, 28*, 206–213.

Craigie, F. C., & Tan, S-Y. (1989). Changing resistant assumptions in Christian cognitive-behavioral therapy. *Journal of Psychology and Theology, 17*, 93–100.

Cunin, B., Cunin, B., & Cunin, S. (1992). Psychotherapy with Orthodox Jewish patients: On clarifying distortions and conflicts. *Journal of Psychology and Judaism, 16*, 123–131.

Dambort, F., & Reep, D. C. (1993). Overview of feminist therapy: Treatment of choice for contemporary women. *The Journal of Training & Practice in Professional Psychology, 7*, 10–25.

Daniels, M. (1992). *Self-discovery the Jungian way: The watchword technique*. London: Routledge.

Davenport, D. S. (1991). The functions of anger and forgiveness: Guidelines for psychotherapy with victims. *Psychotherapy, 28*, 140–144.

Davies, P. (1992). *The mind of god: The scientific basis for a rational world.* New York: Simon & Schuster.

Davis, J. (1914). *Moral and vocational guidance.* Boston: Ginn.

Davis, Ju. (1988). Mazel tov: The Bar Mitzvah—a multigenerational ritual of change and continuity. In E. Imber-Black, J. Roberts, & R. A. Whiting, *Rituals in families and family therapy* (pp. 177–208). New York: Norton.

Deikman, A. J. (1990). *The wrong way home: Uncovering the patterns of cult behavior in American society.* Boston: Beacon.

Derlega, V. J., Hendrick, S. S., Winstead, B. A., & Berg, J. H. (1991). *Psychotherapy as a personal relationship.* New York: Guilford.

Dersheimer, R. A. (1990). *Counseling the bereaved.* New York: Pergamon.

DeStefano, T. J., & Richardson, P. (1992). The relationship of paper-and-pencil wellness measures to objective physiological indexes. *Journal of Counseling and Development, 71,* 226–230.

DiBlasio, F. A., & Benda, B. B. (1992). Practitioners, religion, and the use of forgiveness in the clinical setting. *Journal of Psychology and Christianity, 11,* 181–187.

DiBlasio, F. A., & Proctor, J. H. (1993). Therapists and the clinical use of forgiveness. *The American Journal of Family Therapy, 21,* 175–184.

Dittes, J. E. (1969). The psychology of religion. In G. Lindzey & E. Aronson (Eds.), *The handbook of social psychology* (vol. 5) (pp. 602–659). Reading, MA: Addison-Wesley.

Donahue, M. J. (1985). Intrinsic and extrinsic religiousness: Review and meta-analysis. *Journal of Personality and Social Psychology, 48,* 400–419.

Dossey, L. (1993). *Healing words: The power of prayer and the practice of medicine.* San Francisco: HarperCollins.

Dworkin, S. H., & Gutiérrez, F. J. (Eds.). (1992). *Counseling gay men and lesbians: Journey to the end of the rainbow.* Alexandria, VA: American Counseling Association.

Edwards, G. R. (1984). *Gay/lesbian liberation: A biblical perspective.* New York: Pilgrim.

Egan, G. (1994). *The skilled helper: A systematic approach to effective helping* (5th ed.). Pacific Grove, CA: Brooks/Cole.

Eimer, K. W. (1989). The assessment and treatment of the religiously concerned psychiatric patient. *The Journal of Pastoral Care, 43,* 231–241.

Eklin C. H., & Roehlkepartain, E. C. (1992). The faith factor: What role can churches play in at-risk prevention. *Search Institute Source, 8*(1), pp. 1–3.

Eliade, M., & Couliano, I. P. (1991). *The Eliade guide to world religions.* San Francisco: HarperCollins.

Elkind, D. (1970). The origins of religion in the child. *Review of Religious Research, 12,* 35–42.

Elkind, D. (1978). *The child's reality: Three developmental themes.* Hillsdale, NJ: Lawrence Erlbaum.

Elkins, D. N., Hedstrom, L. J., Hughes, L. L., Leaf, J. A., & Saunders, C. (1988). Toward a humanistic-phenomenological spirituality. *Journal of Humanistic Psychology, 28,* 5–18.

Ellis, A. (1980). Psychotherapy and atheistic values: A response to A. E. Bergin's "Psychotherapy and Religious Values." *Journal of Consulting and Clinical Psychology, 48,* 635–639.

Ellis, A. (1985). Why Alcoholics Anonymous is probably doing more harm than good by its insistence on a higher power. *Employee Assistance Quarterly, 1,* 95–97.

Ellis, A. (1986). Fanaticism that may lead to a nuclear holocaust: The contributions of scientific counseling and psychotherapy. *Journal of Counseling and Development, 65,* 146–151.

Ellis, A. (1989a). Dangers of transpersonal psychology: A reply to Ken Wilber. *Journal of Counseling and Development, 67,* 336–337.

Ellis, A. (1989b). History of cognition in psychotherapy. In A. Freeman, K. M. Simon, L. E. Beutler, & H. Arkowitz (Eds.), *Comprehensive handbook of cognitive therapy* (pp. 5–19). New York: Plenum.

Ellison, C. G. (1991). Religious involvement and subjective well-being. *Journal of Health and Social Behavior, 32,* 80–99.

Ellison, C. W. (1983). Spiritual well-being: Conceptualization and measurement. *Journal of Psychology and Theology, 11,* 330–340.

Ellison, C. W. (1994). *Spiritual Well-Being Scale.* Nyack, NY: Life Advance.

Ellison, C. W., & Smith, J. (1991). Toward an integrative measure of health and well-being. *Journal of Psychology and Theology, 19,* 35–48.

Elzerman, J. H., & Bolvin, M. J. (1987). The assessment of Christian maturity, personality, and psychopathology among college students. *Journal of Psychology and Christianity, 6,* 50–64.

Enns, C. Z. (1993). Twenty years of feminist counseling and therapy: From naming biases to implementing multifaceted practice. *The Counseling Psychologist, 21,* 3–87.

Enright, R. D., Eastin, D. L., Golden, S., Sarinopoulos, I., & Freedman, S. (1992). Interpersonal forgiveness within the helping professions: An attempt to resolve differences of opinion. *Counseling and Values, 36,* 84–103.

Erikson, E. H. (1958). *Young man Luther: A study in psychoanalysis and history.* New York: Norton.

Erikson, E. H. (1964). *Insight and responsibility: Lectures on the ethical implication of psychoanalytic insight.* New York: Norton.

Erikson, E. H. (1968). *Identity: Youth and crisis.* New York: Norton.

Faiver, C. M., & O'Brien, E. M. (1993). Assessment of religious beliefs form. *Counseling and Values, 37,* 176–178.

Farran, C. J., Fitchett, G., Quiring-Emblen, J. D., & Burck, R. (1989). Development of a model for spiritual assessment and intervention. *Journal of Religion and Health, 28,* 185–194.

Fassinger, R. E. (1991). The hidden minority: Issues and challenges in working with lesbian women and gay men. *The Counseling Psychologist, 19,* 157–176.

Feinsilver, M. (1960). *In search of religious maturity.* Yellow Springs, OH: Antioch Press.

Fields, R. (1992). *How the swans came to the lake: A narrative history of Buddhism in America* (3rd ed.). Boston: Shambhala.

Fleischman, P. R. (1986). Release: A religious and psychotherapeutic issue. *The Journal of Transpersonal Psychology, 18,* 99–122.

Fleischman, P. R. (1989). *The healing spirit: Explorations in religion and psychotherapy*. New York: Paragon House.

Fortunato, J. E. (1987). *AIDS, the spiritual dilemma*. San Francisco: Perennial Library, Harper & Row.

Foster, R. J. (1992). *Prayer: Finding the heart's true home*. San Francisco: HarperCollins.

Fowler, J. (1981). *Stages of faith: The psychology of human development and the quest for meaning*. San Francisco: Harper & Row.

Fowler, J. (1991). Stages in faith consciousness. In F. K. Oser & W. G. Scarlett (Eds.), Religious development in childhood and adolescence [Special issue]. *New Directions for Child Development, 52,* 27–45.

Frank, J. D. (1973). *Persuasion and healing: A comparative study of psychotherapy* (rev. ed.). Baltimore: The Johns Hopkins University Press.

Frank, J. D. (1985). Therapeutic components shared by all. In M. J. Mahoney & A. Freeman (Eds.), *Cognition and psychotherapy* (pp. 49–80). New York: Plenum.

Frankl, V. E. (1984). *Man's search for meaning*. New York: Touchstone Book-Simon and Schuster. (Original work published 1946)

Franks, K., Templer., D. I., Cappelletty, G. G., & Kauffman, I. (1990). Exploration of death anxiety as a function of religious variables in gay men with and without AIDS. *Omega Journal of Death and Dying, 22,* 43–50.

Freud, S. (1950). *Totem and taboo*. New York: Norton. (Original work published 1913)

Freud, S. (1958). *Moses and monotheism*. New York: Vintage. (Original work published 1939)

Freud, S. (1962). *Civilization and its discontents*. New York: Norton. (Original work published 1930)

Freud, S. (1964). *The future of an illusion*. Garden City, NY: Anchor. (Original work published 1927)

Friedman, M. (1992). *Religion and psychology: A dialogical approach*. New York: Paragon House.

Fromm, E. (1947). *Man for himself: An inquiry into the psychology of ethics*. New York: Rinehart.

Fromm, E. (1950). *Psychoanalysis and religion*. New Haven, CT: Yale University Press.

Fromm, E. (1992). *The art of being*. New York: Continuum.

Galanter, M. (Ed.). (1989a). *Cults and new religious movements*. Washington: American Psychiatric Association.

Galanter, M. (1989b). Cults and new religious movements. In M. Galanter (Ed.), *Cults and new religious movements* (pp. 25–40). Washington: American Psychiatric Association.

Galanter, M. (1989c). *Cults: Faith, healing, and coercion*. New York: Oxford University Press.

Gallup, G., Jr., & Castelli, J. (1989). *The people's religion: American faith in the 90s*. New York: Macmillan.

Gallup, G. H., Jr., & Bezilla, R. (1994, January 22). More find religion important. *The Washington Post*, p. G10.

Garnets, L., Hancock, K. A., Cochran, S. D., Goodchilds, J. & Peplau, L. A. (1991). Issues in psychotherapy with lesbians and gay men. *American Psychologist, 46,* 964–972.

Gartner, J., Larson, D. B., & Allen, G. D. (1991). Religious commitment and mental health: A review of empirical literature. *Journal of Psychology and Theology, 19,* 6–25.

Gawler, I. (1989). *Peace of mind: How you can learn to meditate and use the power of your mind.* Garden City Park, NY: Avery.

Gelso, C. J., & Carter, J. A. (1985). The relationship in counseling and psychotherapy. *The Counseling Psychologist, 13*(5), 155–243.

Gelso, C. J., & Carter, J. A. (1994). Components of the psychotherapy relationship: Their interaction and unfolding during treatment. *Journal of Counseling Psychology, 41,* 296–306.

Genia, V. (1990). Religious development: A synthesis and reformulation. *Journal of Religion and Health, 29,* 85–99.

Genia, V. (1992). Religious imagery of a schizotypal patient. *Journal of Religion and Health, 31,* 317–326.

Genia, V. (1994). Secular psychotherapists and religious clients: Professional considerations and recommendations. *Journal of Counseling and Development, 72,* 395–398.

Genia, V. (in press). *Counseling and psychotherapy of religious clients: A developmental approach.* Westport, CT: Praeger.

Ghayur, M. A. (1993). Muslims in the United States: Settlers and visitors. In M. E. Marty (Ed.), *Modern American Protestantism: New and intense movements* (pp. 264–277). New York: K. G. Saur.

Gibson, W. C., & Herron, W. G. (1990). Psychotherapists' beliefs and their perception of the psychotherapy process. *Psychological Reports, 66,* 3–9.

Giglio, J. (1993). The impact of patients' and therapists' religious values on psychotherapy. *Hospital and Community Psychiatry, 44,* 768–771.

Gilbert, L. A. (1992). Gender and counseling psychology: Current knowledge and directions for research and social action. In S. D. Brown & R. W. Lent (Eds.), *Handbook of counseling psychology* (2nd ed.) (pp. 383–416). New York: John Wiley & Sons.

Gilbert, L. A. (1993). The third decade of feminist therapy and the personal is still political. *The Counseling Psychologist, 21,* 97–102.

Goldman, L. (1990). Qualitative assessment. *The Counseling Psychologist, 18,* 205–213.

Goleman, D. (1988). *The meditative mind.* Los Angeles: Tarcher.

Gorsuch, R. L. (1988). Psychology of religion. *Annual Review of Psychology, 39,* 201–221.

Gorsuch, R. L., & McPherson, S. E. (1989). Intrinsic/extrinsic measurement: I/E-revised and single-item scales. *Journal for the Scientific Study of Religion, 28,* 348–354.

Gorsuch, R. L., & Smith, C. G. (1983). Attributions of responsibility to God: An interaction of religious belief and outcomes. *Journal for the Scientific Study of Religion, 22,* 340–352.

Greenberg, D. (1987). The behavioral treatment of religious compulsions. *Journal of Psychology and Judaism, 11,* 41–47.

Griffin, G. A., Gorsuch, R. L., & Davis, A-L. (1987). A cross-cultural investigation of religious orientation, social norms, and prejudice. *Journal for the Scientific Study of Religion, 26*, 358–365.

Griffith, J. L. (1986). Employing the God-family relationship in therapy with religious families. *Family Process, 25*, 609–618.

Grof, S., & Grof, C. (1989). *Spiritual emergency: When personal transformation becomes a crisis.* Los Angeles: Tarcher.

Grossman, B. R. (1992). Faith and personal development: A renewed link for Judaism. *Journal of Psychology and Judaism, 16*, 19–29.

Guidano, V. F. (1991). *The self in process: Toward a post-rationalist cognitive therapy.* New York: Guilford.

Hadaway, C. K., Marler, P. L., & Chaves, M. (1993). What the polls don't show: A closer look at U.S. church attendance. *American Sociological Review, 58*, 741–752.

Haddad, Y. Y. , & Lummis, A. T. (1987). *Islamic values in the United States.* New York: Oxford University Press.

Haldeman, D. C. (1994). The practice and ethics of sexual orientation conversion therapy. *Journal of Consulting & Clinical Psychology, 62*, 221–227.

Haneef, S. (1979). *What everyone should know about Islam and Muslims.* Chicago: Kazi Publications.

Harris, M. (1989). *Dance of the spirit: The seven steps of women's spirituality.* New York: Bantam.

Harvey, J. F. (1993). Homosexuality: Challenges for change and and reorientation [Special issue]. *The Journal of Pastoral Counseling, 28.*

Hathaway, W. L., & Pargament, K. I. (1990). Intrinsic religiousness, religious coping, and psychosocial competence: A covariance structure analysis. *Journal for the Scientific Study of Religion, 29*, 323–441.

Haughen, M. L., Tyler, J. D., & Clark, J. A. (1991). Mental health values of psychotherapists: How psychologists, psychiatrists, psychoanalysts, and social workers conceptualize good mental health. *Counseling and Values, 36*, 24–36.

Hay, M. W. (1989). Principles of building assessment tools. *The American Journal of Hospice Care, 6*, 25–31.

Heisig, J. W. (1979). *Imago dei.* Lewisburg, PA: Bucknell University.

Herlihy, B., & Golden, L. (1990). *AACD ethical standards casebook.* Alexandria, VA: American Counseling Association.

Hillowe, B. V. (1985). The effect of religiosity of therapist and patient on clinical judgement of patients. (Doctoral dissertation, Adelphi University, 1985). *Dissertation Abstracts International, 46*, 1687B.

Hoare, C. H., & Nashman, H. W. (1994). *AIDS care in six Washington, D. C. area hospices: Satisfactions and stresses among professional caregivers* (Occasional Paper 12). Washington, DC: George Washington University, Center for Washington Area Studies.

Hood, A. B., & Johnson, R. W. (1991). *Assessment in counseling: A guide to the use of psychological assessment procedures.* Alexandria, VA: American Counseling Association.

Houts, A. C., & Graham, K. (1986). Can religion make you crazy? Impact of client and therapist religious values on clinical judgments. *Journal of Consulting and Clinical Psychology, 54*, 267–271.

Human Development Study Group. (1991). Five points on the construct of forgiveness with psychotherapy. *Psychotherapy, 28*, 493–496.

Humphreys, K. (1993). Psychotherapy and the Twelve Step approach for substance abusers: The limits of integration. *Psychotherapy, 30*, 207–213.

Idler, E. L., & Kasl, S. V. (1992). Religion, disability, depression, and the timing of death. *American Journal of Sociology. 97*, 1052–1079.

Imber-Black, E., & Roberts, J. (1992). *Rituals for our times: Celebrating, healing, and changing our lives and our relationships.* New York: HarperCollins.

Imber-Black, E., Roberts, J, & Whiting, R. A. (1988). *Rituals in families and family therapy.* New York: Norton.

Imbrie, G. S. (1985). Untwisting the illusion. *Journal of Orthomolecular Psychiatry, 14*, 143–145.

Ingersoll, R. E. (1994). Spirituality, religion, and counseling: Dimensions and relationships. *Counseling and Values, 38*, 98–111.

Ingram, B. L., & Lowe, D. (1989). Counseling activities and referral practices of rabbis. *Journal of Psychology and Judaism, 13*, 133–148.

Ivey, A. E. (1986). *Developmental therapy: Theory into practice.* San Francisco: Jossey-Bass.

Ivey, A. E. (1994). *Intentional interviewing and counseling: Facilitating client development in a multicultural society* (3rd ed.). Pacific Grove, CA: Brooks/Cole.

Iwata, E. (1993, December 26). Some executives are trying to make companies heed a higher authority. *The Washington Post*, p. H2.

Jacoby, M. (1991). *Shame and the origins of self-esteem: A Jungian approach.* London: Routledge.

Jacques, F. (1991). *Subjectivity and difference.* (A. Rothwell, Trans.). New Haven, CT: Yale University Press. (Original work published 1982)

Jafari, M. F. (1993). Counseling values and objectives: A comparison of Western and Islamic perspectives. *The American Journal of Islamic Social Studies, 3*, 326–339.

James, W. (1961). *The varieties of religious experience.* New York: Macmillan Collier Books. (Original work published 1902)

Jensen, J. P., & Bergin, A. E. (1988). Mental health values of professional therapists: A national interdisciplinary survey. *Professional Psychology: Research and Practice, 19*, 290–297.

Johnson, R. A., Sandler, K. R., & Griffin-Shelley, E. (1987). Spirituality and the regulation of self-esteem. *Alcoholism Treatment Quarterly, 4*, 1–12.

Johnson, S. E. (1987). *After a child dies: Counseling bereaved families.* New York: Springer.

Johnson, W. B., Devries, R., Ridley, C. R., Pettorini, D., & Peterson. (1994). The comparative efficacy of Christian and secular rational-emotive therapy with Christian clients. *Journal of Psychology and Theology, 22*, 130–140.

Johnson, W. B. & Ridley, C. R. (1992). Brief Christian and non-Christian rational-emotive therapy with depressed Christian clients: An exploratory study. *Counseling and Values, 36*, 220–229.

Jones, J. W. (1991). *Contemporary psychoanalysis and religion*. New Haven, CT: Yale University.

Jones, S. L. (1994). A constructive relationship for religion with the science and profession of psychology: Perhaps the boldest model yet. *American Psychologist, 49*, 184–199.

Julian, R. (1992). The practice of psychotherapy and spiritual direction. *Journal of Religion and Health, 31*, 309–315.

Jung, C. G. (1933). *Modern man in search of a soul*. New York: Harcourt, Brace & World-Harvest.

Jung, C. G. (1966). *Psychology and religion*. New Haven, CN: Yale University Press. (Original work published 1938)

Jung, C. G. (1968). *The archetypes and the collective unconscious* (2nd ed.). London: Routledge & Kegan Paul. (Revised German edition 1954)

Jung, C. G. (1977). *The practice of psychotherapy*. Princeton, NJ: Princeton University. (Original work published 1954)

Jung, C. G. (1981). *The structure and dynamics of the psyche*. Princeton, NJ: Princeton University. (Original work published 1960)

Kabat-Zinn, J. (1993). Mindfulness meditation: Health benefits of an ancient Buddhist practice. In D. Goleman & J. Gurin (Eds.), *Mind-body medicine: How to use your mind for better health* (pp. 259–275). Yonkers, NY: Consumer Reports Books.

Kahn, M. (1991). *Between therapist and client*. New York: W. H. Freeman.

Kass, J. D., Friedman, R., Leserman, J., Zuttermeister, P. C., & Benson, H. (1991). Health outcomes and a new index of spiritual experience. *Journal for the Scientific Study of Religion, 30*, 203–211.

Kegan, R. (1982). *The evolving self*. Cambridge, MA: Harvard University Press.

Kelly, E. W., Jr. (1990). Counselor responsiveness to client religiousness. *Counseling and Values, 35*, 69–72.

Kelly, E. W., Jr. Religion in family therapy journals: A review and analysis. (1992). In L. A. Burton (Ed.), *When God enters the system: Religion and family therapy*. New York: Haworth.

Kelly, E. W., Jr. (1994a). *Relationship-centered counseling: An integration of art and science*. New York: Springer.

Kelly, E. W., Jr. (1994b). The role of religion and spirituality in counselor education: A national survey. *Counselor Education and Supervision, 33*, 227–237.

Kelly, E. W., Jr. (in press). Counselor values: A national survey. *Journal of Counseling and Development*.

Kelly, G. A. (1963). *A theory of personality: The psychology of personal constructs*. New York: Norton. (Original work published 1955)

Kelly, T. A. (1990). The role of values in psychotherapy: A critical review of process and outcome effects. *Clinical Psychology Review, 10*, 171–186.

Kelly, T. A., & Strupp, H. H. (1992). Patient and therapist values in psychotherapy: Perceived changes, assimilation, similarity, and outcome. *Journal of Clinical and Consulting Psychology, 60*, 34–40.

Keyser, D. J., & Sweetland, D. J. (1994). *Test critiques: (Vol. 10)*. Austin, TX: Pro-Ed.

Khantzian, E. J., & Mack, J. E. (1994). How AA works and why it's important for clinicians to understand. *Journal of Substance Abuse Treatment, 11*, 77–92.

Khouj, A. M. (1986). *The relevance of the Qur'an to human nature.* Washington: The Islamic Center.

Kierkegaard, S. (1959). *The Journals.* (A. Dru, Trans. and Ed.). London: Oxford University Press. (Original work published 1909)

Kinsolving, C. (1992, February 22). Gallup finds spiritual 'miracles' amid data. *The Washington Post*, p. B6.

Kirkpatrick, L. A., & Hood, R. W., Jr. (1990). Intrinsic-extrinsic religious orientation: The boon or bane of contemporary psychology of religion? *Journal for the Scientific Study of Religion, 29*, 442–462.

Kirschenbaum, H., & Henderson, V. L. (1989). *The Carl Rogers reader.* Boston: Houghton Mifflin.

Knox, D. H. (1985). Spirituality: A tool in the assessment and treatment of Black alcoholics and their families. *Alcoholism Treatment Quarterly, 2*, 31–44.

Kovacs, G. (1990). *The question of God in Heidegger's phenomenology.* Evanston, IL: Northwestern University Press.

Kramer, J. J., & Conoley, J. C. (1992). *The eleventh mental measurements yearbook.* Lincoln, NE: Buros Institute of Mental Measurements, University of Nebraska-Lincoln.

Kung, H. (1981). *Does God exist? An answer for today.* New York: Vintage.

Kurtz, E. (1988). *A.A.: The story.* San Francisco: Harper & Row.

Kus, R. J. (1992). Spirituality and everyday life: Experiences of gay men of Alcoholics Anonymous. *Alcoholism Treatment Quarterly, 9*, 49–66.

Lattin, D. (1993, July 17). The new seekers showing similar needs, survey says. *The Washington Post*, p. C8.

Lawrence, C. (1983). Redecision and repentance: Reframing redecision work for the religious client. *Transactional Analysis Journal, 13*, 158–162.

Lea, G. (1982). Religion, mental health, and clinical issues. *Journal of Religion and Health, 21*, 336–351.

Ledbetter, M. F., Smith, L. A., Fischer, J. D., Vosler-Hunter, W. L., & Chew, G. P. (1991). An evaluation of the construct validity of the spiritual well-being scale: A confirmatory factor analytic approach. *Journal of Psychology and Theology, 19*, 94–102.

Ledbetter, M. F., Smith, L. A., Vosler-Hunter, W. L., & Fischer, J. D. (1991). An evaluation of the clinical usefulness of the spiritual well-being scale. *Journal of Psychology and Theology. 19*, 49–55.

Lehman, C. (1993, January 30). Faith-based counseling gains favor. *The Washington Post*, pp. B7–8.

Lescoe, F. J. (1974). *Existentialism: With or without God.* New York: Alba House.

Levine, S. V. (1989). Life in the cults. In M. Galanter (Ed.), *Cults and new religious movements* (pp. 95–107). Washington: American Psychiatric Association.

Liddon, S. C. (1989). *The dual brain, religion, and the unconscious.* Buffalo, NY: Prometheus Books.

Lindenthal, J. J., Myers, J. K., Pepper, M. P., & Stern, M. S. (1970). Mental status and religious behavior. *Journal for the Scientific Study of Religion, 9*, 143–149.

Little, T. H., & Price, S. G. (1985). Assessment based on religious history in a child and adolescent service. *Cura Animarum*, *37*, 28–35.

Long, R. E., & Clark, J. M. (1992). *AIDS, God, and faith: Continuing the dialogue on constructing gay theology*. Las Colinas, TX: Monument.

Lovinger, R. J. (1990). *Religion and counseling*. New York: Continuum.

Lovinger, R. J. (1984). *Working with religious issues in therapy*. New York: Jason Aronson.

Luborsky, L., Crits-Christoph, P., Mintz, J., & Auberbach, A. (1988). *Who will benefit from psychotherapy? Predicting therapeutic outcomes*. New York: Basic Books.

Ludwick, C., & Peake, T. H. (1982). Adapting a clinical religious history format for pastoral intervention with adolescents in psychiatric treatment. *Journal of Psychology and Christianity*, *1*, 9–15.

Mahoney, M. J. (1985). Psychotherapy and human change processes. In M. J. Mahoney & A. Freeman (Eds.), *Cognition and psychotherapy* (pp. 3–48). New York: Plenum.

Malony, H. N. (1985a). Assessing religious maturity. In E. M. Stern (Ed.), *Psychotherapy and the religiously committed patient*, (pp. 25–33). New York: Haworth.

Malony, H. N. (1985b). The use of the Jewish/Christian scriptures in counseling. *Journal of Pastoral Counseling*, *20*, 116–124.

Malony, H. N. (1988). The clinical assessment of optimal religious functioning. *Review of Religious Research*, *30*, 3–17.

Malony, H. N. (1992). Religious diagnosis in evaluations of mental health. In J. F. Schumaker (Ed.), *Religion and mental health* (pp. 247–258). New York: Oxford University Press.

Malony, H. N. (1993a). The relevance of "Religious Diagnosis" for counseling. In E. L. Worthington (Ed.). *Psychotherapy and religious values* (pp. 105–120). Grand Rapids, MI: Baker Book House.

Malony, H. N. (1993b). The uses of religious assessment in counseling. In L. B. Brown (Ed.), *Religion, personality, and mental health* (pp. 16–28). New York: Plenum.

Malony, H. N. (in press). "Theological functioning" and mental health. In V. Demarinis & O. Wickstrom (Eds.), *The clinical psychology of religion*. Uppsala, Sweden: University of Uppsala.

Malony, H. N., & Spilka, B. (Eds.). (1991). *Religion in psychodynamic perspective: The contributions of Paul W. Pruyser*. New York: Oxford University Press.

Mamiya, L. H. (1993). From Black Muslim to Bilalian: The evolution of a movement. In M. E. Marty (Ed.), *Native American religion and Black Protestantism* (pp. 151–165). New York: K. G. Saur.

Marcel, G. (1960). *The mystery of being: Volume II: Faith and reality*. (R. Hague, Trans.). Chicago: Gateway. (Original work published 1951)

Martin, C., & Nichols, R. C. (1962). Personality and religious belief. *Journal of Social Psychology*, *56*, 3–8.

Marty, M. E. (Ed.). (1993). *Native American religion and Black Protestantism*. New York: K. G. Saur.

Marty, M. E., & Appleby, R. S. (1991). *Fundamentalisms observed*. Chicago: University of Chicago Press.

Marziali, E., & Alexander, L. (1991). The power of the therapeutic relationship. *American Journal of Orthopsychiatry, 61*, 383–391.

Maslow, A. (1968). *Toward a psychology of being* (2nd ed.). New York: Van Nostrand Reinhold.

Maslow, A. (1970). *Motivation and personality* (2nd ed.). New York: Harper & Row.

Maslow, A. (1980). *Religion, values, and peak-experiences.* Harmondsworth, UK: Penguin. (Original work published 1968)

Massey, D. E. (1988). *The factor analytic structure of the Religious Status Inventory.* Unpublished doctoral dissertation, Fuller Theological Seminary, Pasadena, CA.

Maton, K. I. (1989). The stress-buffering role of spiritual support: Cross-sectional and prospective investigations. *Journal for the Scientific Study of Religion, 28*, 310–323.

May, G. G. (1982a). *Care of mind, care of spirit.* San Francisco: Harper & Row.

May, G. G. (1982b). *Will and spirit: A contemplative psychology.* San Francisco: Harper & Row.

May, R. (1969). *Love and will.* New York: Norton.

Mazumdar, S., & Mazumdar, S. (1993). Sacred place and place attachment. *Journal of Environmental Psychology, 13*, 231–242.

McCullough, M. E., & Worthington, E. L. (1994). Encouraging clients to forgive people who have hurt them: Review, critique, and research prospectus. *Journal of Psychology and Theology, 22*, 3–20.

McNeill, J. J. (1988). *Taking a chance on God: Liberating theology for gays, lesbians, and their lovers, families, and friends.* Boston: Beacon.

McNeill, J. J. (1993). *The church and the homosexual* (4th ed.). Boston: Beacon.

Melton, J. G. (1993). *Encyclopedia of American religions* (4th ed.). Detroit, MI: Gale Research.

Meng, J., & Freud, E. L. (Eds.). (1963). *Psychoanalysis and faith: The letters of Sigmund Freud and Oskar Pfister* (E. Mosbacher, Trans.). New York: Basic Books. (Original work published 1963) *Merriam-Webster's Collegiate Dictionary* (10th ed.). (1993). Springfield, MA: Merriam-Webster.

Mickley, J. R., Soeken, K., & Belcher, A. (1992). Spiritual well-being, religiousness and hope among women with breast cancer. *IMAGE: Journal of Nursing Scholarship, 24*, 267–272.

Midelfort, C. F. (1962). Use of members of the family in the treatment of schizophrenia. *Family Process, 1*, 114–118.

Miller, W. R. (1988). Including clients' spiritual perspectives in cognitive-behavioral therapy. In W. R. Miller & J. E. Martin (Eds.), *Behavior therapy and religion: Integrating spiritual and behavioral approaches to change* (pp. 43–55). Newbury Park, CA: Sage.

Miller, W. R., & Martin, J. E. (1988). Spirituality and behavioral psychology: Toward integration. In W. R. Miller & J. E. Martin (Eds.), *Behavior therapy and religion: Integrating spiritual and behavioral approaches to change* (pp. 11–23). Newbury Park, CA: Sage.

Millison, M., & Dudley, J. R. (1992). Providing spiritual support: A job for all hospice professionals. *The Hospice Journal, 8*(4), 49–66.

Moberg, D. O. (1984). Subjective measures of spiritual well-being. *Review of Religious Research, 25,* 351–364.

Mooney, R. L. (1950). *Mooney Problem Check List.* San Antonio, TX: The Psychological Corporation.

Moore, J., & Herlihy, B. (1993). Grief groups for students who have had a parent die. *The School Counselor, 41,* 54–59.

Moos, R. H., & Moos, B. S. (1981). *Manual for the Family Environment Scale.* Palo Alto, CA: Consulting Psychologist Press.

Moyers, J. C. (1990). Religious issues in the psychotherapy of former fundamentalists. *Psychotherapy, 27,* 42–45.

National Wellness Institute. (1983). *Lifestyle Assessment Questionnaire* (2nd ed.). Stevens Point, WI: University of Wisconsin-Stevens Point Institute for Lifestyle Improvement.

Nelson, J. B. (1982). Religious and moral issues in working with homosexual clients. *Journal of Homosexuality, 7,* 163–175.

Norcross, J. C., & Wogan, M. (1987). Values in psychotherapy: A survey of practitioners' beliefs. *Professional Psychology: Research and Practice, 18,* 5–7.

North, J. (1987). Wrongdoing and forgiveness. *Philosophy, 62,* 499–508.

Odajnyk, V. W. (1993). *Gathering the light: A psychology of meditation.* Boston: Shambhala.

Ofman, W. V. (1976). *Affirmation and reality: Fundamentals of humanistic existential therapy and counseling.* Los Angeles: Western Psychological Services.

Oldenburg, D. (1994, November 17). The spiritual crisis mode. *The Washington Post,* p. D5.

Olson, F. (1993). The development and impact of ritual in couple counseling. *Counseling and Values, 38,* 12–20.

Ondrovik, J. & Hamilton, D. (1992). Is therapy science or religion, logic or faith? A response to Shaffer & Cozolino, Gould & Cozolino, and Friesen. *Journal of Psychology and Theology, 20,* 210–212.

Orlinsky, D. E., & Howard, K. I. (1986). Process and outcome in psychotherapy. In S. L. Garfield & A. E. Bergin (Eds.), *Handbook of psychotherapy and behavior change* (pp. 311–381). New York: Wiley.

Oser, F. K. (1991). The development of religious judgment. In F. K. Oser & W. G. Scarlett (Eds.), Religious development in childhood and adolescence [Special issue]. *New Directions for Child Development, 52,* 5–25.

Owens, S. A. A., Aoto, S. Y., & Prouty, P. S. (1993, October). *Does prayer impact life satisfaction ratings as a function of age?* Paper presented at the meeting of the society for the Scientific Study of Religion, Raleigh, NC.

Owens, S. A. A., Berg, A., & Rhone, R. L. (1993, October). *Religion, optimism, and older adults.* Paper presented at the annual meeting of Society for the Scientific Study of Religion, Raleigh, NC.

Owens, S. A. A., & McClain, S. L. (1992, November). *The effects of religion as a coping mechanism on life satisfaction of older adults.* Paper presented at the annual scientific meeting of the Gerontological Society of America, Washington, DC.

Owens, S. A. A., Ward, C. L., & McLeod-Winder, J. S. (1992, April). *The relationship between cognitive status and religiosity in older adults.* Paper presented at the meeting of Western Psychological Conference for Undergraduate Research. Santa Clara, CA.

Palombi, B. J. (1992). Psychometric properties of wellness instruments. *Journal of Counseling and Development, 71*, 221–225.

Paloutzian, R. F., & Ellison, C. W. (1982). Loneliness, spiritual well-being and the quality of life. In L. A. Peplau & D. Perlman (Eds.), *Loneliness: A sourcebook of current theory, research and therapy* (pp. 224–237). New York: Wiley-Interscience.

Pargament, K. I., Kennell, J., Hathaway, N., Grevengoed, N., Newman, J., & Jones, W. (1988). Religion and the problem-solving process: Three styles of coping. *Journal for the Scientific Study of Religion. 27*, 90–104.

Parker, R. J. (1990). The relationship between dogmatism, orthodox Christian beliefs, and ethical judgment. *Counseling and Values, 34*, 213–216.

Parsons, F. (1909). *Choosing a vocation*. Boston: Houghton Mifflin.

Parsons, F. (1911). *Legal doctrine and social progress*. New York: B. W. Huebsch.

Pattison, E. M. (1982). Management of religious issues in family therapy. *International Journal of Family Therapy, 4*, 140–163.

Pax, C. (1972). *An existential approach to God: A study of Gabriel Marcel*. The Hague: Martinus Nijhoff.

Payne, B. P. (1990). Research and theoretical approaches to spirituality and aging. *Generations, 14*, 11–14.

Payne, I. R., Bergin, A. E., Bielema, K. A., & Jenkins, P. H. (1991). Review of religion and mental health: Prevention and the enhancement of psychosocial functioning. *Prevention in Human Services, 9*, 11–40.

Payne, I. R., Bergin, A. E., & Loftus, P. E. (1992). A review of attempts to integrate spiritual and standard psychotherapy techniques. *Journal of Psychotherapy Integration, 2*, 171–192.

Pfister, O. (1923). *Some applications of psychoanalysis*. London: George Allen & Unwin.

Poloma, M. M., & Gallup, G. H. (1991). *Varieties of prayer: A survey report*. Philadelphia: Trinity.

Poloma, M. M., & Pendleton, B. F. (1991). The effects of prayer and prayer experiences on measures of general well-being. *Journal of Psychology and Theology, 19*, 71–83.

Pope, K. S. (1991). *Ethics in psychotherapy and counseling: A practical guide for psychologists*. San Francisco: Jossey-Bass.

Prest, L. A., & Keller, J. F. (1993). Spirituality and family therapy: Spiritual beliefs, myths, and metaphors. *Journal of Marital and Family Therapy, 19*, 137–148.

Pronk, P. (1993). *Against nature? Types of argumentation regarding homosexuality*. (J. Vriend, Trans.). Grand Rapids, MI: William B. Eerdmans.

Propst, L. R. (1988). *Psychotherapy in a religious framework*. New York: Human Sciences.

Propst, L. R. (1992). Spirituality and the avoidant personality. *Theology Today, 49*, 165–172.

Propst, L. R., Ostrom, R., Watkins, P., Dean, T., & Mashburn, D. (1992). Comparative efficacy of religious and nonreligious cognitive-behavioral therapy for the treatment of clinical depression in religious individuals. *Journal of Consulting and Clinical Psychology, 60,* 94–103.

Pruyser, P. W. (1968). *A dynamic psychology of religion.* New York: Harper & Row.

Pruyser, P. W. (1976). *The minister as diagnostician.* Philadelphia: Westminster.

Pruyser, P. W. (1991). Assessment of the patient's religious attitudes in the psychiatric case study. In H. N. Malony & B. Spilka (Eds.), *Religion in psychodynamic perspective: The contributions of Paul W. Pruyser* (pp. 119–140). New York: Oxford University. (Original work published 1971)

Pruyser, P. W. (1991). The seamy side of current religious belief. In H. N. Malony & B. Spilka (Eds.), *Religion in psychodynamic perspective: The contributions of Paul W. Pruyser.* New York: Oxford University. (Original work published 1977)

Pruyser, P. W. (1991). Forms and functions of the imagination in religion. In H. N. Malony & B. Spilka (Eds.), *Religion in psychodynamic perspective: The contributions of Paul W. Pruyser* (pp. 179–188). New York: Oxford University. (Original work published 1985)

Quackenbos, S., Privette, G. & Klentz, B. (1985). Psychotherapy: Sacred or secular? *Journal of Counseling and Development, 63,* 290–293.

Richards, P. S. (1991). Religious devoutness in college students: Relations with emotional adjustment and psychological separation from parents. *Journal of Counseling Psychology, 38,* 189–194.

Richards, P. S., Smith, S. A. & Davis, L. F. (1989). Healthy and unhealthy forms of religiousness manifested by psychotherapy clients: An empirical investigation. *Journal of Research in Personality, 23,* 506–524.

Riina, G. (1995). *God imagery and religious development in late adolescence and early adulthood: Implications for counseling.* Unpublished doctoral dissertation, The George Washington University, Washington, DC.

Riordan, R. J., & Walsh, L. (1994). Guidelines for professional referral to Alcoholics Anonymous and other twelve step groups. *Journal of Counseling and Development, 72,* 351–355.

Ritter, K. Y., & O'Neill, C. W. (1989). Moving through loss: The spiritual journey of gay men and lesbian women. *Journal of Counseling and Development, 68,* 9–15.

Rizvi, S. A. A. (1989). *Muslim tradition in psychotherapy and modern trends.* Lahore, Pakistan: Institute of Islamic Culture.

Rizzuto, A. M. (1979). *The birth of the living God.* Chicago: University of Chicago Press.

Rizzuto, A. M. (1991). Religious development: A psychoanalytic point of view. In F. K. Oser & W. G. Scarlett (Eds.), Religious development in childhood and adolescence [Special issue]. *New Directions for Child Development, 52,* 47–60.

Rogers, C. R. (1957). The necessary and sufficient conditions of therapeutic personality change. *Journal of Consulting Psychology, 21,* 95–103.

Rogers, C. R. (1989). A client-centered/person-centered approach to therapy. In H. Kirschenbaum & V. L. Henderson, *The Carl Rogers reader* (pp. 135–152). Boston: Houghton Mifflin (Original work published 1986)

Rogers, M. L. (1992). A call for discernment—natural and spiritual: An introductory editorial to a special issue on SRA. *Journal of Psychology and Theology, 20,* 175–186.

Rokeach, M. (1960). *The open and closed mind.* New York: Basic Books.

Rosenthal, J. (1990). The meditative therapist. *Family Therapy Networker, 15*(5), 38–41, 70–71.

Rosenak, C. M., & Harnden, G. M. (1992). Forgiveness in the psychotherapeutic process: Clinical applications. *Journal of Psychology and Christianity, 11,* 188–197.

Rudolph, J. (1989). The impact of contemporary ideology and AIDS on the counseling of gay clients. *Counseling and Values, 33,* 96–108.

Sansone, R. A., Khatain, K., & Rodenhauser, P. (1990). The role of religion in psychiatric education. *Academic Psychiatry, 14,* 34–38.

Sanua, V. D. (1969). Religion, mental health, and personality: A review of empirical studies. *American Journal of Psychiatry, 125,* 1203–1213.

Sappington, D., & Wilson, F. R. (1992). Toward an assessment of spirituality: A critique of measurement tools. *Christian Education Journal, 12,* 46–68.

Sartre, J. P. (1960). *Existentialism and humanism.* (P. Mairet, Trans.). London: Methuen. (Original work published 1948)

Schachter-Shalomi, Z. M. (1991). *Spiritual intimacy: A study of counseling in Hasidism.* Northvale, NJ: Jason Aronson.

Schimmel, A. (1992). *Islam: An introduction.* Albany, NY: State University of New York Press.

Schmidt, P. F. (1983). *Manual for use of the character assessment scale* (2nd ed.). Shelbyville, KY: Institute for Character Development.

Schopen, A., & Freeman, B. (1992). Meditation: The forgotten Western tradition. *Counseling and Values, 36,* 123–134.

Schumaker, J. F. (Ed.). (1992). *Religion and mental health.* New York: Oxford University Press.

Schwab, R., & Petersen, K. U. (1990). Religiousness: Its relation to loneliness, neuroticism, and subjective well-being. *Journal for the Scientific Study of Religion, 29,* 335–345.

Scroggs, R. (1983). *The New Testament and homosexuality: Contextual background for contemporary debate.* Philadelphia: Fortress.

Serow, R. C., & Dreyden, J. I. (1990). Community service among college and university students: Individual and institutional relationships. *Adolescence, 25,* 553–566.

Sexton, T. L., & Whiston, S. C. (1994). The status of the counseling relationship: An empirical review, theoretical implications, and research directions. *The Counseling Psychologist, 22,* 6–78.

Shafii, M. (1985). *Freedom from the self: Sufism, meditation and psychotherapy.* New York: Human Sciences Press.

Shafranske, E. P., & Gorsuch, R. L. (1984). Factors associated with the perception of spirituality in psychotherapy. *Journal of Transpersonal Psychology, 16,* 231–241.

Shafranske, E. P., & Malony, H. N. (1990a). California psychologists' religiosity and psychotherapy. *Journal of Religion and Health, 29,* 219–223.

Shafranske, E. P., & Malony, H. N. (1990b). Clinical psychologists' religious and spiritual orientation and their practice of psychotherapy. *Psychotherapy*, 27, 72–78.

Shannon, J. W., & Woods, W. J. (1991). Affirmative psychotherapy for gay men. *The Counseling Psychologist*, 19, 197–215.

Sirkin, M. I. (1990). Cult involvement: A systems approach to assessment and treatment. *Psychotherapy*, 27, 116–123.

Smedes, L. (1984). *Forgive and forget: Healing the hurts we don't deserve.* New York: Harper and Row.

Smith, D. C. (1993). Exploring the religious-spiritual needs of the dying. *Counseling and Values*, 37, 71–77).

Smith, D. E. (1994). AA recovery and spirituality: An addiction medicine perspective. *Journal of Substance Abuse Treatment*, 11, 111–112.

Smith, D. E., Buxton, M. E., Bilal, R., & Seymour, R. B. (1993). Cultural points of resistance to the 12-step recovery process. *Journal of Psychoactive Drugs*, 25, 97–108.

Smith, Do. E. (1986). The Christian Life Assessment Scales: Christian self-perception. *Journal of Psychology and Christianity.* 5(3), 46–61.

Smith, H. (1991). *The world's religions* (rev. ed.). New York: HarperCollins.

Speck, P. (1989). Cultural and religious aspects of dying. In L. Sherr (Ed.), *Death, dying, and bereavement* (pp. 36–47). Oxford, UK: Blackwell Scientific Publications.

Spero, M. H. (1981). Countertransference in religious therapists of religious patients. *American Journal of Psychotherapy*, 35, 565–575.

Spero, M. H. (1985). Diagnostic guidelines for psychotherapy of the religious patient. In M. H. Spero (Ed.), *Psychotherapy of the religious patient* (pp. 19–59). Springfield, IL: Charles C. Thomas.

Spero, M. H. (1992). *Religious objects as psychological structures.* Chicago: University of Chicago Press.

Spinks, G. S. (1963). *Psychology and religion: An introduction to contemporary views.* London: Methuen.

Spong, J. S. (1988). *Living in sin? A bishop rethinks sexuality.* Nashville, TN: Abingdon.

Stallwood, J., & Stoll, R. (1975). Spiritual dimensions of nursing practice. In I. L. Beland & J. Y. Passos (Eds.), *Clinical Nursing: Pathophysiological & psychosocial approaches* (3rd ed.) (pp. 1086–1097). New York: Macmillan.

Starbuck, E. D. (1899). *The psychology of religion.* New York: Scribner's.

Stark, R. (1971). Psychopathology and religious commitment. *Review of Religious Research*, 12, 165–176.

Steenbarger, B. N. (1992). Toward science-practice integration in brief counseling and therapy. *The Counseling Psychologist*, 20, 403–450.

Steenbarger, B. N. (1993). A multicontextual model of counseling: Bridging brevity and diversity. *Journal of Counseling and Development*, 72, 8–150.

Stern, E. M. (Ed.). (1985). *Psychotherapy and the religiously committed patient.* New York: Haworth.

Stoll, R. I. (1979). Guidelines for spiritual assessment. *American Journal of Nursing*, 79, 1574–77.

Stone, C. L. (1991). Estimate of Muslims living in America. In Y. Y. Haddad (Ed.), *The Muslims of America* (pp. 25–36). New York: Oxford University Press.

Stoudenmire, J., Batman, D., Pavlov, M., & Temple, A. (1985). Validation of a Holistic Living Inventory. *Psychological Reports, 57,* 303–311.

Stoudenmire, J., Batman, D., Pavlov, M., & Temple, A. (1986). The Holistic Living Inventory: Correlations with MMPI. *Psychological Reports, 58,* 577–578.

Stroebe, M. S., Stroebe, W., & Hansson, R. O. (1993). *Handbook of bereavement: Theory, research, and intervention.* Cambridge, Eng.: Cambridge University Press.

Strunk, O., Jr. (1965). *Mature religion: A psychological study.* New York: Abingdon.

Suplee, C. (February 23, 1992). A divinity that shapes our ends. *The Washington Post Book World,* 4, 6.

Sweet, M. J., & Johnson, C. G. (1990). Enhancing empathy: The interpersonal implications of a Buddhist meditation technique. *Psychotherapy, 27,* 19–29.

Tan, S-Y. (1987). Cognitive-behavior therapy: A biblical approach and critique. *Journal of Psychology and Theology, 15,* 103–112.

Tillich, P. (1984). The meaning of health. In P. LeFevre, *The meaning of health: Essays in existentialism, psychoanalysis, and religion: Paul Tillich* (pp. 165–173). Chicago, IL: Exploration. (Original work published 1961)

Tjeltveit, A. C. (1986). The ethics of value conversion in psychotherapy: Appropriate and inappropriate therapist influence on client values. *Clinical Psychology Review, 6,* 515–537.

Travis, J. W. (1981). *The Wellness Inventory.* Mill Valley, CA: Wellness Associates.

Trout, S. S. (1990). *To see differently: Personal growth and being of service through attitudinal healing.* Washington, DC: Three Roses.

Turner, A. (1987, February). *Multicultural considerations: Working with families of developmentally disabled and high-risk children: The Black perspective.* Paper presented at the meeting of the National Center for Clinical Infant Programs, Los Angeles, CA.

Vanderburg, W. H. (1985). *The growth of minds and cultures: A unified theory of the structure of human experience.* Toronto: University of Toronto Press.

Vaughn, F. (1991). Spiritual issues in psychotherapy. *The Journal of Transpersonal Psychology, 23,* 105–119.

Veach, T. L., & Chappel, J. N. (1992). Measuring spiritual health: A preliminary study. *Substance Abuse, 13,* 139–147.

Verge, C. (1992). Foundations for a spiritually based psychotherapy. In L. A. Burton (Ed.), *Religion and the family: When God helps* (pp. 41–59). New York: Haworth Pastoral Press.

Wadsworth, J. D., & Checketts, K. T. (1980). Influence of religious affiliation on pyschodiagnosis. *Journal of Consulting and Clinical Psychology, 48,* 234–240.

Wagner, G., Serafini, J., Rabkin, J., Remien, R., & Williams, J. (1994). Integration of one's religion and homosexuality: A weapon against internalized homophobia? *Journal of Homosexuality, 26,* 91–110.

Warner, R. (1993). Work in progress toward a new paradigm for the sociological study of religion in the United States. *American Journal of Sociology, 98,* 1044–1093.

Watkins, C. E., Jr., & Campbell, V. L. (1990). *Testing in counseling practice.* Hillsdale, NJ: Lawrence Erlbaum.

Wax, M. L., & Wax, R. H. (1993). Religion among Native Americans. In M. E. Marty (Ed.), *Native American religion and Black Protestantism* (pp. 3–15). New York: K. G. Saur.

Weinhold, B., & Hendricks, G. (1993). *Counseling and psychotherapy: A transpersonal approach* (2nd ed.). Denver: Love.

Weisbord, A., Sherman, M. F., & Hodinko, B. A. (1988). Impact of precounseling information: Therapist counseling style and similarity of religious values on religious Jewish clients. *Journal of Psychology and Judaism, 12,* 60–78.

Whipple, V. (1987). Counseling battered women from fundamentalist churches. *Journal of Marital and Family Therapy, 13,* 251–258.

Wilber, K. (1986). Treatment modalities. In K. Wilber, J. Engler, & D. P. Brown, *Transformations of consciousness* (pp. 127–159). Boston: Shambala.

Wilber, K., Engler, J., & Brown, D. P. (1986). *Transformation of consciousness.* Boston: Shambala.

Witmer, J. (1988). Older order Amish: Culturally different by religion. In N. A. Vacc, J. Wittmer, & S. B. DeVaney (Eds.), *Experiencing and counseling multicultural and diverse populations* (2nd ed.) (pp. 29–59). Muncie, IN: Accelerated Development.

Witmer, J. M., Sweeney, T. J., & Myers, J. E. (1994). *Wellness Evaluation of Lifestyle: The WEL Inventory.* Palo Alto, CA: Mind Garden.

Witmer, J. M., & Sweeney, T. J. (1992). A holistic model of wellness and prevention over the life span. *Journal of Counseling and Development, 71,* 140–148.

Wolfe, B. E., & Goldfried, M. R. (1988). Research on psychotherapy integration: Recommendations and conclusions from an NIMH Workshop. *Journal of Consulting and Clinical Psychology, 56,* 448–451.

Wolpe, J. (1990). *The practice of behavior therapy* (4th ed.). New York: Pergamon.

Worthington, E. L., Jr. (1986). Religious counseling: A review of published empirical research. *Journal of Counseling and Development, 64,* 421–431.

Worthington, E. L., Jr. (1989). Religious faith across the life span: Implications for counseling and research. *The Counseling Psychologist, 17,* 555–612.

Worthington, E. L., Jr. (1991). Psychotherapy and religious values: An update. *Journal of Psychology and Christianity, 10,* 211–223.

Worthington, E. L., Jr., & Scott, G. G. (1983). Goal selection for counseling with potentially religious clients by professional and student counselors in explicitly Christian or secular settings. *Journal of Psychology and Theology, 11,* 318–329.

Wulff, D. M. (1991). *Psychology of religion: Classic and contemporary views.* New York: Wiley.

Wuthnow, R. (1994). *Sharing the journey: Support groups and America's new quest for community.* New York: Free Press.

Wyatt, S. C., & Johnson, R. W. (1990). The influence of counselors' religious values on clients' perceptions of the counselor. *Journal of Psychology and Theology, 18,* 158–165.

Yalom, I. (1980). *Existential psychotherapy.* New York: Basic Books.

Yalom, I. D. (1985). *The theory and practice of group psychotherapy* (3rd ed.). New York: Basic Books.

Yost, J. L. (1986). For God, country, and family: A personal tribute to Christian Fredrik Midelfort, M.D. *Family Process, 25,* 149–151.

Zuesse, E. M. (1983). The absurdity of ritual. *Psychiatry, 46,* 40–50.

Index